The Home of Cambridge Glass

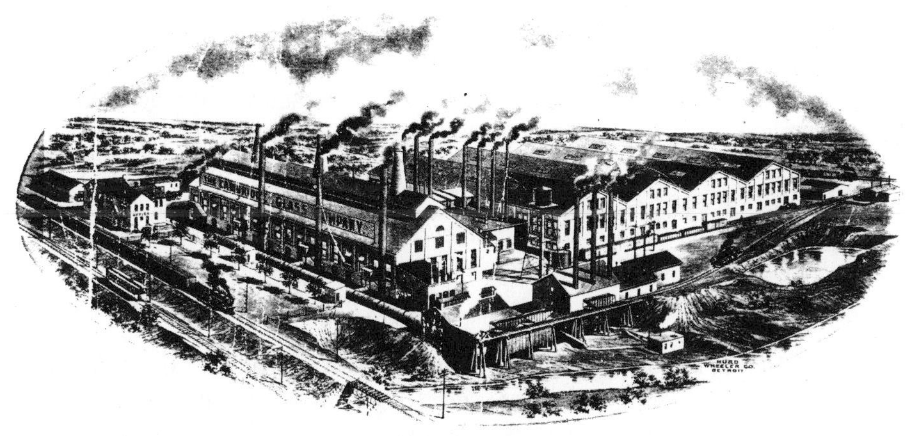

THE CAMBRIDGE GLASS COMPANY

Capital $1,500,000.00

Incorporated 1901

CAMBRIDGE, OHIO, U. S. A.

National Cambridge Collectors, Inc. of Cambridge, Ohio, takes great pleasure in presenting this additional chapter in the total knowledge of a great glassware. National Cambridge Collectors is a non-profit organization dedicated to the preservation and collection of the products of The Cambridge Glass Company of Cambridge, Ohio. The object of this organization is to establish a permanent museum in or near Cambridge for the purpose of display and study of this glassware.
For your assistance in using this catalog we offer this brief explanation regarding the page numbering that has been used:

The frontispiece, pictures, general information, index, and pages 1 – 71 comprise that portion which was the original 1930 issue and was probably issued in January of 1930.

Pages 72 – 82	*Addition of Summer of early Fall 1930*
Pages A – K	*Addition of late Fall 1930*
Pages 31-1 – 31-34	*Addition of early 1931*
Pages 32-1 – 32-36	*Addition of early 1932*
Pages 33-1 – 33-36	*Addition of early 1933*
Pages 33-29A and 33-29B	*Addition of mid 1933*
Pages 33-B-1 – 33-B-11	*Addition of mid to late 1933*

(This is a Bar Ware section that was added in an effort to capture some of the newly opening market that was being created by the repeal of the Prohibition amendment.)

Pages 34-1 – 34-25	*Addition of early 1934*

We also wish to point out that items pictured on a page may or may not have been a completely new item at that time. It may have been a new shape addition or a new treatment to an existing shape that is represented. It is also important to bear in mind that many of these shapes and decorations were carried in production for long periods of time. In many instances the shapes and/or the decorations were continued in new colors that were added to the production.
Those of you wishing to further your knowledge in this fine glassware are cordially invited to seek membership in our organization.
We wish to extend grateful acknowledgment to THE IMPERIAL GLASS CO. of Bellaire, Ohio (a subsidiary of LENOX, Inc.) for the use of the original catalog which made this reprint possible.

COLLECTOR BOOKS
P.O. Box 3009 • Paducah, KY 42002-3009

National Cambridge Collectors, Inc.
P.O. Box 416 • Cambridge, Ohio 43725

3400 Line Plate Etched "744" Apple-Blossom

3400/647 Candlestick

3400/2-12½" Bowl

3400/647 Candlestick

3400/1-13" Bowl

3400/10-11" Hdl. Sandwich Tray

3400/6-11½" Cheese and Cracker

3400 Dinnerware Plate Etched "744" Apple-Blossom

3400/3-11" Low Footed Bowl

3400/11 3 Pc. Mayonnaise Set

3400/9-7" Candy Box and Cover

3400/1186-12½" Sandwich Plate

3400/15-4" Comport

3400/14-7" Tall Comport

3400 Line Plate Etched "744" Apple-Blossom

3400/646 Candlestick

3400/4-12" Bowl

3400/646 Candlestick

3400/1240-12" Bowl "Oval"

3400/638 Candelabra

3400/638 Candelabra

3400/1185-10" Bowl

3400 Dinnerware Plate Etched "744" Apple-Blossom

3400/53-6″ Cereal

3400/68 Sugar

3400/68 Cream

3400/54 Cup and Saucer

3400/55 Cream Soup and Saucer

3400/18 Salt and Pepper

3400/67-12″ Celery and Relish Service

3400/62-8½″ Plate

3400/51-10″ Baker

3400/1174 Bread and Butter Plate
3400/1176 Salad Plate
3400/1177 Dinner Plate
3400/1178 Service Plate

3400 Dinnerware Plate Etched "744" Apple Blossom

3400/52-5½" Butter and Cover

3400/16 6 oz. Ftd. Sugar and Cream

3400/56-5½" Fruit Saucer

3400/60-6" Bread and Butter Plate

3400/59-9" Pickle Tray

3400/57-11½" Platter

3400/8-11½" Two handled Sandwich Plate

3400 Dinnerware Plate Etched "744" Apple Blossom

3400/61-7½" Tea Plate

3400/63-9½" Dinner Plate

3400/1177 Dinner Plate

3400/58-13½" Platter

3400/66-10" Club Luncheon Plate

3400/1188-11" Fruit Bowl

3135 Stemware Plate Etched "744" Apple-Blossom

10 oz. Footed Tumbler

Finger Bowl and Plate

8 oz. Goblet

6 oz. Low Sherbet

3 oz. Cocktail

12 oz. Footed Tumbler

6 oz. Tall Sherbet

711-76 oz. Ftd. Jug and Cover

8 oz. Footed Tumbler

5 oz. Footed Tumbler

3130 Stemware Plate Etched "744" Apple-Blossom

Finger Bowl and Plate

12 oz. Footed Tumbler

5 oz. Footed Tumbler

10 oz. Footed Tumbler

8 oz. Footed Tumbler

1205-64 oz. Jug

3 oz. Cocktail

8 oz. Goblet

6 oz. Low Sherbet

6 oz. Tall Sherbet

3400 Line Plate Etched "744" Apple-Blossom

3400/1179-5½" Bon Bon

3400/1180-5¼" Bon Bon

3400/1181-6" Plate

3400/1182-6" Basket

2½ oz. Footed Tumbler

6 oz. Footed Sherbet

9 oz. Footed Tumbler

12 oz. Footed Tumbler

3400-50 oz. Ftd. Jug

9 oz. Lunch Goblet

Decagon Dinnerware Plate Etched "Cleo"

865 Cup and Saucer

867 Cream

1075 Cream Soup and Saucer

867 Sugar

1011-6" Cereal

811-9½" Dinner Plate

1082-9" Pickle Tray

1078-12" Service Tray Oval

983-5" 3 Pc. Mayonnaise Set

866 2 Hdl. Bouillon and Saucer

760-7" 2 Hdl. Basket

758-5½" 2 Hdl. Bon Bon

749-6¼" 2 Hdl. Bon Bon

193-6 oz. Oil

759-7" 2 Hdl. Plate

1091 Sauce Boat and Stand

1087-9½" Vegetable Oval

3077 Stemware Plate Etched "Cleo"

10 oz. Footed Tumbler

Finger Bowl and Plate

6 oz. Low Sherbet

9 oz. Goblet

2½ oz. Cocktail

12 oz. Footed Tumbler

8 oz. Footed Tumbler

5 oz. Footed Tumbler

6 oz. Tall Sherbet

3077/10-63 oz. Jug and Cover

3115 Stemware Plate Etched "Cleo"

9 oz. Goblet

6 oz. Fruit Salad

Fingerbowl and Plate

8 oz. Footed Tumbler

3½ oz. Cocktail

1090-7" Tall Comport

10 oz. Footed Tumbler

6 oz. Tall Sherbet

5 oz. Footed Tumbler

12 oz. Footed Tumbler

Plate Etching "Cleo"

984-10" Bowl

971-8½" Bowl

977-11" Basket

972-11" Plate

Plate Etching "739"

627-4" Candlestick

855-11" Bowl

627-4" Candlestick

1240-12" Refectory Bowl. Oval

638 Candelabra

638 Candelabra

Decagon Dinnerware Plate Etched "739"

809-6¼" Bread and Butter Plate

1075 Cream Soup and Saucer

865 Cup and Saucer

917/1167 Gravy Boat and Stand

1085-9" Vegetable Dish "Round"

1263 French Dressing Bottle

1068-11" 2 Part Relish

1200-10" Club Luncheon Plate

3130 Stemware Plate Etched "739"

10 oz. Footed Tumbler

Fingerbowl and Plate

6 oz. Low Sherbet

3 oz. Cocktail

8 oz. Goblet

12 oz. Footed Tumbler

935 64 oz. Jug

6 oz. Tall Sherbet

8 oz. Footed Tumbler

5 oz. Footed Tumbler

3120 Stemware Plate Etched "739"

9 oz. Goblet

3 oz. Cocktail

4½ oz. Oyster Cocktail

Fingerbowl and Plate

8 oz. Footed Tumbler

6 oz. Tall Sherbet

5 oz. Footed Tumbler

1090-7" Tall Comport

12 oz. Footed Tumbler

10 oz. Footed Tumbler

Decagon Line Plate Etched "738"

977-11" Basket

627-4" Candlestick

856-11" Bowl

627-4" Candlestick

1090-7" Tall Comport

877-11½" Comport

878-4" Candlestick

855-11" Bowl

878-4" Candlestick

873 3 Pc. Mayonnaise Set

971-8½" Bowl

842-12" Bowl

984-10" Bowl

867 Sugar

867 Cream

868-11" Cheese and Cracker

972-11" Plate

870-11" Hdl. Sandwich Tray

Decagon Dinnerware

1102-3¾" Cranberry Flat Rim

1099-5¾" Fruit Flat Rim

807-6" Cereal Flat Rim

1096 Cream

1101-3½" Cranberry Belled

1096 Sugar

1098-5½" Fruit Belled

1011-6" Cereal Belled

865 Cup and Saucer

1075 Cream Soup and Saucer

866 Bouillon Cup and Saucer

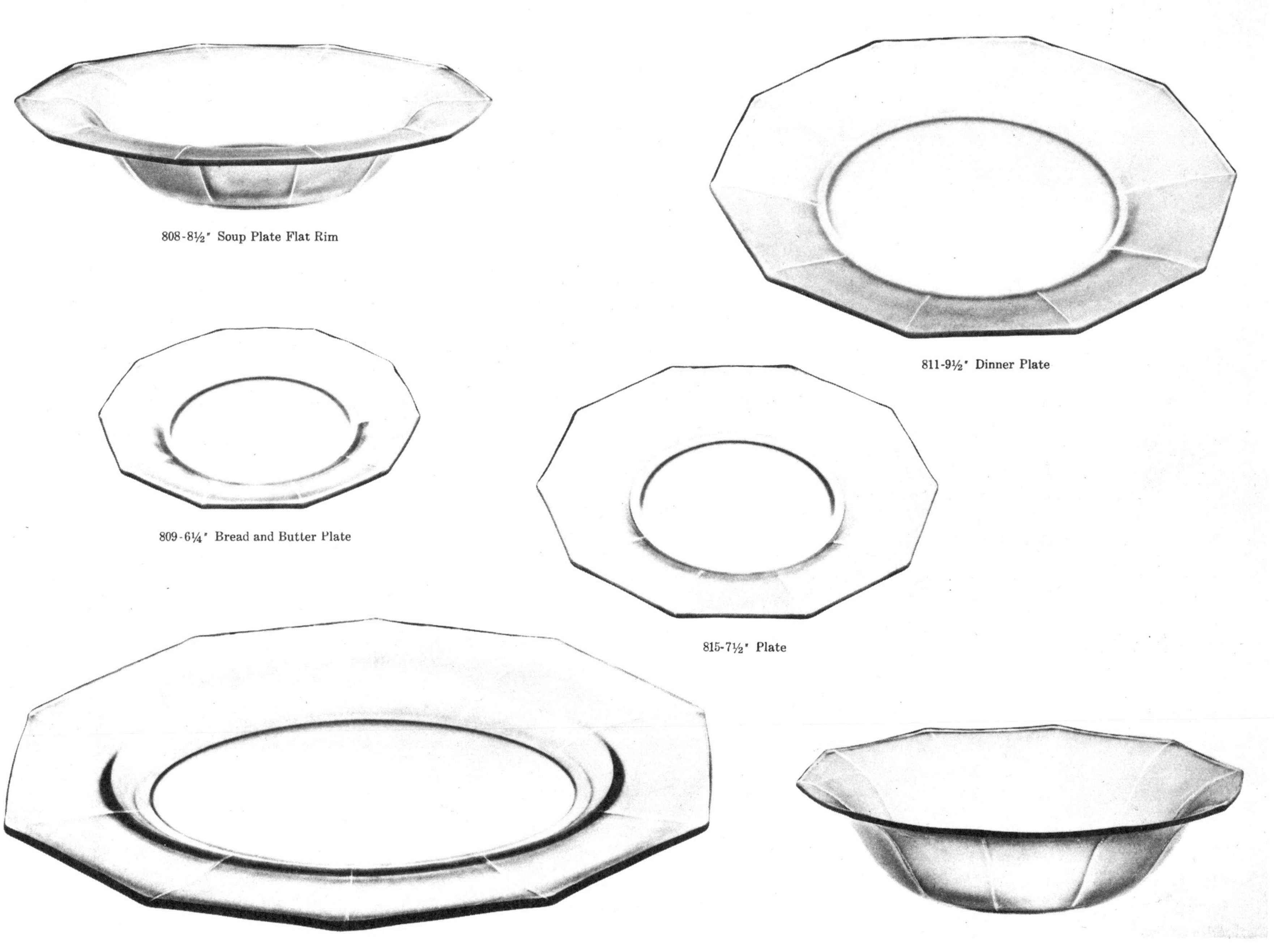

808-8½″ Soup Plate Flat Rim

811-9½″ Dinner Plate

809-6¼″ Bread and Butter Plate

815-7½″ Plate

1078-12″ Service Tray Oval
1077-11″ " " "
1079-15″ " " "

1012-8½″ Soup Plate

Decagon Dinnerware

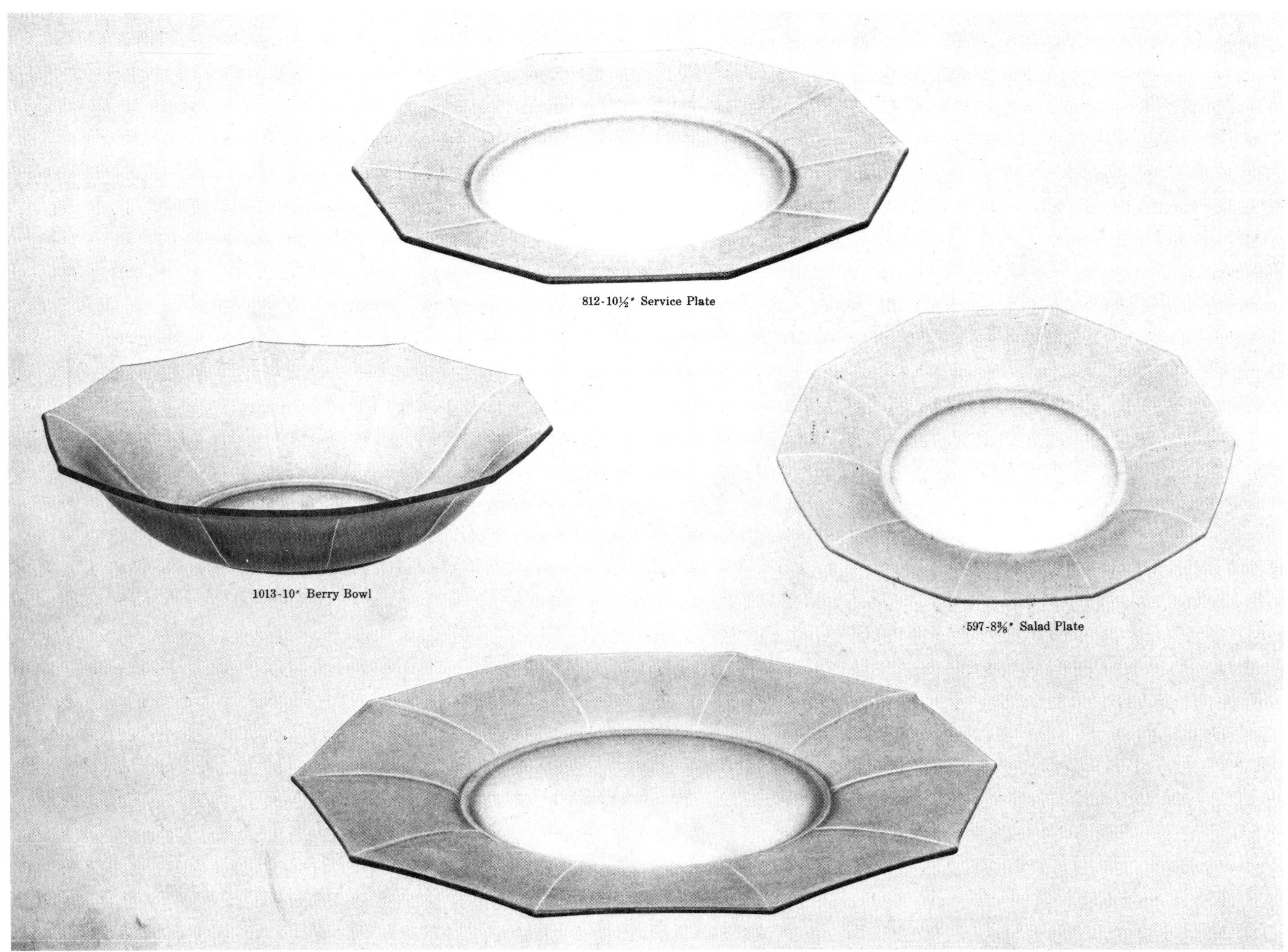

812-10½" Service Plate

1013-10" Berry Bowl

597-8⅜" Salad Plate

598-12½" Plate

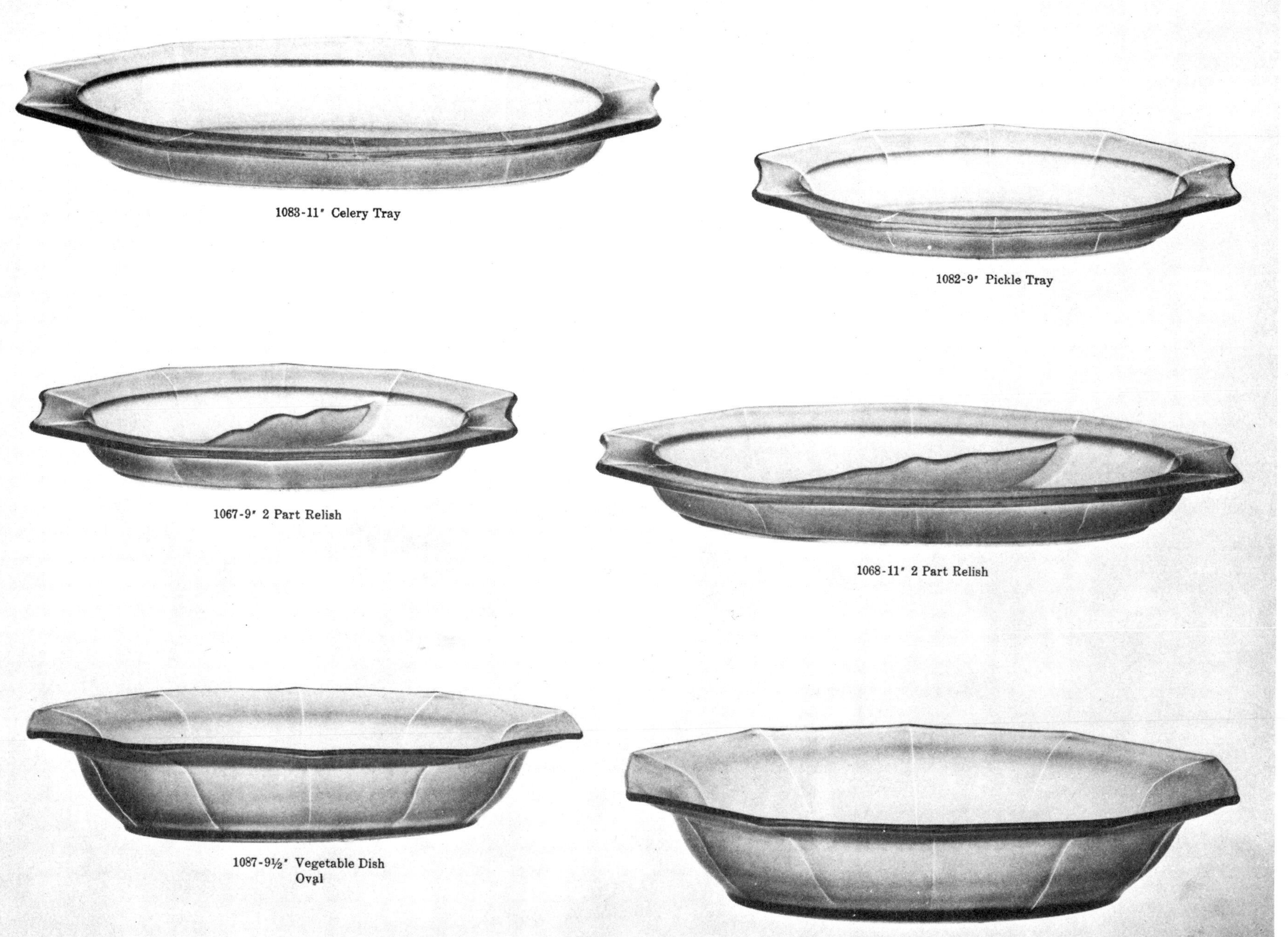

1083-11" Celery Tray

1082-9" Pickle Tray

1067-9" 2 Part Relish

1068-11" 2 Part Relish

1087-9½" Vegetable Dish Oval

1088-10½" Vegetable Dish Oval

Decagon Dinnerware

979 Sugar

979 Cream

873 3 Pc. Mayonnaise Set

867 Cream

867 Sugar

1094 Cream

1094 Sugar

983-5" 3 Pc. Mayonnaise Set

917/1167 Gravy Boat and Stand

193 6 oz. Oil

197 6 oz. Oil

1091 Sauce Boat and Stand

1263 French Dressing Bottle
Engraved "Oil and Vinegar"

1261 French Dressing Bottle
Engraved "Oil and Vinegar"

758/759/445 3 Pc. Mayonnaise Set

Decagon Dinnerware

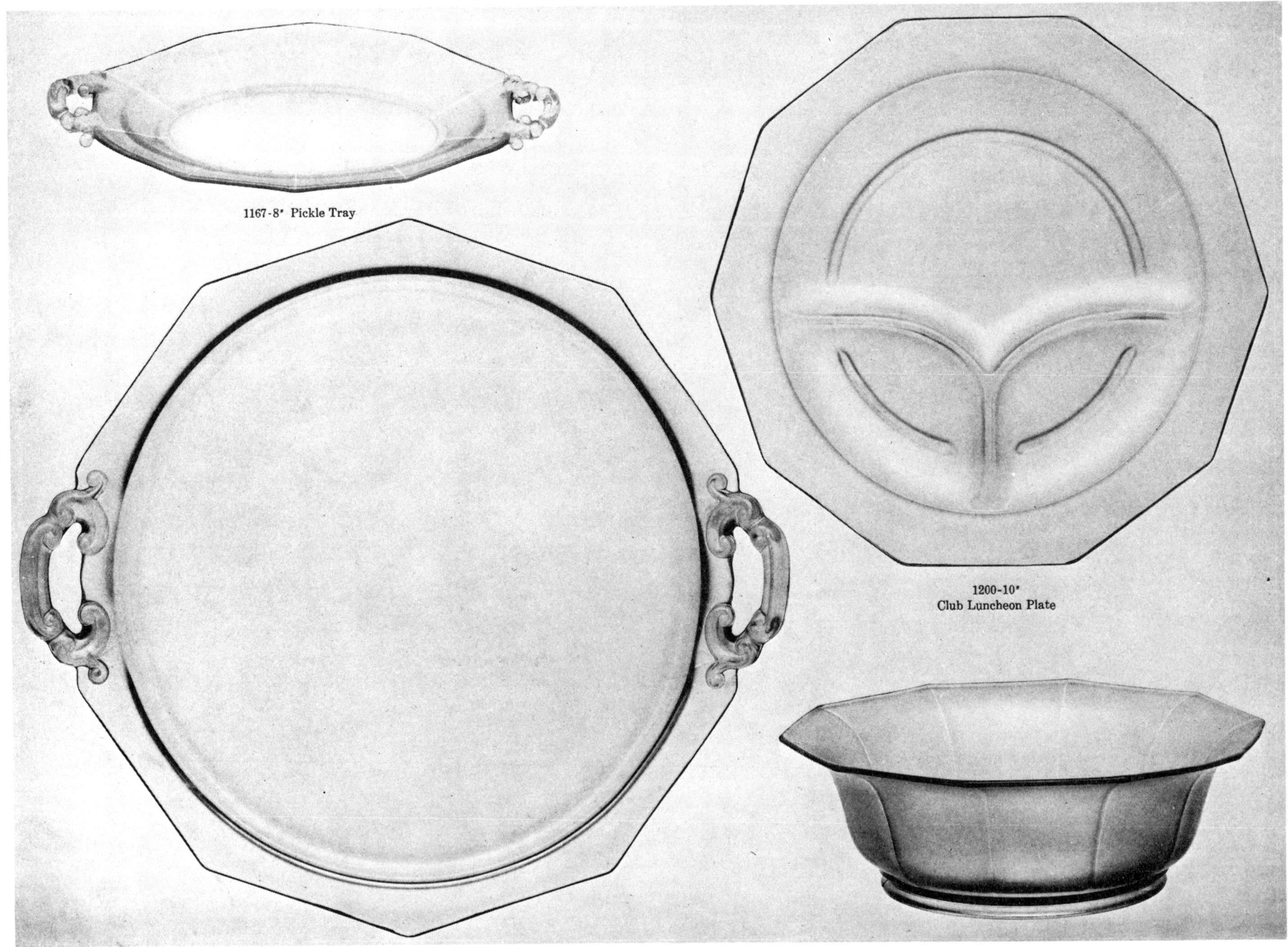

1167-8″ Pickle Tray

1200-10″
Club Luncheon Plate

1084-13″ Service Tray

1085-9″ Vegetable Dish Round
1086-11″ " " "

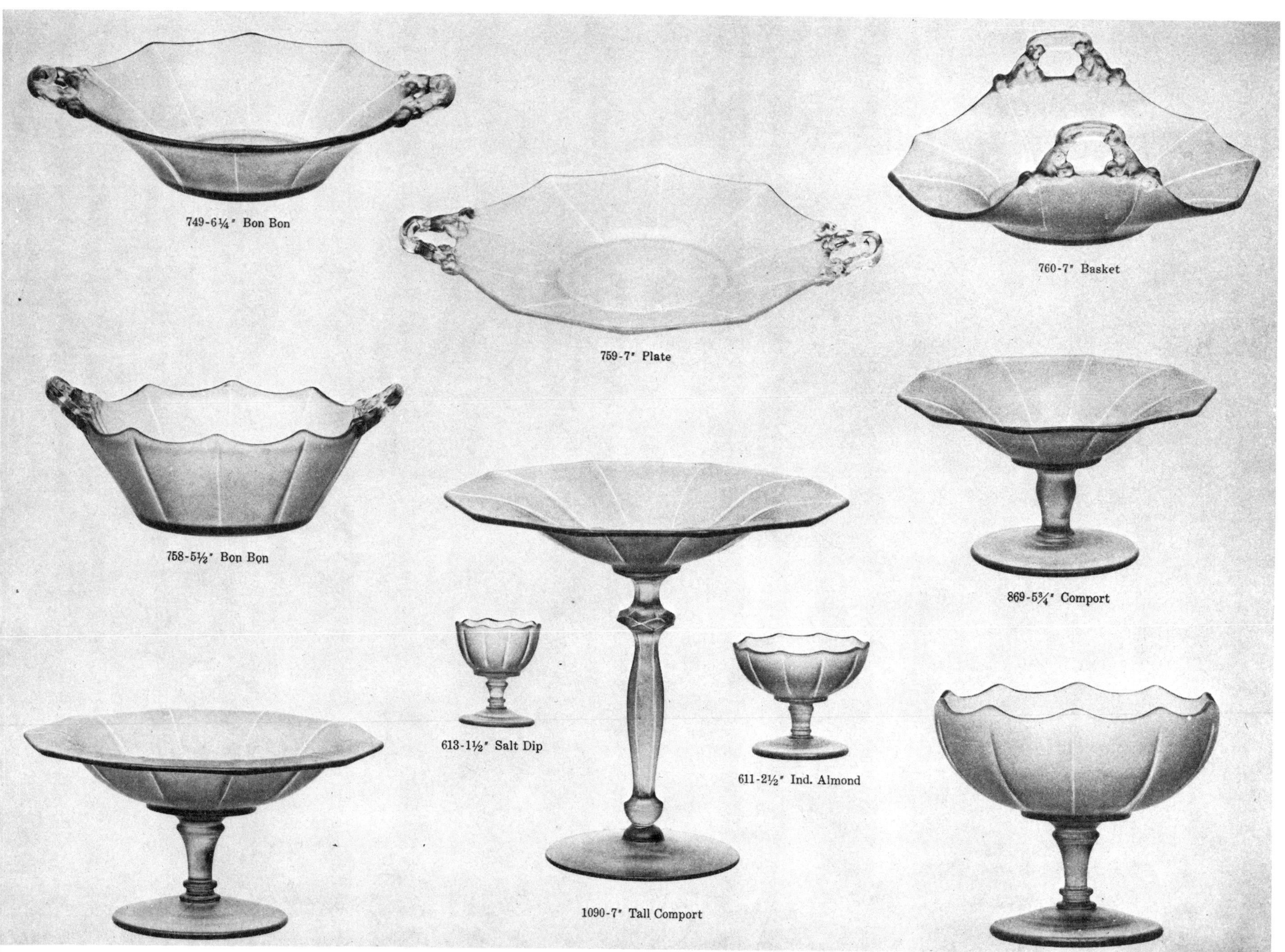

749-6¼" Bon Bon

759-7" Plate

760-7" Basket

758-5½" Bon Bon

869-5¾" Comport

613-1½" Salt Dip

611-2½" Ind. Almond

1090-7" Tall Comport

608-6½" Comport

612-6" Ftd. Almond

Round Dinnerware Plate Etched "732"

933 Cup and Saucer

922 Cream Soup and Saucer

944 Cream

944 Sugar

810-9½" Dinner Plate

193 6 oz. Oil

907-9" Pickle Tray

381-8½" Soup Plate

914-12" Open Dish Oval

3130 Stemware Plate Etched "732"

10 oz. Footed Tumbler

Fingerbowl and Plate

8 oz. Goblet

6 oz. Low Sherbet

3 oz. Cocktail

12 oz. Footed Tumbler

955-62 oz. Jug

6 oz. Tall Sherbet

8 oz. Footed Tumbler

5 oz. Footed Tumbler

3120 Stemware Plate Etched "732"

8 oz. Footed Tumbler

Fingerbowl and Plate

6 oz. Tall Sherbet

9 oz. Goblet

1 oz. Cordial

12 oz. Footed Tumbler

712-76 oz. Jug

3 oz. Cocktail

6 oz. Fruit Salad

2½ oz. Footed Tumbler

Plate Etching "732"

628-3½" Candlestick

676-11½" Bowl

628-3½" Candlestick

531-7¼" Tall Comport

441-10½" Comport

533 3 Pc. Mayonnaise Set

300-6" Candy Box

487-12" Cheese and Cracker "Oval"

674-13" Bowl

168-10" Hdl. Sandwich Tray

135-10" Cheese and Cracker

173-12" Hdl. Sandwich Tray "Oval"

Round Dinnerware Plate Etched "520"

928-5¼" Fruit Saucer

934 2 Hdl. Bouillon and Saucer

933 Cup and Saucer

138 Sugar

138 Cream

197-6 oz. Oil

466-6½" Cereal or Grape Fruit

810-9½" Dinner Plate

3060 Stemware Plate Etched "520"

7 oz. Fruit Salad

3 oz. Footed Tumbler

Finger Bowl and Plate

9 oz. Goblet

2½ oz. Cocktail

5 oz. Footed Tumbler

6 oz. Tall Sherbet

531-7¼" Tall Comport

2½ oz. Wine

10 oz. Footed Tumbler

Round Dinnerware

138 Sugar

138 Cream

925 After Dinner
Cup and Saucer

494 Footed
Cup and Saucer

933 Cup and Saucer

495 Footed Bouillon
Cup and Saucer

3½ Ovide
Cup and Saucer

934 Bouillon Cup and Saucer

920 Butter and Cover
with Drainer

922 Cream Soup and Saucer

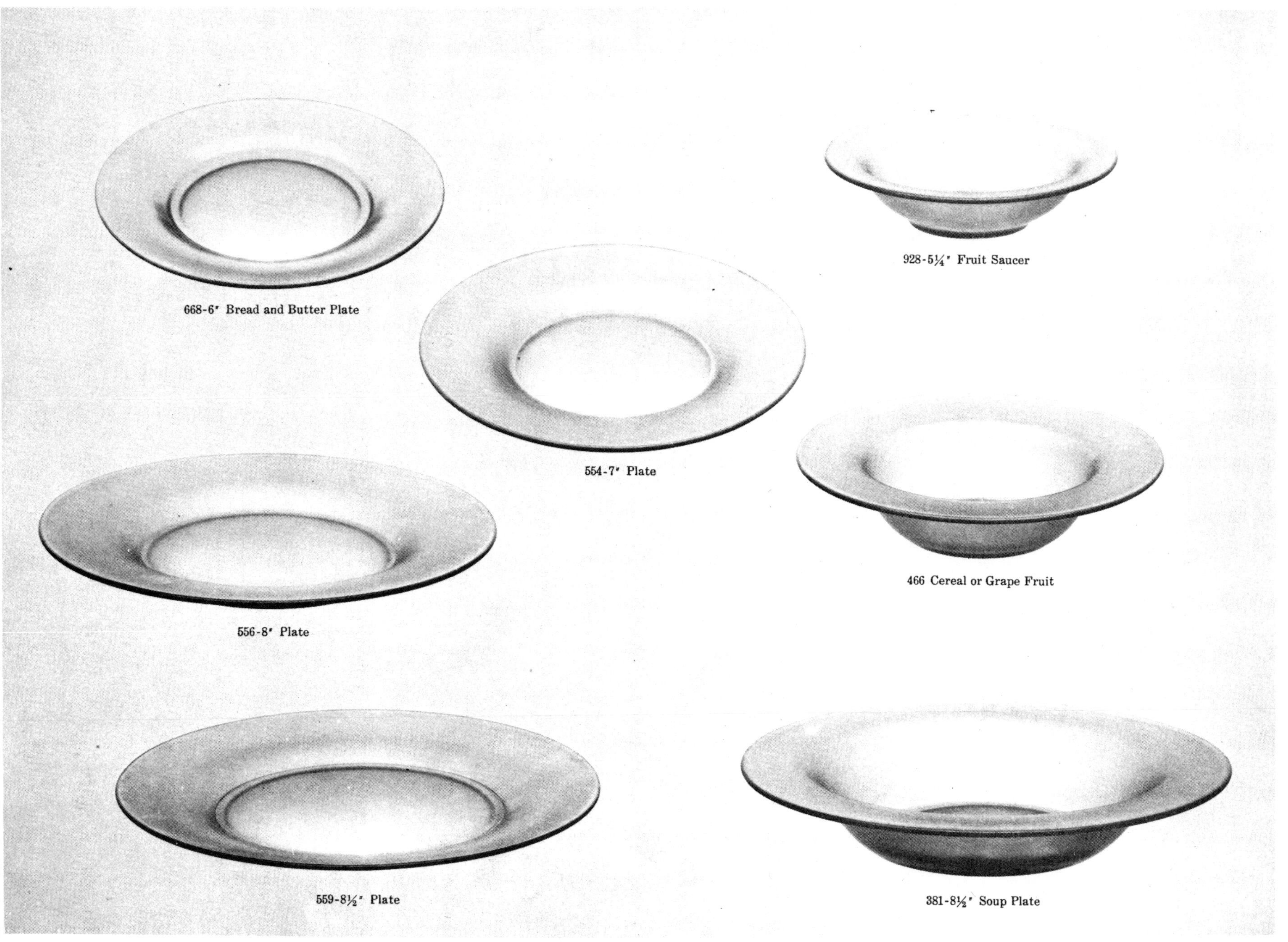
668-6″ Bread and Butter Plate

928-5¼″ Fruit Saucer

554-7″ Plate

466 Cereal or Grape Fruit

556-8″ Plate

559-8½″ Plate

381-8½″ Soup Plate

Round Dinnerware

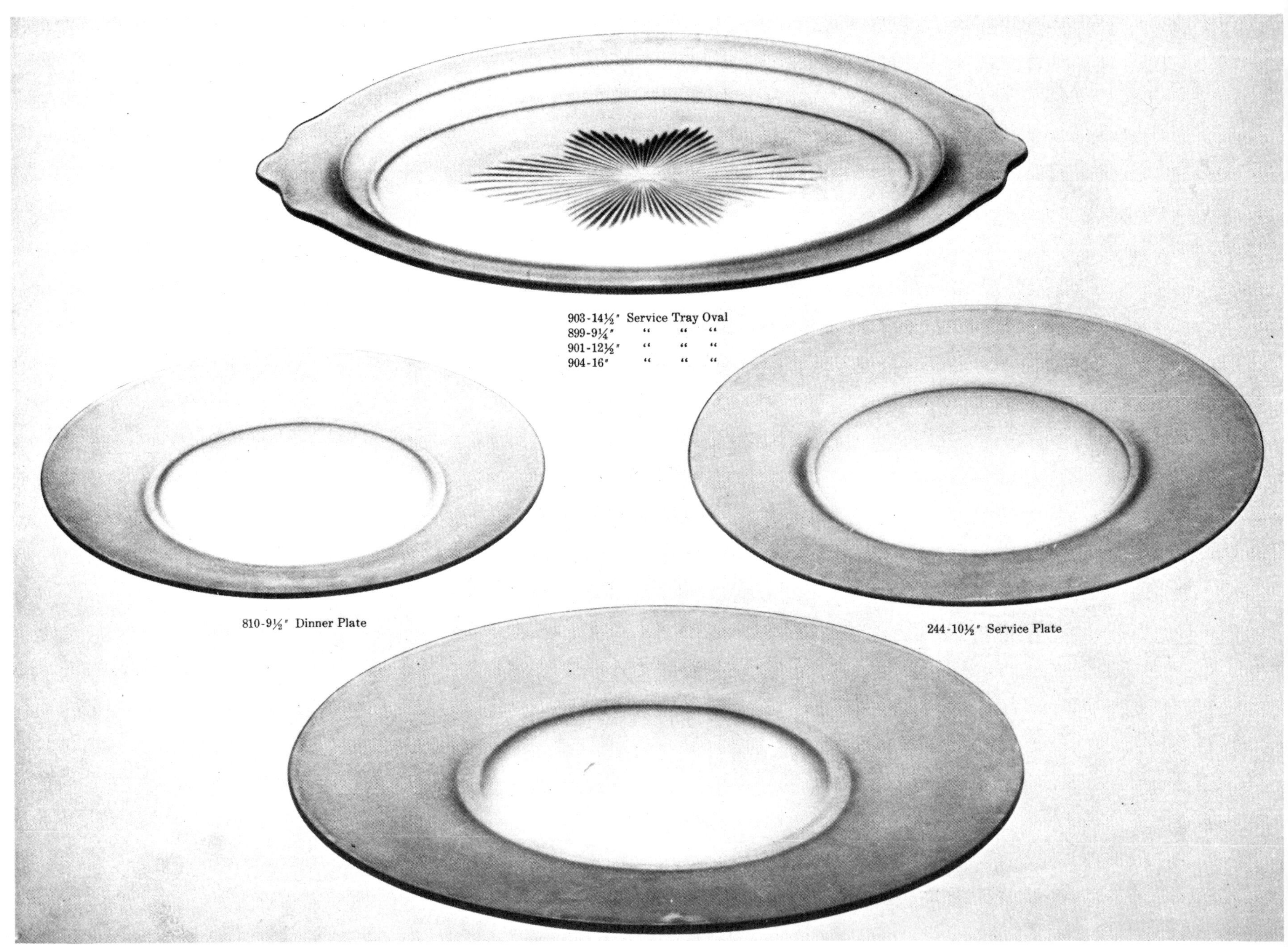

903-14½" Service Tray Oval
899-9¼" " " "
901-12½" " " "
904-16" " " "

810-9½" Dinner Plate

244-10½" Service Plate

242-13½" Plate

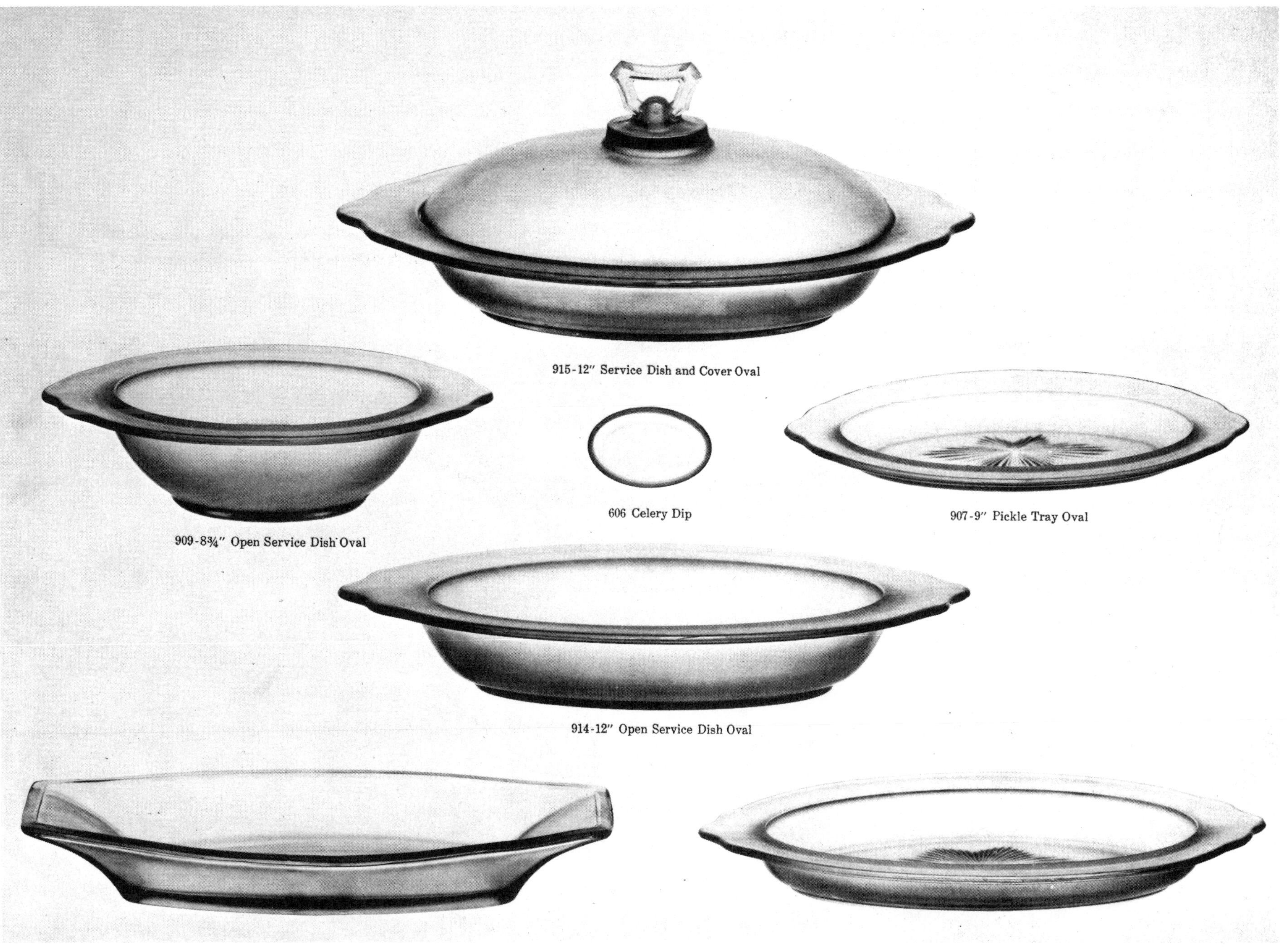

915-12″ Service Dish and Cover Oval

909-8¾″ Open Service Dish Oval

606 Celery Dip

907-9″ Pickle Tray Oval

914-12″ Open Service Dish Oval

652-11″ Celery Tray

908-11″ Celery Tray Oval

Round Dinnerware

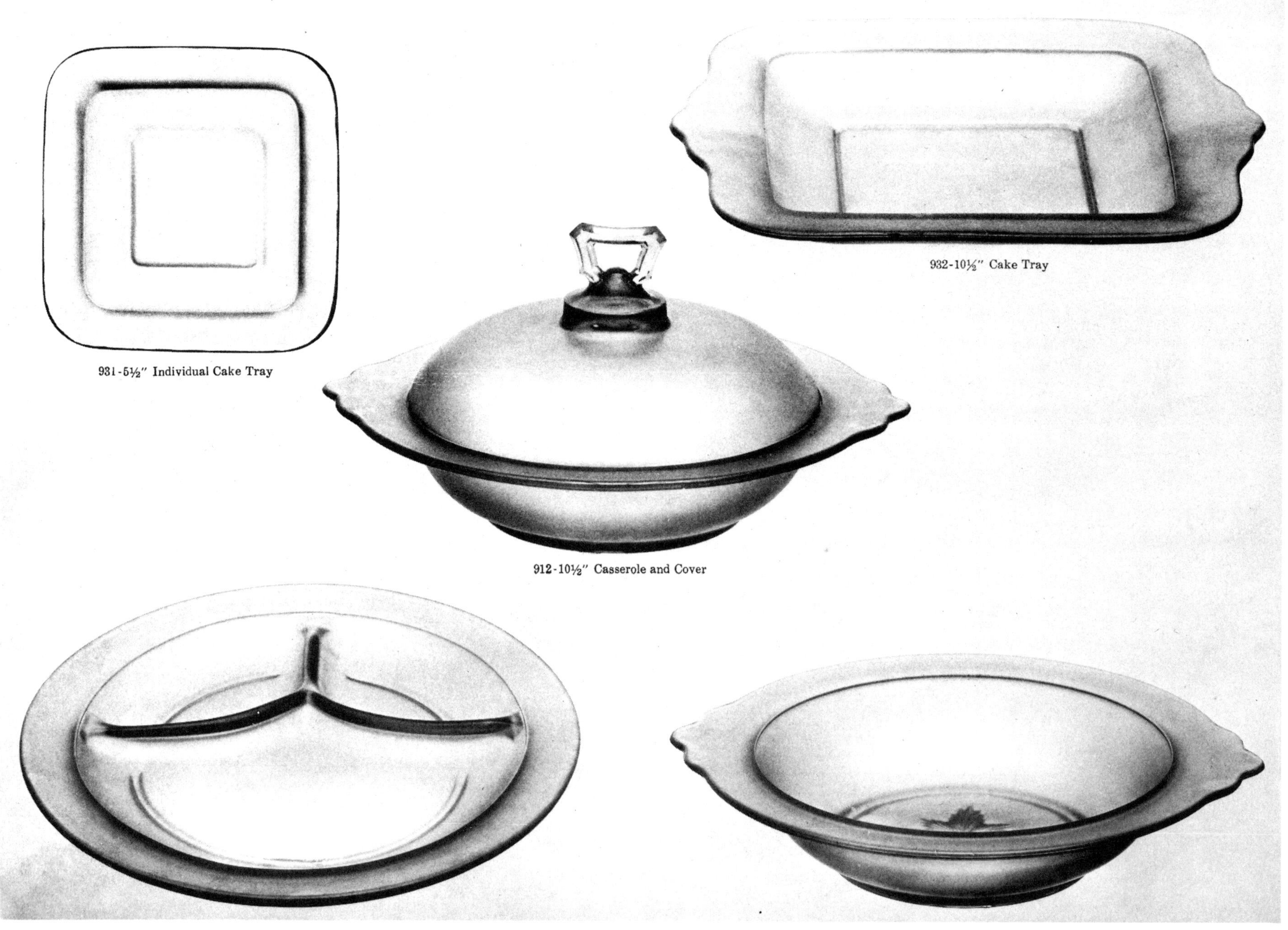

931-5½" Individual Cake Tray

932-10½" Cake Tray

912-10½" Casserole and Cover

380-10" Club Luncheon Plate
378-11" Club Luncheon Plate

911-10½" Open Service Dish

752 Egg Cup

942 Sugar and Cover

941 Sugar

943 Cream

944 Sugar

944 Cream

961 Sugar

961 Cream

193-6 oz. Oil

1263 French Dressing Bottle
Engraved Oil and Vinegar

1261 French Dressing Bottle
Engraved Oil and Vinegar

197-6 oz. Oil

Round Dinnerware

400 Ind. Salt

398

397

396

395

158 Marmalade and Cover

940 Ind. Sugar

940 Ind. Cream

137 Sugar

137 Cream

960 Sugar

960 Cream

174-9 oz. Syrup Metal Top
602-5¼″ Plate

175-8 oz. Syrup and Cover
602-5¼″ Plate

170 9 oz. Syrup Metal Top
602-5¼″ Plate

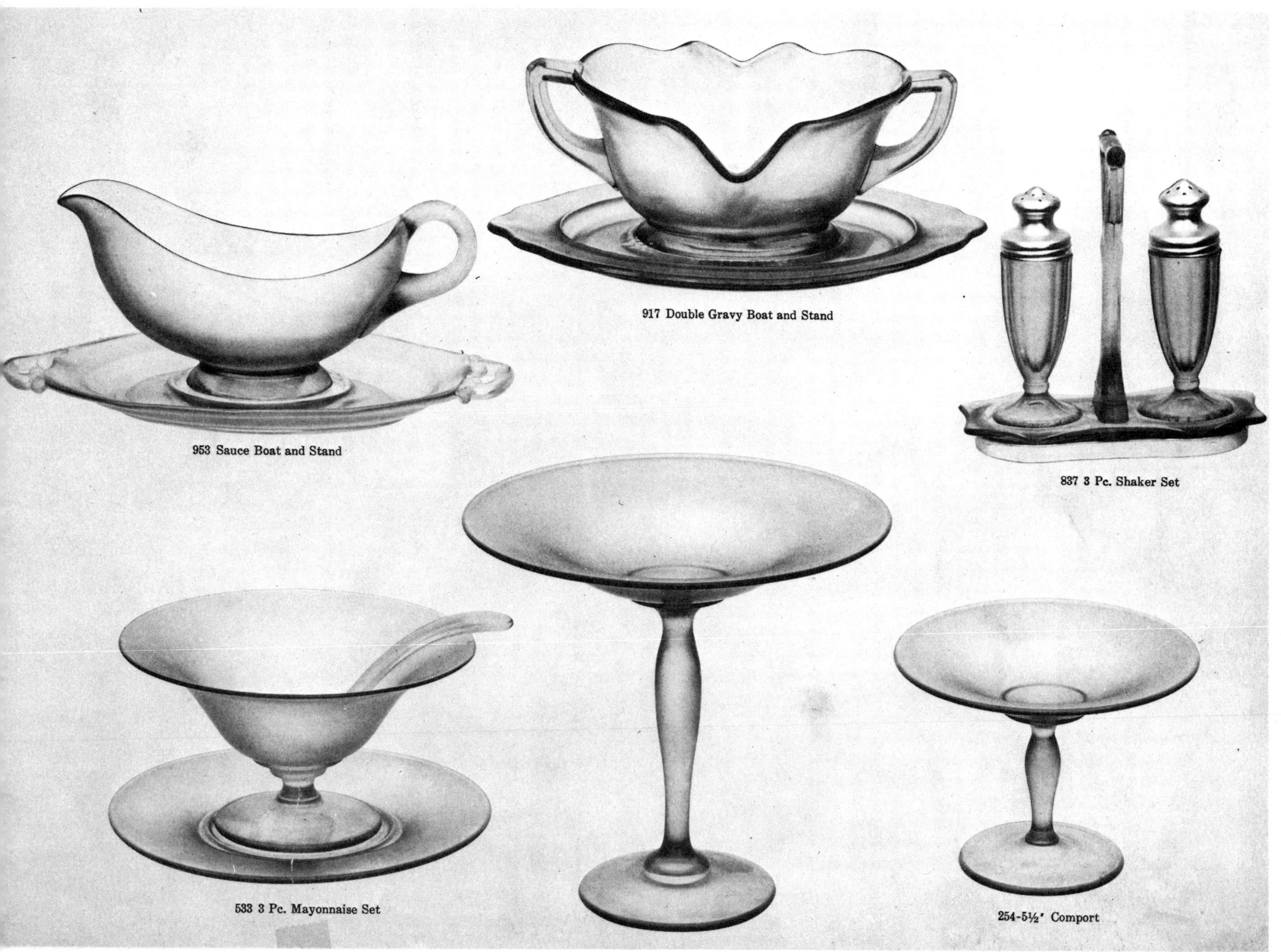

917 Double Gravy Boat and Stand

953 Sauce Boat and Stand

837 3 Pc. Shaker Set

533 3 Pc. Mayonnaise Set

254-5½' Comport

531-7½' Comport
532-6½' Comport

Miscellaneous Items

1110 Dessert Mold

703 Flower Holder
3" Block

3077 Cheese Dish and Cover

816 Tall Cream

813 Sugar Sifter
Silver Plated Top

1220 Ind. Shaker
Glass Top

102 Ind. Salt

833 Oil Bottle

1215/1094 3 Pc.
Sugar and Cream Set

1215/619 3 Pc.
Oil and Vinegar Set

396 Shaker
Silver Plated Top

829 7 Pc. Set

1095 3 Pc. Sugar and Cream Set

830 5 Pc. Set

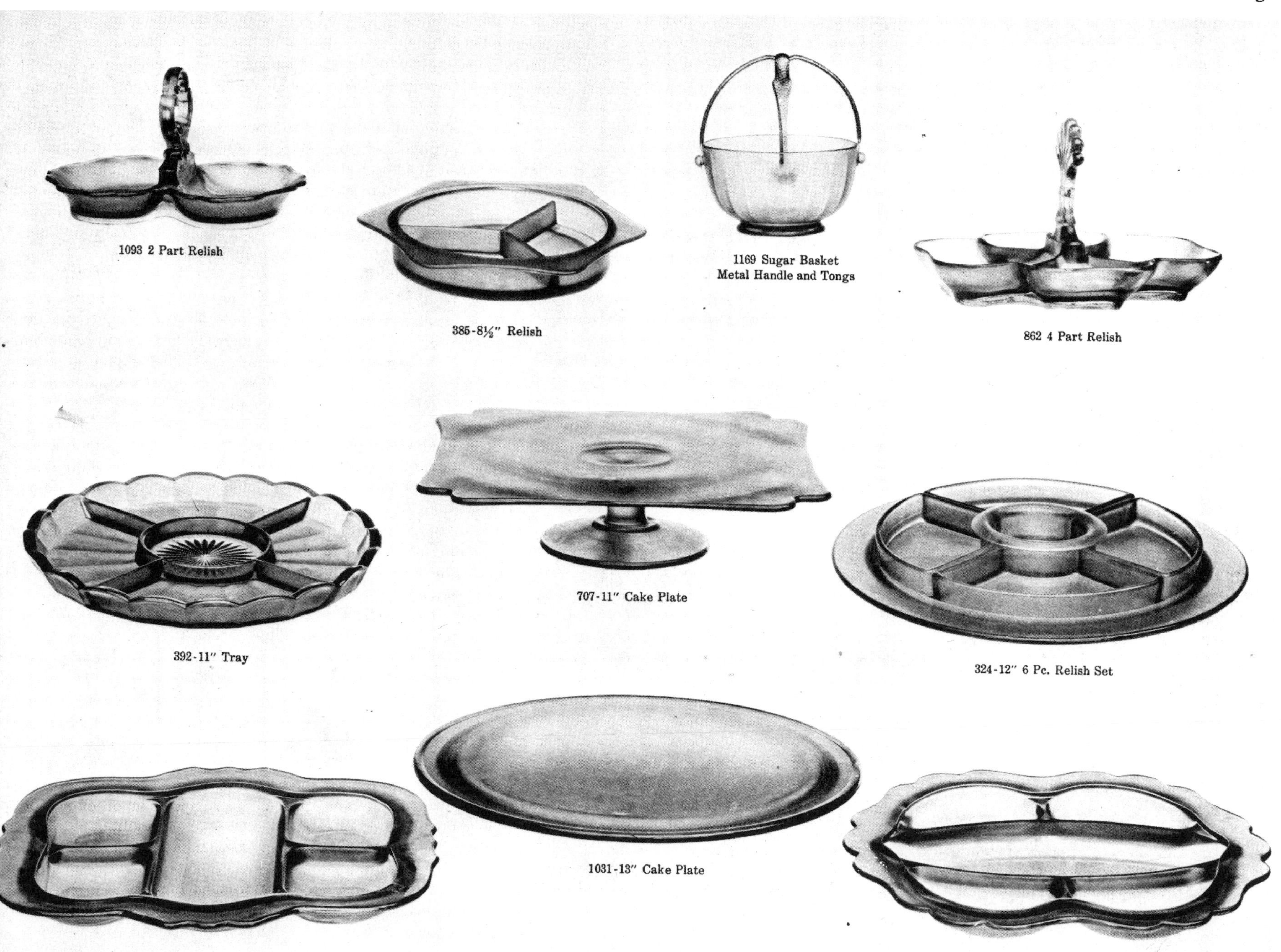

1093 2 Part Relish

385-8½" Relish

1169 Sugar Basket
Metal Handle and Tongs

862 4 Part Relish

707-11" Cake Plate

392-11" Tray

324-12" 6 Pc. Relish Set

1031-13" Cake Plate

397 Celery and Relish Tray

3400/67-12" Celery and Relish Service

Tumblers and Coasters   Sea Food or Fruit Cocktails   Hotel and Tea Room Glassware

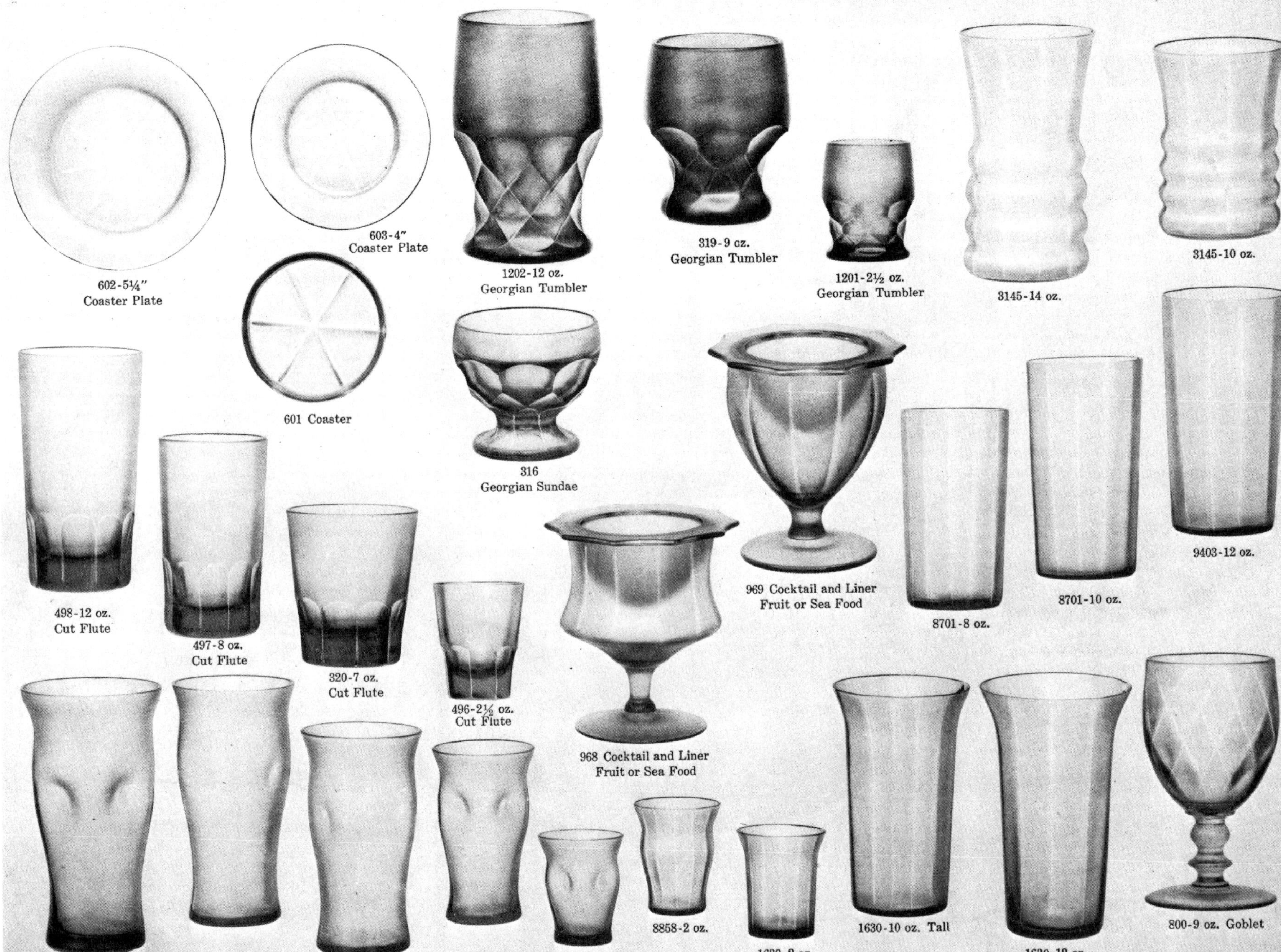

1070 PINCH TUMBLERS

1106-2½ oz. Tumbler

1105-34 oz. Cocktail Shaker Silver Top, 2 Lip

820 Serving Tray

1 Keg Set

693 2 Pc. Set (3077-3 oz. Tumbler)

1020-34 oz. Cocktail Shaker Silver Top

1021-2½ oz. Tumbler

3145-2½ oz. Tumbler

3145-32 oz. Decanter

1070-36 oz. Pinch Bottle Decanter

315-28 oz.
315-16 oz.
Decanters

3145-14 oz. Tumbler

3145-84 oz. Jug Ice Lip

Ice Pails, Candy Boxes and Bridge Sets

103-7" Candy Box
Plate Etched "725"

973/8701 5 Pc. Bridge Set
Plate Etched "726"

880/881 5 Pc. Bridge Set
Plate Etched "Golf Scene"

300-6" Candy Box
Plate Etched "520"

1215/8701 3 Pc. Set

730-½ lb. Candy Jar
Plate Etched "732"

847 Ice Tub
Plate Etched "718"

1147 Ice Tub
Plate Etched "739"

1122 Ice Tub
Plate Etched "Tulip"

864 Candy Box
Plate Etched "Cleo"

851 Ice Pail
Plate Etched "Cleo"

1121 Ice Pail
Plate Etched "Chrys"
Metal Handles and Tongs

957 Ice Pail
Plate Etched "732"

845 Ice Bucket
Metal Handle and Tongs

Ice Tea and Water Sets

1630-10 oz.
E 732

955-62 oz.
E 732

9403-12 oz.
E Cleo

124-68 oz.
E Cleo

1630-12 oz.
E "Chrys"

107-76 oz.
E "Chrys"

3077-12 oz. Ftd.
E 718

3077/10-63 oz.
E 718

1630-10 oz.
E 739

935-64 oz.
E 739

1630-12 oz.
E Tulip

119-83 oz.
E Tulip

1630-12 oz.
E 695

937-68 oz.
E 695

9403-12 oz.
E 520

937-68 oz.
E 520

SWANS

1043—8½″
This size popular for Celery Holder or Bon Bons. Makes fine Centerpiece with 2¼ in. Flower Block.

1042—6½″
This size sold either with 2¼ in. Flower Block for small Centerpiece, or with Ladle to make Mayonnaise Set. Used also as Candy Dish.

1045—13″
Table Centerpiece
with 3½ in. Flower Block.

1041 Candy Dish
1041/1050 Candle Holder

1040—3″
Individual Nut or Mint

1044—10″
Table Decoration with or without 3 in. Flower Block.

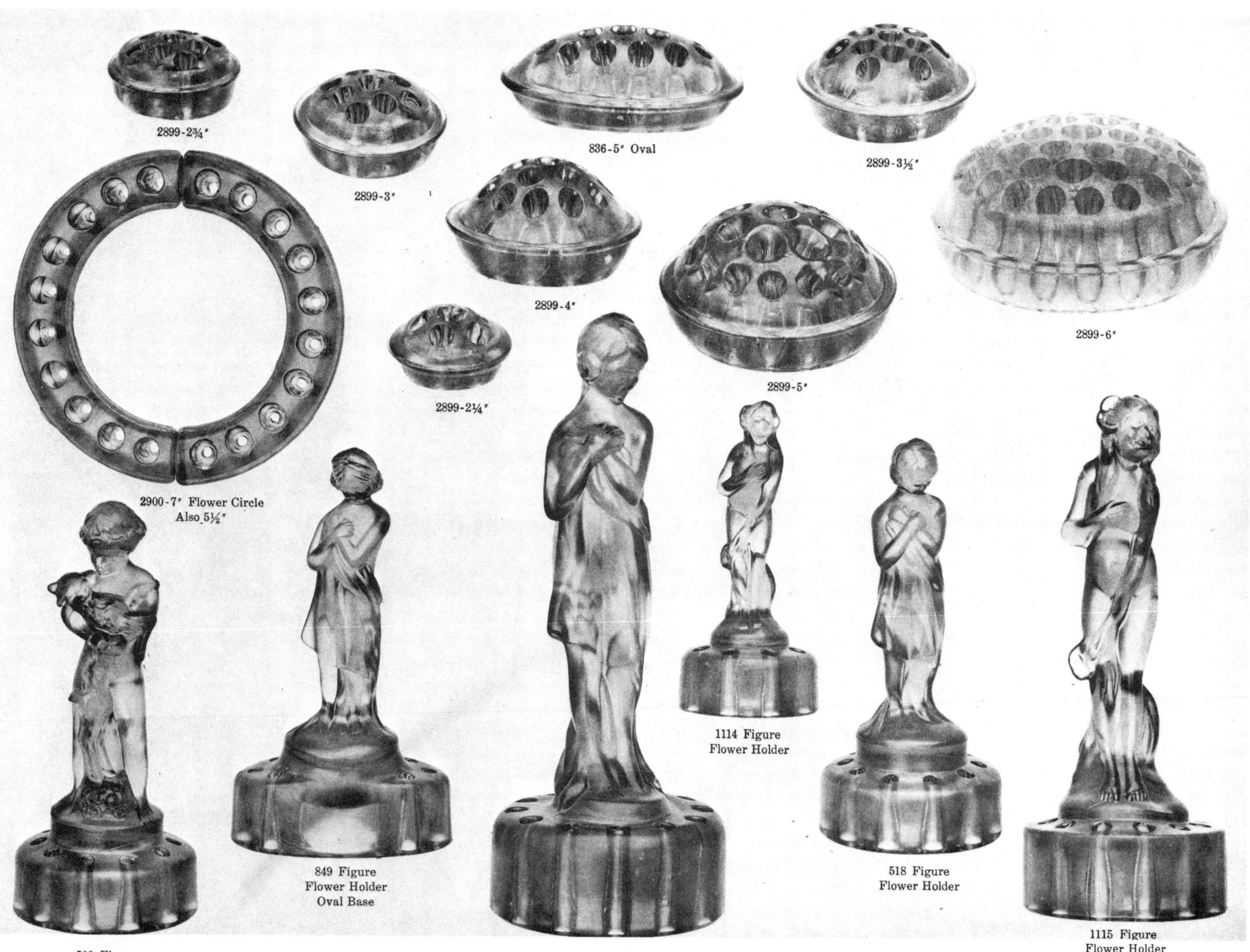
2899-2¾"
2899-3"
836-5" Oval
2899-3½"
2899-4"
2899-5"
2899-6"
2899-2¼"
2900-7" Flower Circle
Also 5½"
1114 Figure
Flower Holder
849 Figure
Flower Holder
Oval Base
518 Figure
Flower Holder
509 Figure
Flower Holder
513 Figure
Flower Holder
1115 Figure
Flower Holder

Vases

1002 1½ Gal. Aquarium
Etched "736"

277-9"
Etched "737"

1130-11"

779-14"
Etched "Dragon"

797-8"
Etched "Martha"

1023-9½"
Etched "741"

275-10″
Etched "724"

276-10″
Etched "724"

272-10″
Etched "743"

274-10″
Etched "743"

280-12″
Etched "724"

281-12″
Etched "724"

278-11″
Etched "724"

84-12″
Etched "724"

Vases

1005-6½″
Etched "732"

279-13″
Etched "742"

1037-10″
Etched "725/737"

782-8″
Etched "717"

402-12″
Etched "741"

639
687
646
747
624
625
627
630
227½
647
638
878
636-9½"
628

Smokers Articles

212 Match Holder

117 Ash Tray "Oval"

112 Ash Tray

Moistener for Humidor

130 Ind. Ash Tray

617 Cigarette Jar

1025 Cigar Humidor
Ash Tray Cover

885 Cigarette Jar
Ash Tray Cover

387-2½" Ash Tray
388-4" " "

390-6" Ash Tray
391-8" " "

882 Tobacco Humidor
Ash Tray Cover

616 Cigarette Box

615 Cigarette Box

883 Ash Tray
Use in sets with 885 Jar

607 Cigarette Box

1208 Cigarette Box
2 Compartment

430 Cigarette Box

605 Cigarette Box

Bathroom Bottles

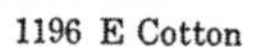
1196 E Cotton

897 E Epsom Salts

895 E Toilet Water

894 E Boric Acid

896 E Bath Salts

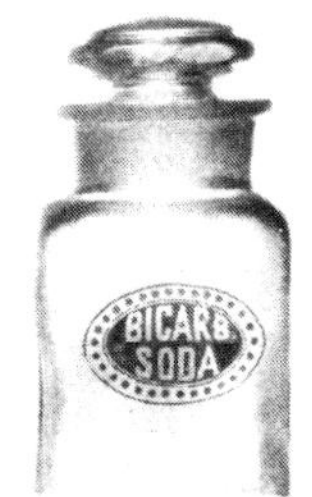

1194 E Bicarb. Soda

1195 E Witch Hazel

1198 Tray 6″ x 6″

1197 Tray 15″ x 3½″

1197 Tray
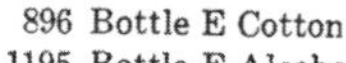
1194 Bottle E Bicarb. Soda
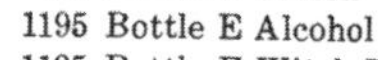
1194 Bottle E Boric Acid
896 Bottle E Cotton
1195 Bottle E Alcohol
1195 Bottle E Witch Hazel

1198 Tray
896 E Bath Salts
1195 E Hand Lotion
1195 E Toilet Water
1195 E Mouth Wash

1198 Tray
1196 E Bath Salts
897 E Boric Acid
897 E Bicarb. Soda
897 E Epsom Salts

1197 Tray
895 Bottle E Listerine
895 Bottle E Witch Hazel
1196 Bottle E Cotton
897 Bottle E Epsom Salts
897 Bottle E Boric Acid

3120 Stemware Crystal "Majestic"

628-3½" Candlestick

676-11½" Bowl

628-3½" Candlestick

10 oz. Footed Tumbler

6 oz. Fruit Salad

9 oz. Goblet

4½ oz. Oyster Cocktail

12 oz. Footed Tumbler

5 oz. Footed Tumbler

3 oz. Cocktail

6 oz. Low Sherbet

8 oz. Footed Tumbler

6 oz. Tall Sherbet

556-8" Plate

3400 Line Rock Crystal Engraved "541"

3400/1182-6" Basket

3400/627 Candlestick

3400/2-12½" Bowl

3400/627 Candlestick

3400/13-6" Comport

3400/14-7" Tall Comport

3400/16 Sugar

3400/16 Cream

3400/4-12" Bowl

3400/3-11" Low Ftd. Bowl

3400/9-7" Candy Box

3400/17-12" Vase

3400/11 3 Pc. Mayonnaise Set

3400/851 Ice Pail
Metal Handle and Tongs

3400/1-13" Bowl

3400/1180-5¼" Jelly

3400/6-11½" Cheese and Cracker

3400/1181-6" Plate

3400/1179-5½" Mint

3400/10-11" Hdl. Sandwich Tray

3400 Line Engraved "542"

3400/11 3 Pc. Mayonnaise Set

3400/627 Candlestick

3400/2-12½" Bowl

3400/627 Candlestick

3400/14-7" Tall Comport

3400/16 Sugar

3400/3-11" Low Ftd. Bowl

3400/4-12" Bowl

3400/16 Cream

3400/9-7" Candy Box

3400/1185-10" Bowl

3400/1188-11" Bowl

3400/1-13" Bowl

3400/8-11½" Sandwich Plate

3400/6-11½" Cheese and Cracker

3400/1186-12½" Plate

3400/10-11" Hdl. Sandwich Tray

3130 Stemware Rock Crystal Engraving "538"

8 oz. Goblet

Fingerbowl and Plate

597-8" Plate

6 oz. Tall Sherbet

6 oz. Low Sherbet

3 oz. Cocktail

2½ oz. Footed Tumbler

5 oz. Footed Tumbler

8 oz. Footed Tumbler

10 oz. Footed Tumbler

12 oz. Footed Tumbler

Engraved "538" Crystal

628-3½" Candlestick

676-11½" Bowl

628-3½" Candlestick

441-10½" Comport

944 Sugar

674-13" Bowl

278-11" Vase

104-6" Candy Box and Cover

533 3 Pc. Mayonnaise Set

944 Cream

532-6½" Tall Comport

135-10" Cheese and Cracker

168-10" Hdl. Sandwich Tray

173-12" Hdl. Sandwich Tray "Oval"

Rock Crystal Composition Engraving "479"

272-10" Vase

758-5½" Bon Bon

869-5½" Comport

1096 Sugar

1096 Cream

533-6¼" Comport

760-7" Basket

1075-5" Bon Bon

158 Marmalade and Cover

64-5¼" Comport

759-7" Plate

749-6¼" Bon Bon

1917/255 3 Toed Mayonnaise Bowl

1917/92 3 Toed Card Tray

Rock Crystal Bon Bons Engraving "497"

1182-6"

1179-5½"

1180-5¼"

1181-6"

Engraved "515" Crystal

977-11" Basket

627-4" Candlestick

856-11" Bowl

627-4" Candlestick

1090-7" Tall Comport

867 Sugar

867 Cream

873 3 Pc. Mayonnaise Set

877-11½" Comport

971-8½" Bowl

984-10" Bowl

851 Ice Pail
Metal Handle and Tongs

842-12" Bowl

278-11" Vase

972-11" Plate

870-11" Hdl. Sandwich Tray

868-11" Cheese and Cracker

628-3½" Candlestick

676-11½" Bowl

628-3½" Candlestick

674-13" Bowl

300-6" Candy Box and Cover

533 3 Pc. Mayonnaise Set

441-10½" Comport

487-12" Cheese and Cracker "Oval"

135-10" Cheese and Cracker

168-10" Hdl. Sandwich Tray

173-12" Hdl. Sandwich Tray "Oval"

"Springtime"

1250-6" Vase

1251-8" Vase

1252-10" Vase

1009-6" Vase

646-5" Candlestick

1256-11" Oval Bowl
849 Figure Flower Holder
(Oval Base)

646-5" Candlestick

1008-12" Vase

1253-12" Vase

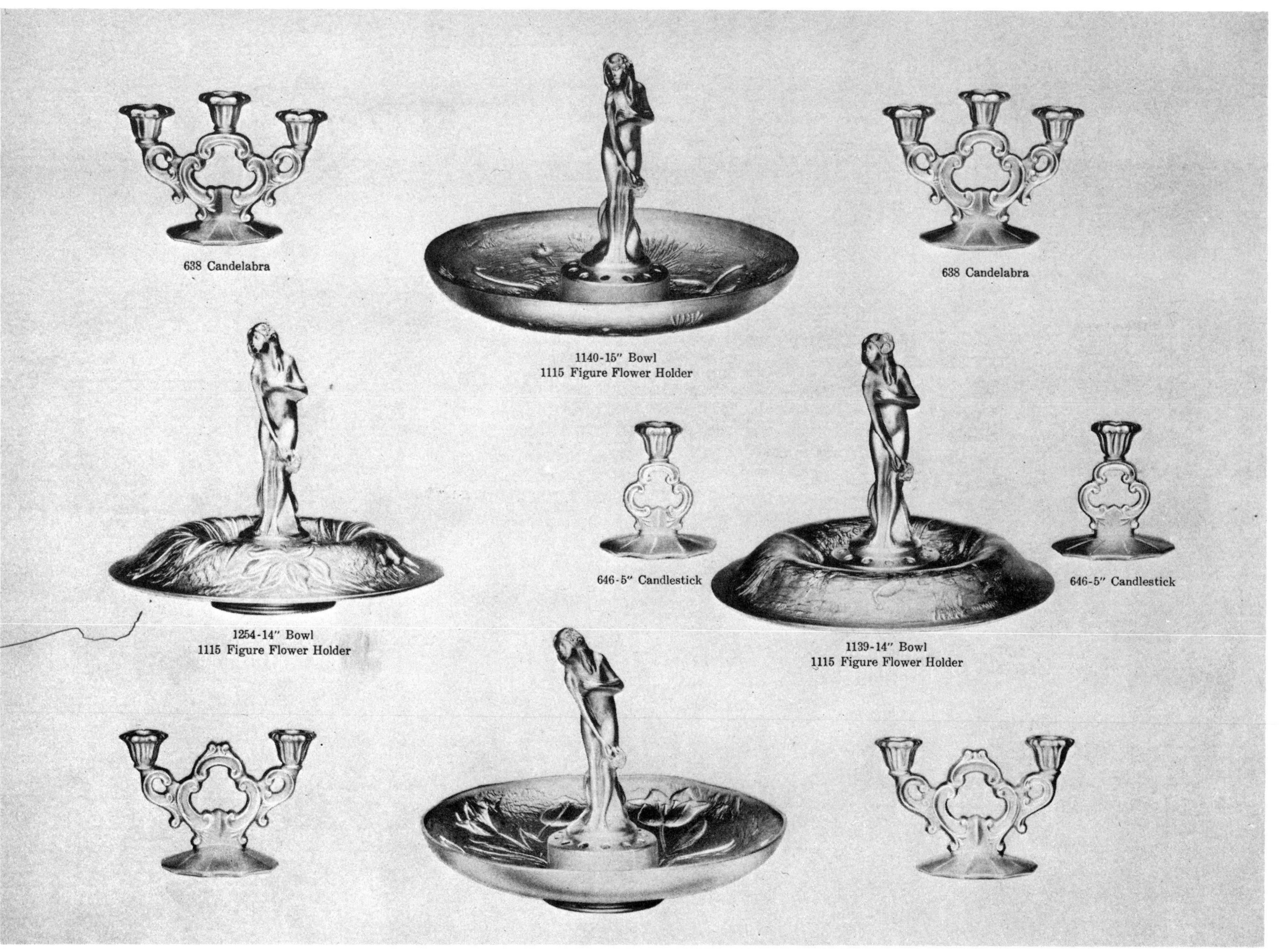

638 Candelabra

1140-15" Bowl
1115 Figure Flower Holder

638 Candelabra

1254-14" Bowl
1115 Figure Flower Holder

646-5" Candlestick

1139-14" Bowl
1115 Figure Flower Holder

646-5" Candlestick

647 Candelabra

1255-15" Bowl
1115 Figure Flower Holder

647 Candelabra

Table Centers

638 Candelabra

1151-12¾" Bowl
518 Figure Flower Holder

638 Candelabra

1152-10" Bowl
1114 Figure Flower Holder

1155 Candlestick

1155 Candlestick

646-5" Candlestick

1153-10½" Bowl
1114 Figure Flower Holder

646-5" Candlestick

647 Candelabra

1150-12½" Bowl
518 Figure Flower Holder

647 Candelabra

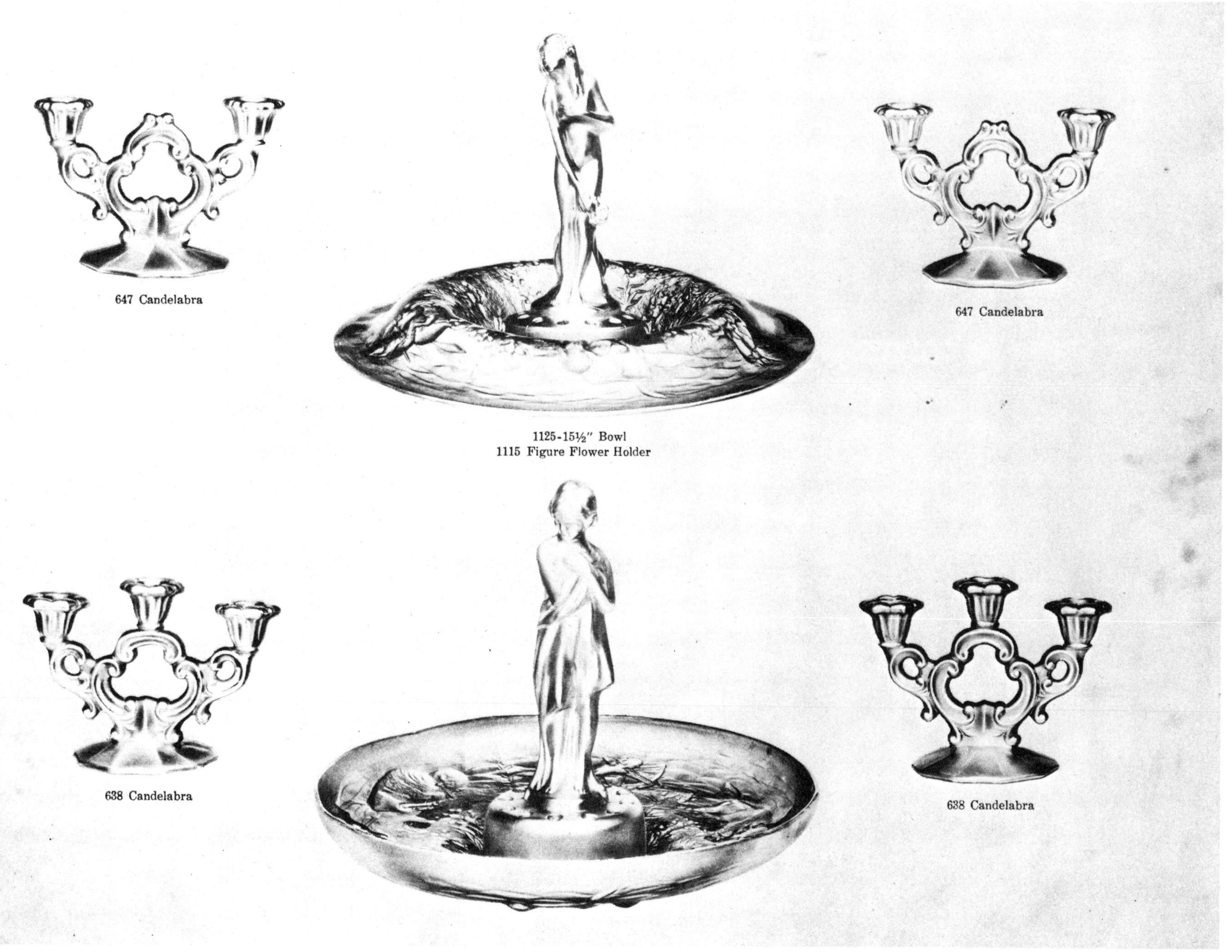

647 Candelabra

647 Candelabra

1125-15½" Bowl
1115 Figure Flower Holder

638 Candelabra

638 Candelabra

1126-16" Bowl
513 Figure Flower Holder

Table Centers

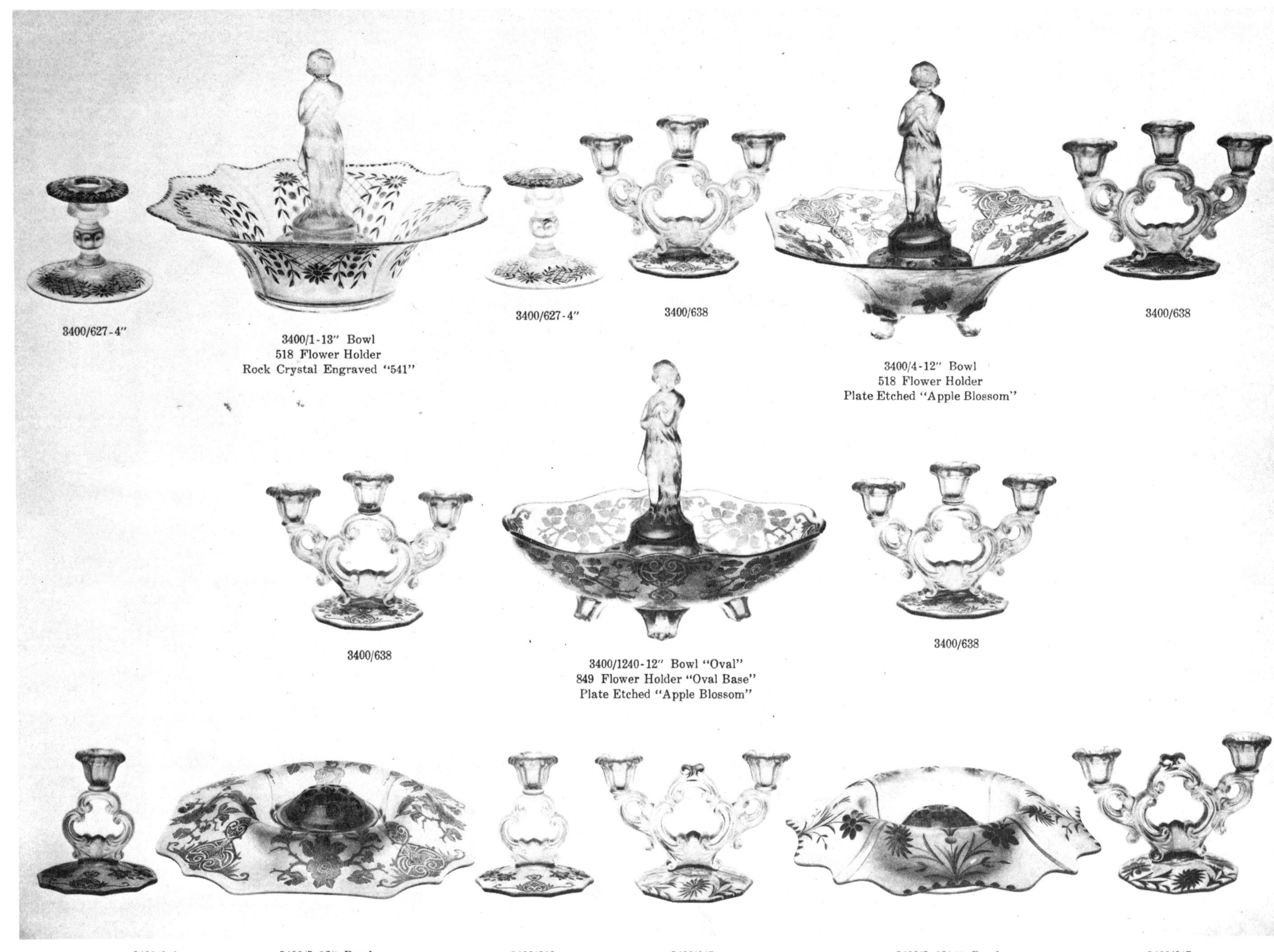

3400/627-4"

3400/1-13" Bowl
518 Flower Holder
Rock Crystal Engraved "541"

3400/627-4"

3400/638

3400/4-12" Bowl
518 Flower Holder
Plate Etched "Apple Blossom"

3400/638

3400/638

3400/1240-12" Bowl "Oval"
849 Flower Holder "Oval Base"
Plate Etched "Apple Blossom"

3400/638

3400/646

3400/5-12" Bowl
2899-3½" Flower Block
Plate Etched "Apple Blossom"

3400/646

3400/647

3400/2-12½" Bowl
2899-3½" Flower Block
Engraved "542"

3400/647

747

732 Refectory Bowl
836-5½" Oval Flower Block
Plate Etched "741"

747

628-3½"

674-13" Bowl
518 Flower Holder
Plate Etched "520"

628-3½"

628-3½"

676-11½" Bowl
2899-3½" Flower Block
Plate Etched "732"

628-3½"

628-3½"

673-15" Bowl
1115 Flower Holder
Plate Etched "704"

628-3½"

Table Centers

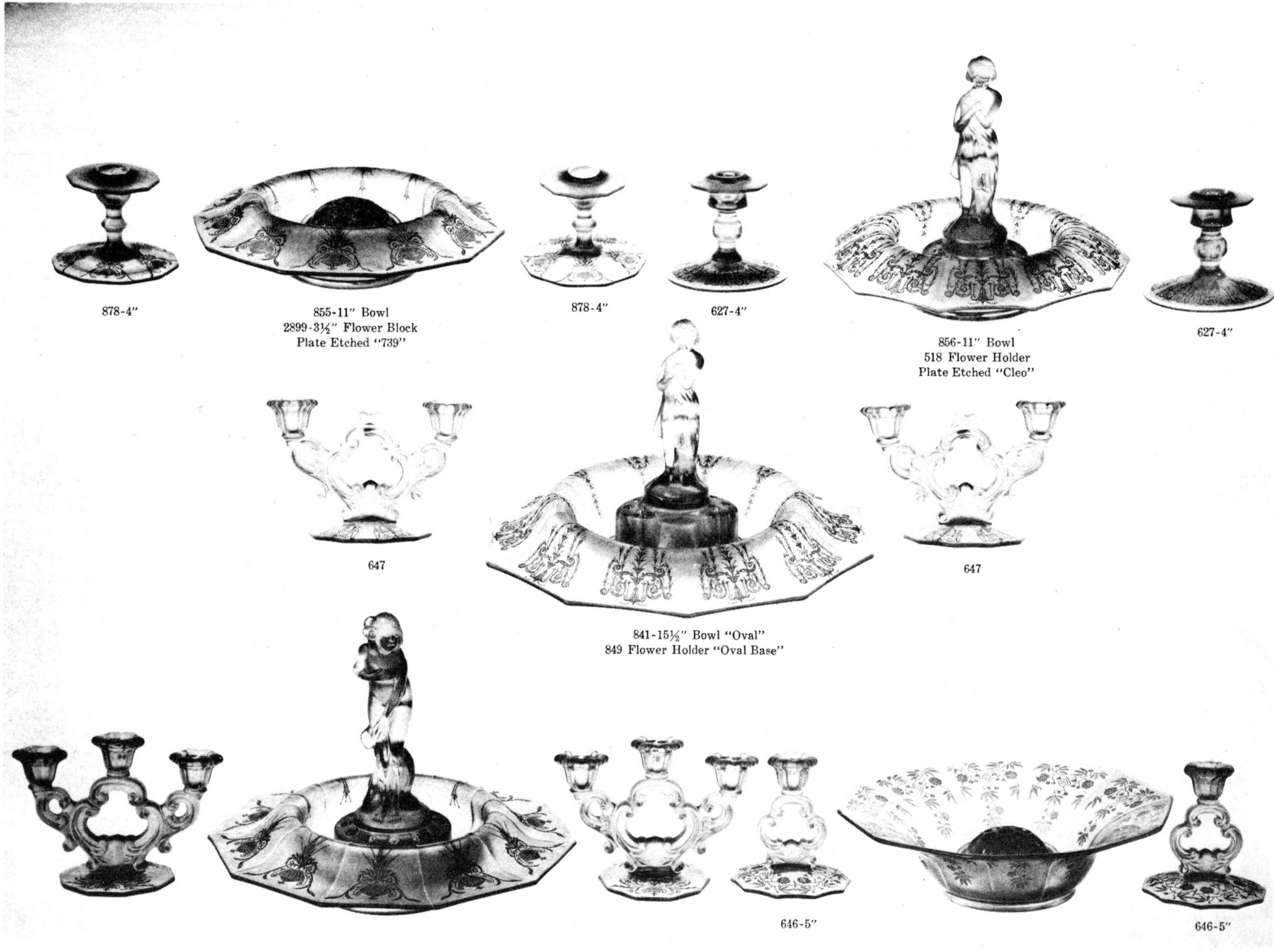

878-4″

855-11″ Bowl
2899-3½″ Flower Block
Plate Etched "739"

878-4″

627-4″

856-11″ Bowl
518 Flower Holder
Plate Etched "Cleo"

627-4″

647

841-15½″ Bowl "Oval"
849 Flower Holder "Oval Base"

647

646-5″

646-5″

638

857-14″ Bowl
1115 Flower Holder
Plate Etched "739"

638

842-12″ Bowl
2899-3½″ Flower Block
Plate Etched "731"

627-4″

842-12″ Bowl
518 Flower Holder

627-4″

1192-6″

1235-9½″ Bowl
518 Flower Holder

1192-6″

630-4″

993-12½″ Bowl
2899-3½″ Flower Block

630-4″

637-3½″

675-9½″ Bowl
2899-2¾″ Flower Block

637-3½″

987-11″ Bowl
1114 Flower Holder

639-4″

3400 Line Plate Etched 746 "Gloria"

3400/627 Candle

3400/5-12" Bowl 4-Toed

3400/627 Candle

3400/1-13" Bowl

3400/10-11" Hdl. Sandwich Tray

3400/6-11½" Cheese and Cracker

3400/15-4" Comport

3400/707-11" Footed Cake Plate

3400/851 Ice Pail
Metal Handle and Tongs.

3400/65-14" Chop or Salad Plate

3400/9-7" Candy Box and Cover

3400/11 3 Pc. Mayonnaise Set

3400 Line Plate Etched 746 "Gloria"

3400/1192-6" Candle

3400/4-12" Bowl

3400/1192-6" Candle

3400/1240-12" Bowl "Oval"

3400/17-12" Vase

3400/1185-10" Bowl

3400/23-10" Vase

3400 Dinnerware Plate Etched 746 "Gloria"

3400/53-6" Cereal

3400/68 Sugar

3400/68 Cream

3400/54 Cup and Saucer

3400/69 After Dinner Cup and Saucer

3400/55 Cream Soup and Saucer

3400/18 Salt and Pepper

3400/67-12" Celery and Relish Service

3400/62-8½" Salad Plate

3400/51-10" Baker

3400/1174 Bread and Butter Plate
3400/1176 Salad Plate
3400/1177 Dinner Plate
3400/1178 Service Plate

3400 Dinnerware Plate Etched 746 "Gloria"

3400/52-5½" Butter and Cover

3400/16-6 oz. Ftd. Sugar and Cream

3400/56-5½" Fruit Saucer

3400/60-6" Bread and Butter Plate

3400/59-9" Pickle Tray

3400/57-11½" Platter

3400/8-11½" Two Hdl. Sandwich Plate

3400/61-7½" Tea Plate

3400/63-9½" Dinner Plate

3400/1177 Dinner Plate

3400/1188-11" Fruit Bowl

3400/22-10" Salad Plate

3400/21-9" Salad Bowl

3400 Line Plate Etched 746 "Gloria"

3400/1179-5½" Bon Bon

3400/1181-6" Plate

3400/1180-5¼" Bon Bon

3400/1182-6" Basket

3400/25-5" Ftd. Bon Bon

3400/1093 Relish Tray

3400/862 Relish Tray

3400/26-5½" Ftd. Bon Bon

3135 Stemware Plate Etched 746 "Gloria"

Finger Bowl and Plate

6 oz. Fruit Salad

4½ oz. Oyster Cocktail

3400/14-7" Tall Comport

6 oz. Low Sherbet

8 oz. Goblet

12 oz. Footed Tumbler

10 oz. Footed Tumbler

5 oz. Footed Tumbler

1 oz. Cordial

6 oz. Tall Sherbet

3130 Stemware Plate Etched 746 "Gloria"

12 oz. Ftd. Tumbler

6 oz. Fruit Salad

2½ oz. Wine

8 oz. Goblet

10 oz. Ftd. Tumbler

2½ oz. Ftd. Tumbler
To be used with Shaker

5 oz. Ftd. Tumbler

3400/78 Cocktail Shaker
Ground in Stopper with
Opening for Pouring.

6 oz. Low Sherbet

6 oz. Tall Sherbet

3120 Stemware Plate Etched 746 "Gloria"

Finger Bowl and Plate

12 oz. Footed Tumbler

1 oz. Cordial

4½ oz. Claret

9 oz. Goblet

10 oz. Footed Tumbler

5 oz. Footed Tumbler

1205-64 oz. Jug and Cover

6 oz. Low Sherbet

6 oz. Tall Sherbet

3115 Stemware Plate Etched "742"

597-8⅜" Salad Plate

6 oz. Fruit Salad

12 oz. Footed Tumbler

9 oz. Goblet

3½ oz. Cocktail

8 oz. Footed Tumbler

10 oz. Footed Tumbler

1205-64 oz. Jug

6 oz. Low Sherbet

6 oz. Tall Sherbet

Round Dinnerware Plate Etched "704"

933 Cup and Saucer

922 Cream Soup and Saucer

944 Cream

925 After Dinner
Cup and Saucer

944 Sugar

556-8″ Plate

901-12½″ Service Tray Oval

652-11″ Celery Tray

3060 Stemware Plate Etched "704"

12 oz. Footed Tumbler

5 oz. Parfait

Finger Bowl and Plate

4½ oz. Oyster Cocktail

6 oz. Tall Sherbet

2 oz. Tumbler

955-62 oz. Jug

9 oz. Goblet

12 oz. Tumbler

10 oz. Tumbler

1098-5½" Fruit

1096 Sugar

1096 Cream

865 Cup and Saucer

1101-3½" Cranberry Dish

1012-8½" Soup Plate

1083-11" Celery Tray

597-8⅜" Plate

3115 Stemware Plate Etched "731"

10 oz. Footed Tumbler

3½ oz. Cocktail

Finger Bowl and Plate

6 oz. Tall Sherbet

9 oz. Goblet

12 oz. Footed Tumbler

8 oz. Footed Tumbler

955-62 oz. Jug

2½ oz. Footed Tumbler

6 oz. Low Sherbet

628-3½" Candlestick

676-11½" Bowl

628-3½" Candlestick

533 3 Pc. Mayonnaise Set

278-11" Vase

532-6½" Tall Comport

441-10½" Comport

674-13" Bowl

135-10" Cheese and Cracker

168-10" Hdl. Sandwich Tray

173-12" Hdl. Sandwich Tray "Oval"

3135 Stemware "Rock Crystal" Engraved "539"

8 oz. Goblet

3 oz. Cocktail

Finger Bowl and Plate

556-8" Plate

2½ oz. Footed Tumbler

5 oz. Footed Tumbler

10 oz. Footed Tumbler

6 oz. Tall Sherbet

6 oz. Low Sherbet

12 oz. Footed Tumbler

627-4" Candlestick

856-11" Bowl

627-4" Candlestick

977-11" Basket

867 Sugar

867 Cream

1090-7" Tall Comport

873 3 Pc. Mayonnaise Set

877-11½" Comport

971-8½" Bowl

984-10" Bowl

851 Ice Pail
Metal Handle and Tongs

278-11" Vase

842-12" Bowl

870-11" Hdl. Sandwich Tray

972-11" Plate

868-11" Cheese and Cracker

Engraved "534" Assortment

867 Sugar

867 Cream

873 3 Pc. Mayonnaise Set

972-11″ Plate

977-11″ Basket

842-12″ Bowl

627 Candlestick

856-11″ Bowl

627 Candlestick

971-8½″ Bowl

984-10″ Bowl

877-11″ Comport

868-11″ Cheese and Cracker

870-11″ Sandwich Tray

Lustre Cut Prism Candlesticks

Patented Lock Bobeche

1270-6½″

1271-7″

1273-10½″

1269-11″

1272-10½″

Miscellaneous

609 Salad Fork

609 Salad Spoon

1257 Shaker Glass Top

1265 Shaker Glass Top

1266 Shaker Glass Top

1260 Shaker Glass Top

1222 Turkey

3200 Punch Cup

1262 Shaker Glass Top

1111 Heron Flower Holder

3200 Punch Bowl and Foot

30 Base for Bowls

214-10″ Handled Tray

1074-17″ Handled Tray

321-9 oz. Tumbler
Cut Flute
Plate Etched "Gloria"

3077-8″ Salad Plate

3140 Footed Sherbet

3140 Hot Coffee Glass

499-21 oz. Tumbler
Cut Flute
Plate Etched "Gloria

1226-10″ 2-Handled Plate
Plate Etched "Lorna"

3140-10 oz.
Footed Tumbler

1225-9″ 2-Handled Bowl
Plate Etched "Lorna"

3400/33-11¼″ Bowl
Plate Etched "Apple Blossom"

1243-10″ Vase
Aero Optic

3400/32-11½″ Bowl
Plate Etched "Apple Blossom"

3015 Stemware Plate Etched "748" Lorna

10 oz. Footed Tumbler

6 oz. Fruit Salad

Finger Bowl and Plate

2½ oz. Cocktail

9 oz. Goblet

6 oz. Low Sherbet

12 oz. Footed Tumbler

935-64 oz. Jug

6 oz. Tall Sherbet

5 oz. Footed Tumbler

2½ oz. Wine

Decagon Dinnerware Plate Etched "748" Lorna

865 Cup and Saucer

867 Sugar

867 Cream

1075 Cream Soup and Saucer

749-6¼" 2-Handled Bon Bon

968/698 Fruit Cocktail Set

1098-5½" Fruit

1087-9½" Vegetable, Oval

597-8⅜" Salad Plate

1068-11" 2-Part Relish

3035 Stemware Plate Etched "746" Gloria

6 oz. Fruit Salad

9 oz. Goblet

2½ oz. Wine

4½ oz. Oyster Cocktail

6 oz. Low Sherbet

12 oz. Footed Tumbler

10 oz. Footed Tumbler

6 oz. Tall Sherbet

3 oz. Cocktail

4½ oz. Claret

5 oz. Footed Tumbler

Plate Etching 746 "Gloria'

3400/76 Shaker Glass Top

3400/77 Shaker Glass Top

1228-9" Vase, Oval

3400/90-8" 2-Handled Relish

3400/91-8" 3-Handled Relish

1242-11" Vase

3400/82-6" Square Cereal

3400/75 Square Cup and Saucer

3400/81-5" Square Fruit Saucer

3400/85 Square Cream Soup and Saucer

3400/74-5" Comport

3400/71-3" Ind. Nut

3400/13-6" Comport

3400/70-3½" Cranberry

3400/83 Square After Dinner Cup and Saucer

3025 Stemware Plate Etched 744 "Apple Blossom"

12 oz. Footed Tumbler

Finger Bowl and Plate

10 oz. Goblet

7 oz. Low Sherbet

4 oz. Footed Tumbler

10 oz. Footed Tumbler

4½ oz. Oyster Cocktail

7 oz. Tall Sherbet

935-64 oz. Jug

1066 Stemware

11 oz. Goblet

5 oz. Claret

3 oz. Cocktail

7 oz. Tall Sherbet

6 oz. Fruit Salad

12 oz. Footed Tumbler

10 oz. Footed Tumbler

8 oz. Footed Tumbler

5 oz. Footed Tumbler

3 oz. Footed Tumbler

"Victorian Period" Glassware

18-12" Footed Vase

41-1 Lb. Candy Jar and Cover

5-10½" Bowl
4-9" Bowl

17-7½" Fan Vase

21-8¼" Salad Plate
23-12½" Plate

1-Sugar

1-Cream

34-8 oz. Goblet

36-6 oz. Footed Sherbet

35-10 oz. Footed Ice Tea

3-10" Candlestick

9-10" Comport

3-10" Candlestick

-4" Candlestick

26-13½" Bowl
25-10½" Bowl

19-Sugar

19-Cream

16-10" Sweet Pea Vase

54-8 oz. Stein
Footed and Handled

55-10 oz. Stein
Footed and Handled

56-12 oz. Stein
Footed and Handled

52-Finger Bowl
53-Finger Bowl Plate

47-7 oz. Fruit Salad

46-5 oz. Footed
Tomato or Orange Juice

48-8 oz. Footed Tumbler

49-10 oz. Footed Tumbler

50-12 oz. Footed Tumbler

10-5½" Comport

6-10" Bowl, Cupped

57-5¼" Fruit Saucer

20-6⅜" Bread and Butter Plate

Miscellaneous

1214-12" Vase

1193-12" Vase

1210-10" Vase

1236 Ivy Ball

1192-6" Candlestick

1191 Candlestick

1209 Candlestick

1211 Candelabra

Vases

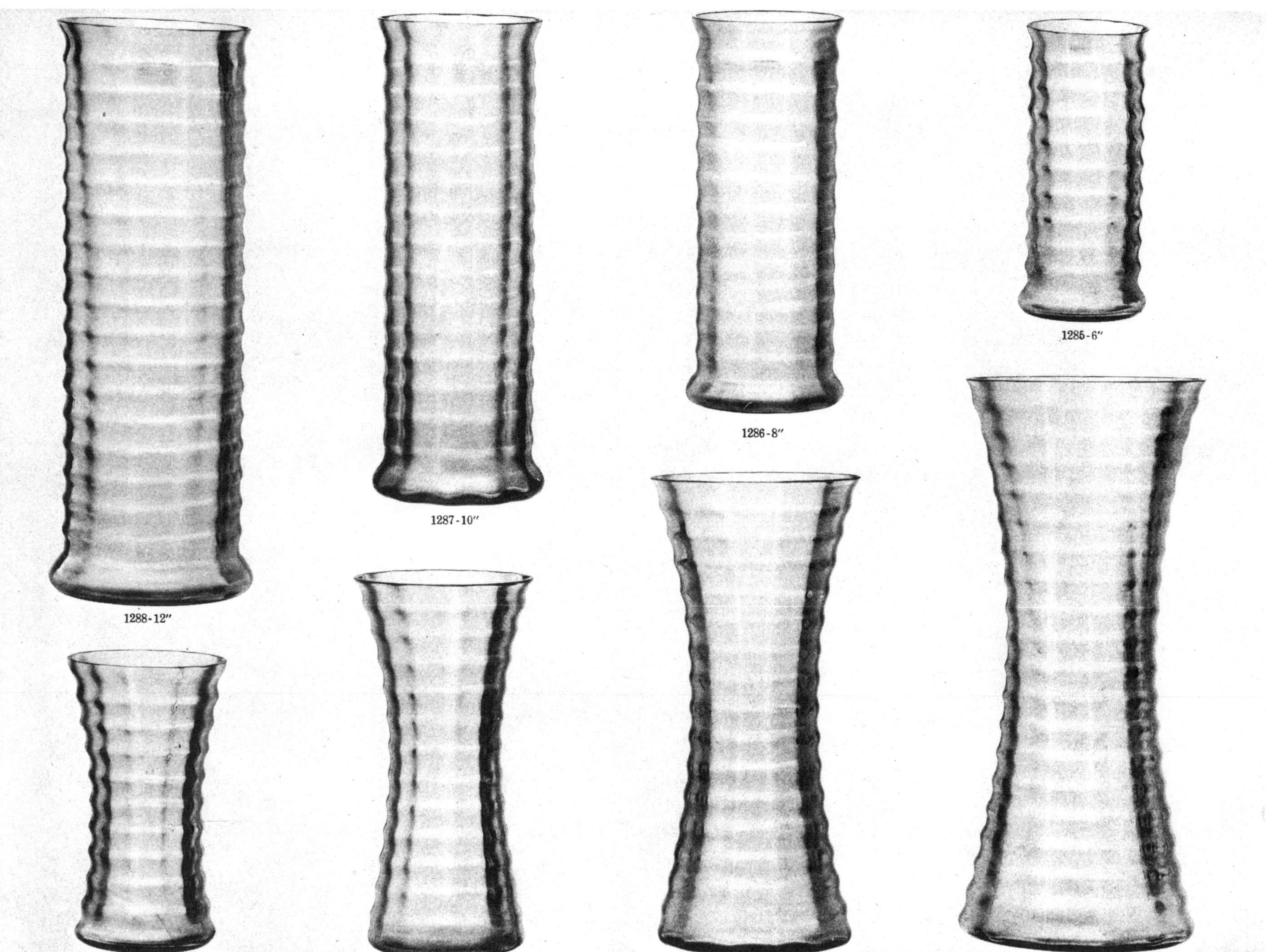

1288-12″

1287-10″

1286-8″

1285-6″

1289-6″

1290-8″

1291-10″

1292-12″

Ebony Silver Decorated Ware

3400/68 Sugar and Cream
D/970-S

1093 2-Compt. Relish
D/970-S

862 4-Compt. Relish
D/973-S

867 Sugar and Cream
D/973-S

1090-7" Comport
D/971-S

1020 Cocktail
Shaker 2-Lip
Chrom. Top
D/970-S

1070 36-oz.
Pinch Bottle
D/970-S

851 Ice Pail
Chrom. Plated Hdl.
D/971-S

935-64 oz. Jug
D/973-S

3400/67 Celery and Relish
D/970-S

1084-13" 2-Hdl. Tray
D/975-S

870-11" Hdl. Sandwich Tray
D/975-S

Ebony Silver Decorated Ware

1228-9″ Oval Vase
D/970-S

638 3-Holder Candelabra
D/971-S

1240-12″ Oval Bowl
D/971-S

646-4″ Candlestick
D/970-S

782-8″ Vase
D/975-S

779-14″ Vase
D/971-S

3400/17-12″ Vase
D/972-S

1242-10″ Vase
D/973-S

274-10″
Bud Vase
D/971-S

1130-11″ Ftd. Vase
D/972-S

402-12″ Vase
D/970-S

Ebony Silver Decorated Ware

856-11" R. E. Bowl
D/973-S

1185-10" 2-Hdl. Bowl
D/970-S

3400/5-12" 4-toed Bowl, F. R. E.
D/971-S

984-10" 2-Hdl. Bowl
D/973-S

3400/4-12" 4-toed Bowl
D/970-S

842-12¼" Bowl, Belled
D/975-S

3400/10-11" Hdl. Sandwich Tray
D/971-S

1186-12½" 2-Hdl. Plate
D/971-S

972-11" 2-Hdl. Plate
D/975-S

3400/10-10" Handled Sandwich Tray
D/971-S

3400/14-7" Tall Comport
D/971-S

3400/1185-10" 2-Hdl. Bowl
D/971-S

646-5" Candlestick
D/971-S

3400/5-12" Bowl
D/971-S

646-5" Candlestick
D/971-S

3400/4-12" Bowl, Flared
D/970-S

1242-10" Vase
D/970-S

1070-36 oz. Pinch Decanter
D/970-S

3400/1186-12½" 2-Hdl. Plate
D/970-S

3400/38-80 oz. Ball Shaped Jug
D/971-S

Ice Tea Sets

3400/38-80 oz. Jug
3400/38-12 oz. Tumbler

3400/38-80 oz. Jug E/Apple Blossom
3400/38-12 oz. Tumbler E/Apple Blossom

3400/38-80 oz. Jug E/Lorna
3400/38-12 oz. Tumbler E/Lorna

3400/38-80 oz. Jug E/Gloria
3400/38-12 oz. Tumbler E/Gloria

3400/27-67 oz. Jug
3400/27-12 oz. Tumbler

3400/27-67 oz. Jug E/Gloria
3400/27-12 oz. Tumbler E/Gloria

3400/27-67 oz. Jug E/Lorna
3400/27-12 oz. Tumbler E/Lorna

3400/27-67 oz. Jug E/Apple Blossom
3400/27-12 oz. Tumbler E/Apple Blossom

1309-5"
E/Apple Blossom

1305-10"
E/Gloria

1233-9½"
E/Lorna

1238-12"
E/Gloria

1237-9"
E/Lorna

1239-14"
E/Gloria

1308-6"
E/Apple Blossom

1234-12"
E/Apple Blossom

Vases

1284-10″
E/Gloria

1300-8″
E/Apple Blossom

1303-7″
E/Lorna

1283-8″
E/Apple Blossom

1295-10″
E/Lorna

1298-13″
E/Lorna

1297-11″
E/Gloria

1299-11″
E/Gloria

1301-10″
E/Apple Blossom

1296-12″
E/Apple Blossom

489 4 Pc. Boudoir Set

1043-8½" Swan with 2¾" Flower Block

397 5 Compt. Celery and Relish

862 4 Compt. Relish

1095 3 Pc. Sugar and Cream Set

955-62 oz. Refrigerator Jug with Flat Cover

1256-11" Oval Bowl

1252-10" Vase

1253-12" Vase

1223-5" Candlestick

1224-11" Oval Bowl

1223-5" Candlestick

Business Stimulators

880/8701 5 Pc. Bridge Set

214-10" Tray

1025 Cigar Humidor and Cover with Moistener.

607 Cigarette Box and Cover

880/8701 5 Pc. Bridge Set E/740

882-Tobacco Humidor with Moistener as shown in cut of 1025.

1070-36 oz. Pinch Decanter
1070-2 oz. Pinch Tumbler

3145-32 oz. Decanter
3145-2½ oz. Tumbler

3145-84 oz. Jug, Ice Lipped
3145-14 oz. Tumbler

3400/90 2 Hdl. 2 Compt. Relish
E/Cleo

1012-8½" Bowl
E/Cleo

608-6½" Low Comport
E/731

3400/13-6" 4 Toed Comport
E/Cleo

3077-22 oz. Jug and Cover
E/Cleo

197-6 oz. Oil, G. S. Tall
E/Cleo

1308-6" Vase
E/731

1147 Ice Tub, Open Handles
E/731

871 2 Hdl. Mayonnaise and Ladle
E/731

532-6½" Comport
E/731

Sport Novelties

9403-14 oz. Tumbler
D/983

9403-12 oz. Tumbler
D/984

9403-14 oz. Tumbler
D/985

9403-12 oz. Tumbler
D/986

9403-12 oz. Tumbler
D/987

9403-14 oz. Tumbler
D/988

9403-12 oz. Tumbler
D/989

320-7 oz. Tumbler
D/983

320-7 oz. Tumbler
D/985

320-7 oz. Tumbler
D/987

320-7 oz. Tumbler
D/989

693/3000 2 Pc. Canape Set
D/983

693/3000 2 Pc. Canape Set
D/985

693/3000 2 Pc. Canape Set
D/987

693/3000 2 Pc. Canape Set
D/989

Miscellaneous

1274-13½" 2-Light
Lustre Cut Prism Candelabrum

1268 2-Light
Lustre Cut Prism Candelabrum

1274-13½" 2-Light
Lustre Cut Prism Candelabrum
Rock Crystal Engraved 560

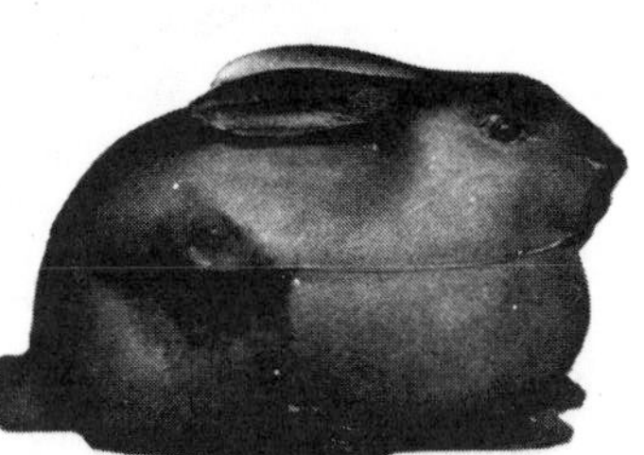

Large "Bunny" Box and Cover

1076 Sugar and Cream
E/Lorna

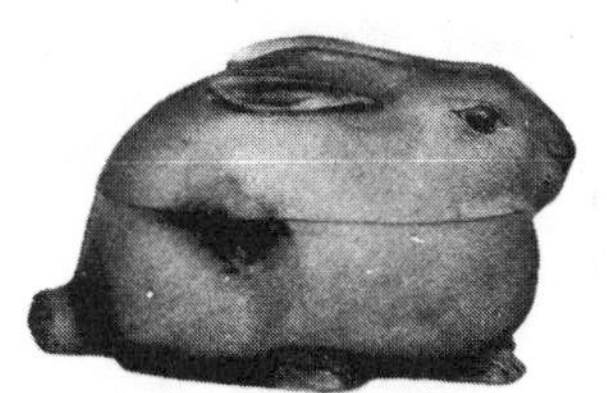

Small "Bunny" Box and Cover

1259 3-Pc. Salt and Pepper
Shaker Set with Glass Tops

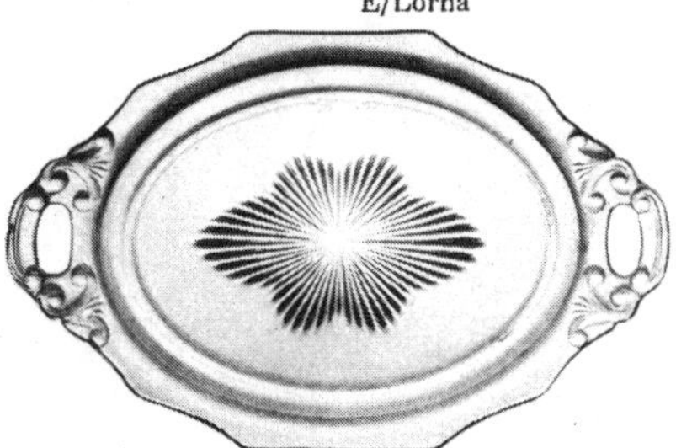

1071-9" 2-Hdl. Tray

1230 Cigarette Box and Ash Tray

Plate Etched 746 "Gloria"

3400/30-9½" 2-Hdl. Footed Bowl

3400/39 Tall Cream or Syrup

3400/40 Sugar Shaker with Glass Top

3400/29-7" Tall Comport

3400/28-7" Low Comport

3400/79 Tall Oil G. S.

3400/50 Square 4-Toed Cup and Saucer

3400/34-9½" 2-Hdl. Bowl

3025 Fingerbowl

1071-9" 2-Hdl. Tray

3400/86-8¾" 2-Hdl. Pickle

3400/35-11" 2-Hdl. Plate

3400/88-8¾" 2-Hdl. 2-Compt. Relish

3011 Stemware Plate Etched "746" Gloria

11 oz. Banquet Goblet

11 oz. Table Goblet

7 oz. Tall Sherbet

3½ oz. Cocktail

7" Comport, flared

3011 Stemware Plate Etched "744" Apple Blossom

11 oz. Banquet Goblet

11 oz. Table Goblet

7 oz. Tall Sherbet

3½ oz. Cocktail

7" Comport, cupped

Early American Glassware

Mount Vernon Pattern

1-9 oz. Goblet

2-6½ oz. Tall Sherbet

3-10 oz. Footed Tumbler

8-Sugar and Cream

12-4½" Footed Rose Bowl

11-7½" Footed Comport

10-7" Footed Bon Bon

9-1 lb. Candy Jar and Cover

7-Cup and Saucer

4-6" Bread and Butter Plate

6-5¼" Fruit Saucer

5-8½" Salad Plate

61-11½" Bowl, shallow cupped

126-10" Bowl, shallow cupped

128-10" Bowl, belled

68-11½" Bowl, belled

13-3 Pint Jug

13-1½ Pint Jug

106-6½" Rose Bowl

107-6½" Squat Vase

105-8½" 2 Handled, 2 Compt. Sweetmeat or Relish

Early American Glassware

Mount Vernon Pattern

46-10" Vase

54-7" Vase

42 ~~45~~-5" Vase

50-6" Vase

58-7" Vase

102-Oval 2 Handled Salt Dip

79-10½" Celery Tray

16-3" Vanity Box and Cover

74-Honey Jar and Cover

65-8" Pickle

100-9" Oval 2 Handled Comport

77-5½" 2 Handled Comport

73-5" Butter Tub and Cover

Ebony Silver Decorated Ware

Sport Novelties

3400/38-80 oz. Jug
D/983-S

1070-36 oz. Decanter
D/985-S

1066-3½ oz. Cocktail
D/985-S

1020-Cocktail Shaker
2-Lip Top
D/987-S

1021-2½ oz. Tumbler
Crystal - Ebony Foot
D/987-S

3400/17-12" Vase
D/990-S

973-5 pc. Bridge Set
D/983 S
Ebony Tray - Crystal Tumblers

3400/38-12 oz. Tumbler
D/983-S

693/1021-2 pc. Canape Set
D/987-S

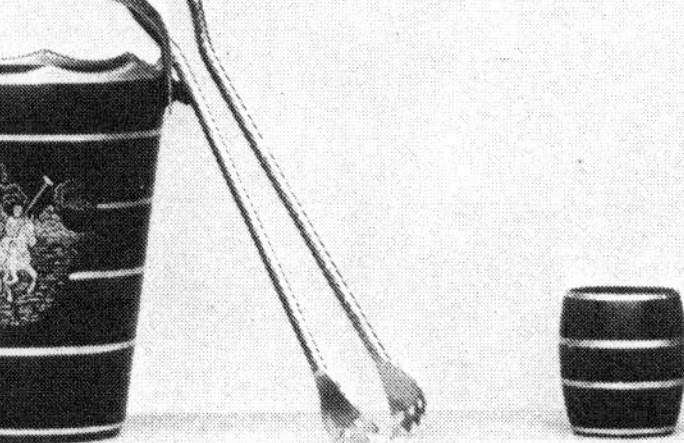
851-Ice Pail with Handle
and Tongs
D/983-S

3400/92-2½ oz. Tumbler
D/983-S

3400/92-32 oz. Decanter
D/983-S

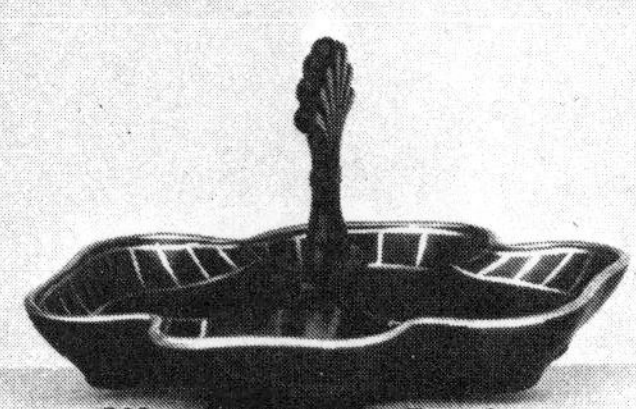
862-4 Compt. Hld. Relish
D/989-S

1095-3-pc. Sugar and Cream Set
D/987-S

3400/68-Sugar and Cream
D/983-S

1093-2 Compt. Hdl. Relish
D/987-S

972-11" 2.Hld. Plate
D/990-S

1179-5½" Bon Bon
D/983-S

1181-6" Plate
D/987-S

103-7" Candy Box and Cover
D/989-S

Ebony Silver Decorated Ware

Sport Novelties

1025 Cigar Humidor
D/985-S

882-Tobacco Humidor
D/990-S

643-6″ Ash Well-2 pc.
D/983-S

885-Cigarette Jar and Cover
D/985-S

1025-Ash Tray
D/989-S

617-Cigarette Jar and Cover
D/983-S

641-4″ Ash Well 2-pc.
D/987-S

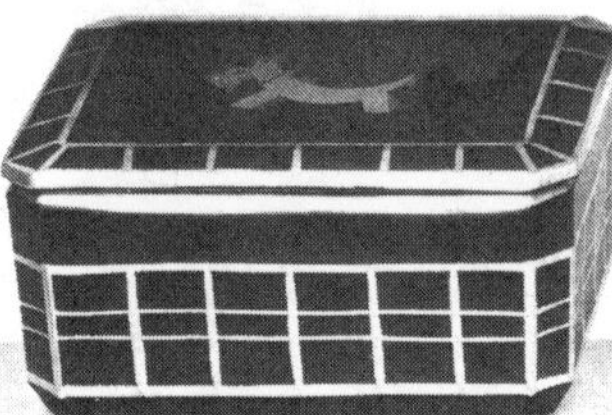

616-Cigarette Box and Cover
D/987-S

615-Cigarette Box and Cover
D/983-S

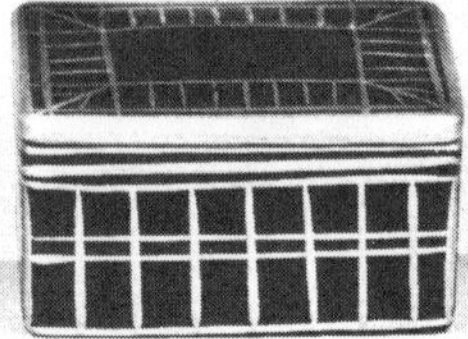

430-Cigarette Box and Cover
D/989-S

413-Cigarette Box and Cover
D/983-S

388-4″ Ash Tray
D/985-S

391-8″ Ash Tray
D/990-S

390-6″ Ash Tray
D/987-S

Sport Novelties — Color Decorations

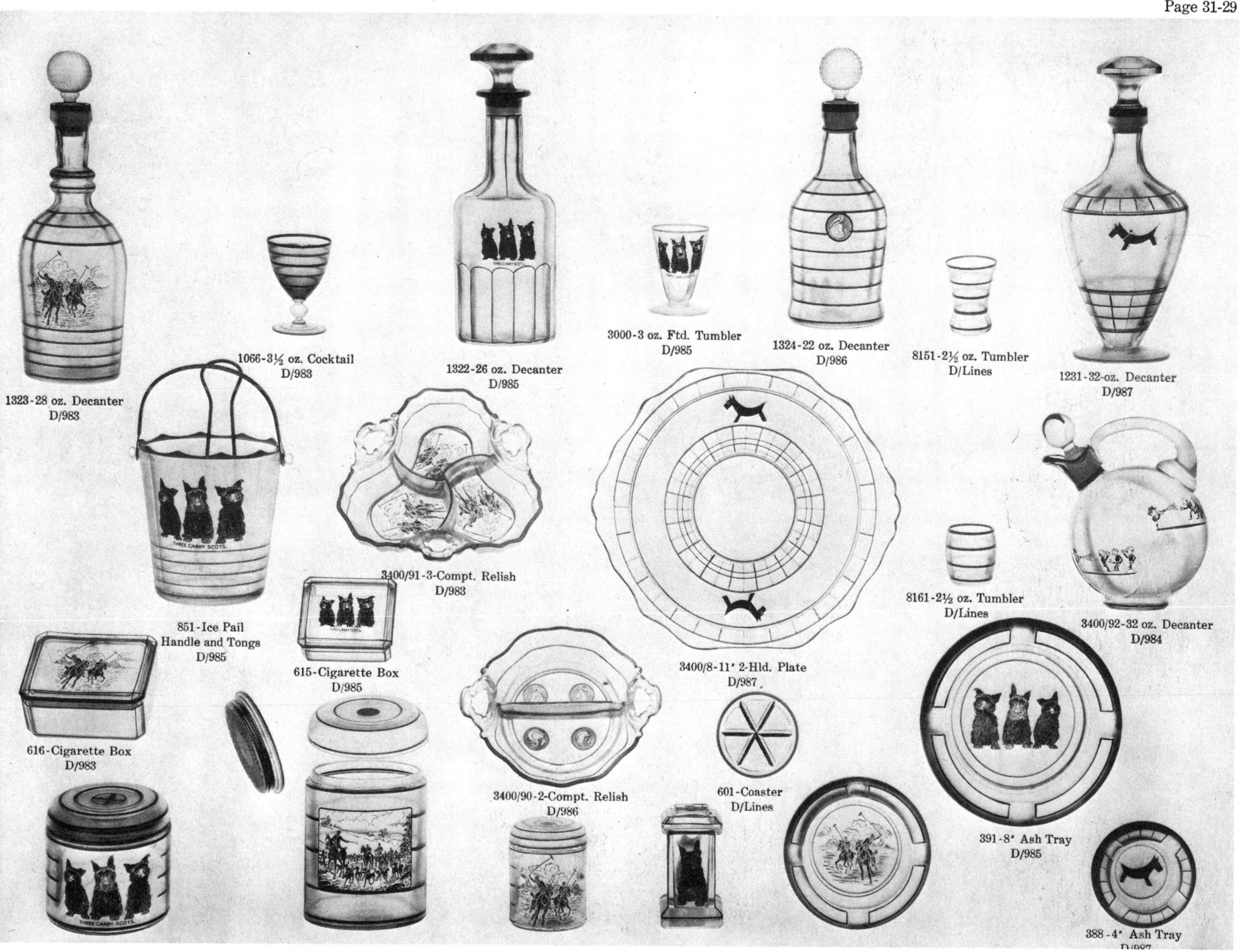

1323-28 oz. Decanter D/983

1066-3½ oz. Cocktail D/983

1322-26 oz. Decanter D/985

3000-3 oz. Ftd. Tumbler D/985

1324-22 oz. Decanter D/986

8151-2½ oz. Tumbler D/Lines

1231-32-oz. Decanter D/987

851-Ice Pail Handle and Tongs D/985

3400/91-3-Compt. Relish D/983

3400/8-11" 2-Hld. Plate D/987

8161-2½ oz. Tumbler D/Lines

3400/92-32 oz. Decanter D/984

616-Cigarette Box D/983

615-Cigarette Box D/985

3400/90-2-Compt. Relish D/986

601-Coaster D/Lines

391-8" Ash Tray D/985

388-4" Ash Tray D/987

882-Tobacco Humidor D/985

1025-Cigar Humidor D/990

617-Cigarette Jar D/983

885-Cigarette Box D/985

390-6" Ash Tray D/983

3122 Stemware Plate Etched "752" Diane

12 oz. Ftd. Tumbler

9 oz. Ftd. Tumbler

7 oz. Low Sherbet

5 oz. Ftd. Tumbler

2½ oz. Ftd. Tumbler

4½ oz. Oyster Cocktail

Fingerbowl and Plate

9 oz. Goblet

7 oz. Tall Sherbet

4½ oz. Claret

2½ oz. Wine

3 oz. Cocktail

1 oz. Cordial

3400 Dinnerware Plate Etched "752" Diane

3400/53-6" Cereal

3400/68-Sugar

3400/68-Cream

3400/54-Cup and Saucer

3400/55-Cream Soup and Saucer

3400/77-Salt and Pepper Shaker Glass Top

3400/58-13½" Platter

3400/62-8½" Plate

3400/51-10" Baker

3400/1174-6" Bread and Butter Plate

3400 Dinnerware Plate Etched "752" Diane

3400/646-Candlestick

3400/45-11" Bowl

3400/646-Candlestick

3400/638-Candelabra

3400/1240-12" Bowl "Oval"

3400/638-Candelabra

3400/647-Candelabra

3400/4-12" 4-toed Bowl

3400/647-Candelabra

1066 Stemware Plate Etched "752" Diane

12 oz. Ftd. Tumbler

9 oz. Ftd. Tumbler

7 oz. Low Sherbet

5 oz. Ftd. Tumbler

3 oz. Ftd. Tumbler

3 oz. Low Cocktail

5 oz. Oyster Cocktail

11 oz. Goblet

7 oz. Tall Sherbet

4½ oz. Claret

3 oz. Wine

3½ oz. Tall Cocktail

1 oz. Cordial

1066 Stemware Plate Etched "752" Diane

12 oz. Ftd. Tumbler (3135)

10 oz. Ftd. Tumbler (3135)

8 oz. Ftd. Tumbler (3135)

5 oz. Ftd. Tumbler (3135)

2½ oz. Ftd. Tumbler (3135)

14 oz. Tumbler Sham Bottom

12 oz. Tumbler Sham Bottom

10 oz. Tumbler Sham Bottom

7 oz. Tumbler "Old Fashioned" Cocktail Sham Bottom

5 oz. Tumbler Sham Bottom

2½ oz. Tumbler Sham Bottom

3126-Stemware Plate Etched "Portia"

9 oz. Goblet

7 oz. Tall Sherbet

7 oz. Low Sherbet

4½ oz Claret

1 oz. Cordial

3 oz. Cocktail

13 oz. Ftd. Tumbler

Finger Bowl and Plate

2½ oz. Wine

10 oz. Ftd. Tumbler

4½ oz. Oyster Cocktail

5 oz. Ftd. Tumbler

2½ oz. Ftd. Tumbler

1 oz. Brandy

3121-Stemware Plate Etched "Portia"

10 oz. Goblet

6 oz. Tall Sherbet

6 oz. Low Sherbet

4½ oz. Claret

1 oz. Cordial

3 oz. Cocktail

12 oz. Ftd. Tumbler

Finger Bowl and Plate

2½ oz. Wine

4½ oz. Oyster Cocktail

10 oz. Ftd. Tumbler

5 oz. Ftd. Tumbler

2½ oz. Ftd. Tumbler

1 oz.

No. 3124 Stemware Plate Etched "Portia"

10 oz. Goblet

7 oz. Tall Sherbet

3 oz. Cocktail

7 oz. Low Sherbet

5 oz. Ftd. Tumbler

10 oz. Ftd. Tumbler

12 oz. Ftd. Tumbler

3 oz. Ftd. Tumbler

4½ oz. Oyster Cocktail

4½ oz. Claret

3 oz. Wine

Finger Bowl and Plate

Plate Etched "Portia"

119
7" Basket

3400/93
5¼" Ivy Ball

3400/98
8 oz. Sugar

3400/98
8 oz. Cream

3400/99
6 oz. Oil

3400/97
2 oz. Cologne

3400/94
3½" Puff Box

193
6 oz.
Oil

3400/80
3½" Cranberry
Square

3400/108
80 oz. Cocktail Shaker
Chrom. Top

652
11" Celery Tray

3400/1176
8½" Salad Plate

3400/89
11" 2 compartment Relish

3400/49
3½" Cranberry

3400/41
3 Pc. Frappe Set

3400/50
Square Cup & Saucer

3400/1188
11" Bowl

3400/109
6" Grape Fruit
or Oyster Bowl

968
Sea Food
or
Fruit Cocktail & Liner

Ten Piece Assortment E/758

531
7¼" Tall Comport

533
3 Pc. Mayonnaise Set

782
8" Vase

168
10½" Hdl. Sandwich Tray

315
28 oz. Decanter

135-10½"
Cheese and Cracker

138
Sugar

138
Cream

676
11½" Bowl

628
3½" Candlestick

988
11¼" Bowl

Ten Piece Assortment E/760

532-6½" Tall Comport

1012-8½" Bowl

1308-6" Vase

1147-Ice Tub

3400/90-8" 2 Part Relish

608-6½" Comport

871-2 Pc. Mayonnaise Set

197-6 oz. Tall Oil G. S.

3400/13-6" 4 Toed Comport

3077-22 oz. Jug and Cover

Decorate 996

Also furnished in Etchings 758-759-760 and Lorna

864 Candy Box and Cover

3400/102-5" Globe Jar

1303-7" Vase

1076 Sugar

1076 Cream

3400/88-8¾" 2 Compt. Relish

1093-6" Hdl. Relish

851 Ice Pail
Metal Handle

1284-10" Vase

3400/87-11" Celery

1225-9" 2 Hdl. Bowl

3400/28-7" Comport

1226-10" 2 Hdl. Plate
D/997

Console Sets

993-12½" Bowl
D/997

1307-Candelabra
D/997

1307-Candelabra
D/999

993-12½" Bowl
D/999

842-12½" Bowl Rock Crystal
Engraved 648

992-12½" Bowl
E/756

842-12½" Bowl
E/755

993-12½" Bowl Rock Crystal
Engraved 649

993-12½" Bowl
D/998

993-12½" Bowl
E/757

"Cambridge" Two Tone "Quick Sellers"

3400/28-7" Comport

1234-12" Vase

627-4" Candlestick

627-4" Candlestick

119-7" Basket
(12" high)

1236-8" Ivy Ball

1070-36 oz. Pinch Decanter

993-12½" Bowl

489-4 Pc. Boudoir Set

1095-3 Pc. Sugar and Cream Set

Miscellaneous

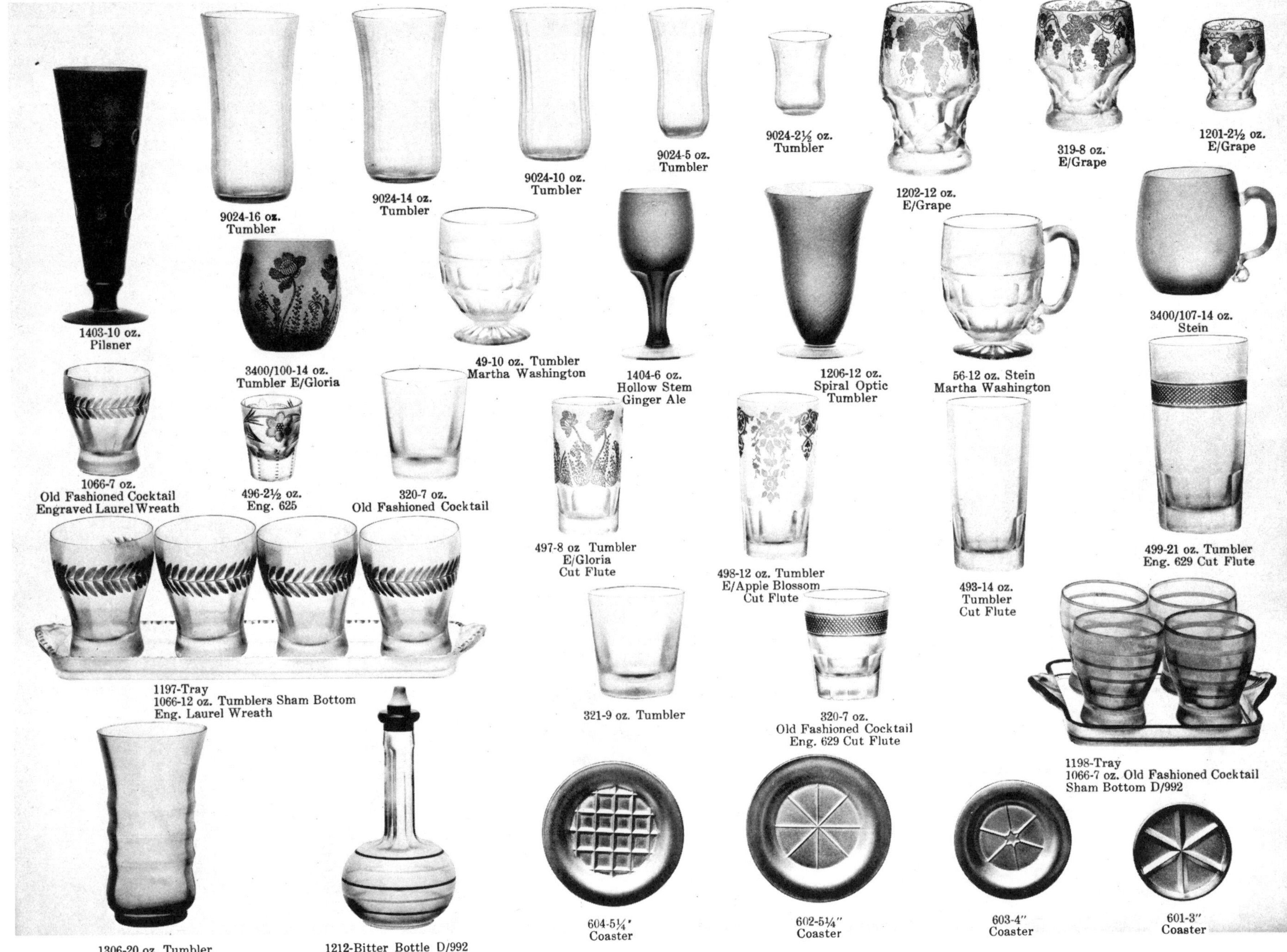
1403-10 oz. Pilsner
9024-16 oz. Tumbler
9024-14 oz. Tumbler
9024-10 oz. Tumbler
9024-5 oz. Tumbler
9024-2½ oz. Tumbler
1202-12 oz. E/Grape
319-8 oz. E/Grape
1201-2½ oz. E/Grape
3400/100-14 oz. Tumbler E/Gloria
49-10 oz. Tumbler Martha Washington
1404-6 oz. Hollow Stem Ginger Ale
1206-12 oz. Spiral Optic Tumbler
56-12 oz. Stein Martha Washington
3400/107-14 oz. Stein
1066-7 oz. Old Fashioned Cocktail Engraved Laurel Wreath
496-2½ oz. Eng. 625
320-7 oz. Old Fashioned Cocktail
497-8 oz Tumbler E/Gloria Cut Flute
498-12 oz. Tumbler E/Apple Blossom Cut Flute
493-14 oz. Tumbler Cut Flute
499-21 oz. Tumbler Eng. 629 Cut Flute
1197-Tray 1066-12 oz. Tumblers Sham Bottom Eng. Laurel Wreath
321-9 oz. Tumbler
320-7 oz. Old Fashioned Cocktail Eng. 629 Cut Flute
1198-Tray 1066-7 oz. Old Fashioned Cocktail Sham Bottom D/992
1306-20 oz. Tumbler
1212-Bitter Bottle D/992
604-5¼" Coaster
602-5¼" Coaster
603-4" Coaster
601-3" Coaster

3400/103-6½″ Vase
Rock Crystal Eng. 640

1330-5″ Sweet
Potato Vase

1319-4½″ Vase

3400/102-5″ Vase
Rock Crystal Engraved 641

1304-11″ Urn
Rock Crystal Engraved 618

1238-12″ Vase
Rock Crystal Engraved 639

1297-11″ Vase
Rock Crystal Engraved 640

1305-10″ Vase
Rock Crystal Engraved 560

1299-11″ Vase
Rock Crystal Engraved 615

1335-12″ Vase
E/758

1318-14″ Urn
Rock Crystal Engraved 639

Stemware and Tumblers Plate Etched "Old Fashioned Grape" 401

1401-10 oz.
Goblet

1401-6 oz.
Tall Sherbet

1401-4½ oz.
Claret

1401-3 oz.
Cocktail

1401-3 oz.
Wine

1401
Finger Bowl

1401-1 oz.
Cordial

1401-5 oz.
Ftd. Tumbler

1401-10 oz.
Ftd. Tumbler

1400-10 oz.
Goblet

1204-14 oz.
Tumbler

1203-14 oz.
Tumbler

1203-12 oz.
Tumbler

1203-10 oz.
Tumbler

1203-2½ oz.
Tumbler

1203-7 oz.
Old Fashioned Cocktail

1203-5 oz.
Orange or
Tomato Juice

1203-8 oz.
Tumbler

Rock Crystal Engraved 643 and 646

1400-Eng. 643
12 oz. Ftd. Tumbler

1400-Eng. 643
1 oz. Cordial

1400-Eng. 643
10 oz. Goblet

1400-Eng. 643
2 oz. Wine

1400-Eng. 643
7 oz. Tall Sherbet

1400-Eng. 643
3½ oz. Cocktail

1400-Eng. 643
5½ oz. Sherbet

1400-Eng. 643
5 oz. Ftd. Tumbler

1404-Eng. 643
6 oz. Hollow Stem
Gingerale

1401-Eng. 646
10 oz. Goblet

1203-Eng. 646
2½ oz. Tumbler

1204-Eng. 646
14 oz. Tumbler

1203-Eng. 646
7 oz. Old Fashioned
Cocktail

1203-Eng. 646
14 oz. Tumbler

1203-Eng. 646
5 oz. Orange Juice

1203-Eng. 646
12 oz. Tumbler

1203-Eng. 646
8 oz. Tumbler

1203-Eng. 646
10 oz. Tumbler

Rock Crystal Engraved Stemware

Rock Crystal Engraved Stemware

3035-Eng. 613

Rock Crystal Engraved 644

1242
10" Vase

984
10" Bowl

1090
7" Tall Comport

627
4" Candlestick

856
11" Bowl

877
9½" Comport

3400/91-8"
3 compartment Relish

1147
Ice Tub

842
12¼" Bowl

873
3 Pc. Mayonnaise Set

647
5½" Candelabrum

1226
10½" Plate

3400/90-8"
2 compartment Relish

1225
9" Bowl

103
7" Candy Box

870
11" Hdl. Sandwich Tray

868
11" Cheese and Cracker

1147-Eng. 650
Ice Pail

3400/88-Eng. 650
8¾"-2 compartment Relish

983-Eng. 650
2 Pc. Mayonnaise Set

864-Eng. 650
Candy Box

871-Eng. 650
5½"-2 Hdl. Comport

3400/90-Eng. 650
7½"-2 compartment Relish

1076-Eng. 650
Sugar and Cream

532-Eng. 650
6½" Tall Comport

639-Eng. 650
4" Candlestick

988-Eng. 650
11½" Bowl

639-Eng. 650
4" Candlestick

3400/102-Eng. 650
5" Vase

1012-Eng. 650
8½" Bowl

1225-Eng. 650
9" Bowl

1226-Eng. 650
10½" Plate

1284-Eng. 650
10" Vase

3400/59-Eng. 650
9" Celery Tray

1226-Eng. 647
10½" Plate

103-Eng. 650
7" Candy Box

489-Eng. 650
22 oz. Jug and Cover

1308-Eng. 650
6" Vase

1169-Eng. 650
Bon Bon Chrom. Hdl. & Tongs

Rock Crystal Engraved

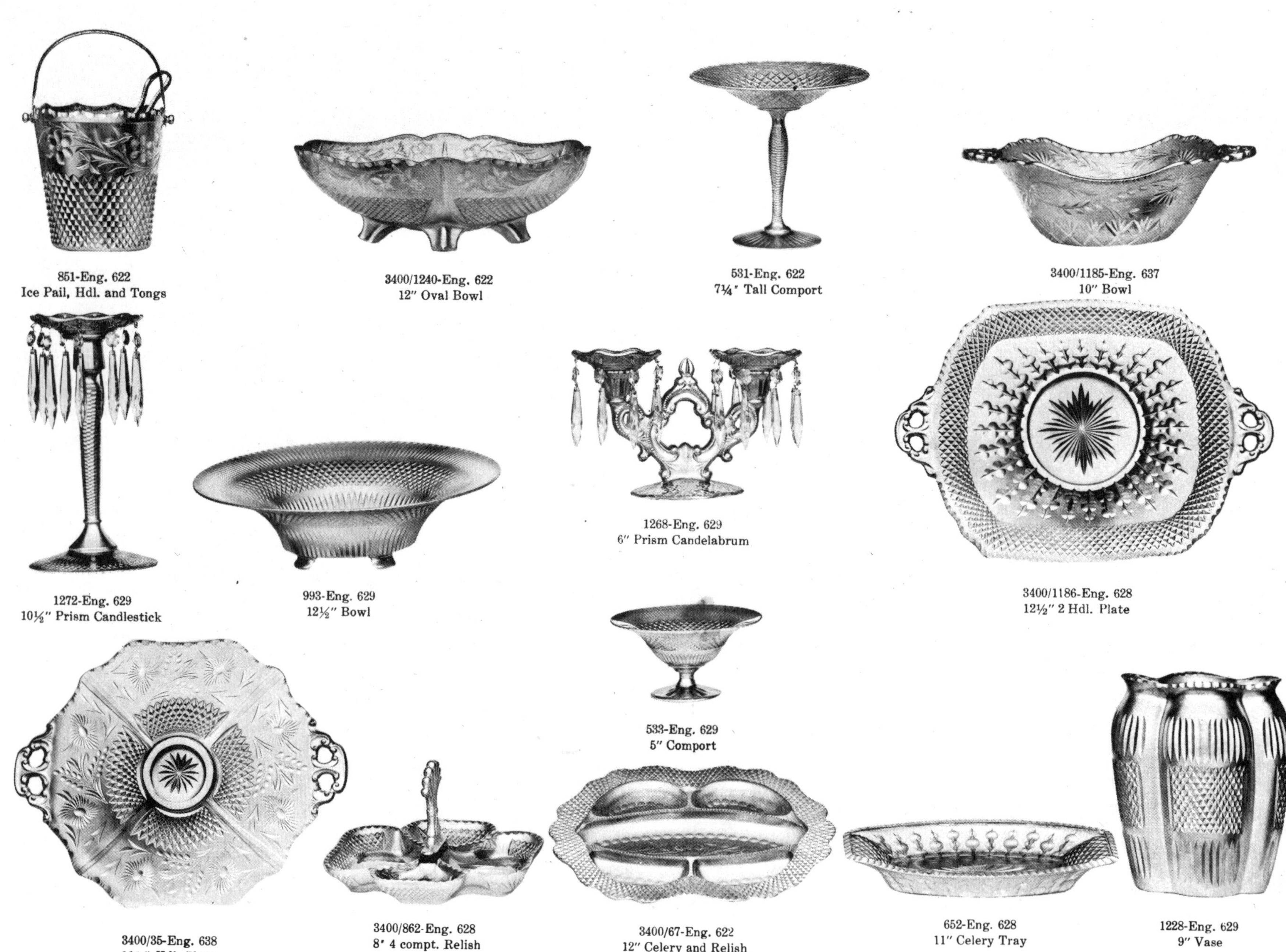

851-Eng. 622
Ice Pail, Hdl. and Tongs

3400/1240-Eng. 622
12" Oval Bowl

531-Eng. 622
7¼" Tall Comport

3400/1185-Eng. 637
10" Bowl

1272-Eng. 629
10½" Prism Candlestick

993-Eng. 629
12½" Bowl

1268-Eng. 629
6" Prism Candelabrum

3400/1186-Eng. 628
12½" 2 Hdl. Plate

533-Eng. 629
5" Comport

3400/35-Eng. 638
11" 2 Hdl. Plate

3400/862-Eng. 628
8" 4 compt. Relish

3400/67-Eng. 622
12" Celery and Relish

652-Eng. 628
11" Celery Tray

1228-Eng. 629
9" Vase

1268-Eng. 621
Lustre Prism Candelabrum

3400/32-Eng. 625
11½" Bowl

3400/4-Eng. 611
12" Bowl

3400/28-Eng. 611
7" L. F. Comport

3400/91-Eng. 624
8" 3 compt. Relish

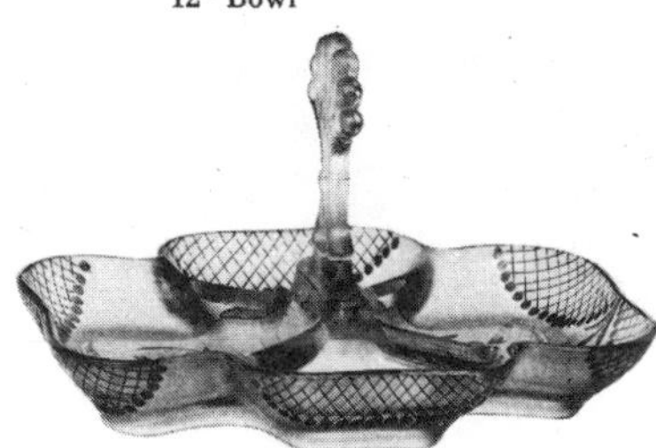

3400/862-Eng. 615
8" Relish

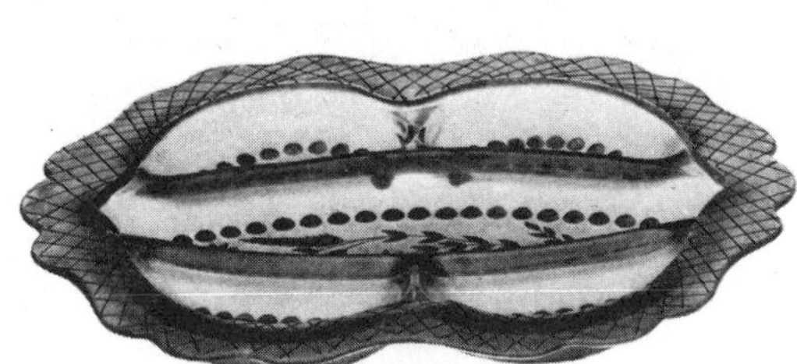

3400/67-Eng. 621
12" Celery and Relish Tray

3400/3-Eng. 560
11" Ftd. Comport

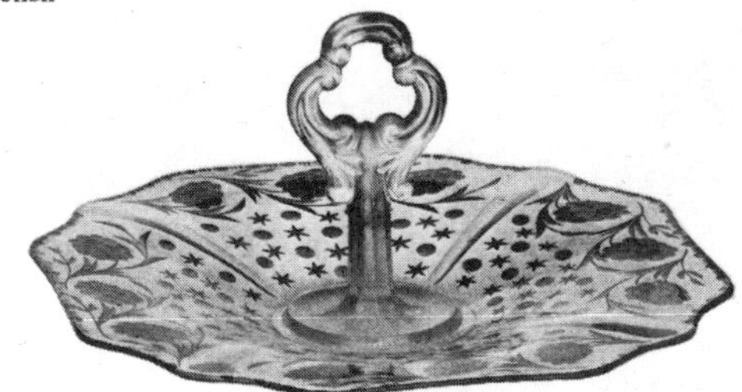

3400/10-Eng. 623
11" Hdl. Sandwich Plate

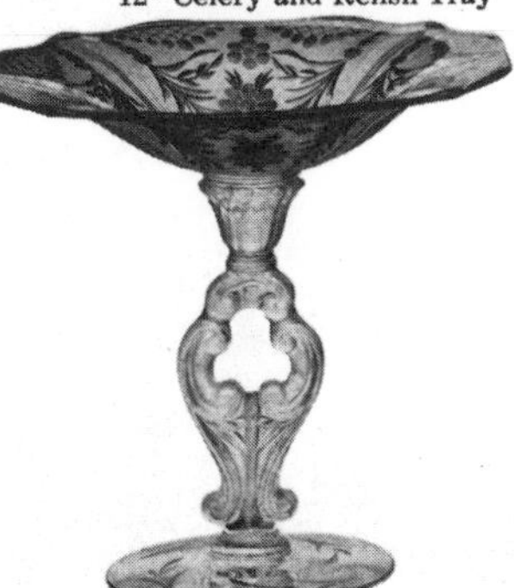

3400/29-Eng. 615
7" Tall Comport

3400/1-Eng. 615
13" Bowl

3400/6-Eng. 624
11½" Cheese and Cracker

Rock Crystal Engraved

1263-Eng. 639
French Dressing
Bottle

1261-Eng. 641
French Dressing
Bottle

3400/79
Eng. 611
6 oz. Oil G. S.

3400/32-Eng. 642
11½" Bowl

3400/36-Eng. 642
Shaker, Chrom.
Top

3400/37-Eng.
641 Shaker
Chrom. Top

3400/14-Eng. 641
7" Tall Comport

3400/18
Eng. 560
Shaker
Chrom. Top.

3400/77-Eng. 642
Shaker, Glass Top.

3400/1093-Eng. 615
Handled Relish

3400/4-Eng. 641
12" Bowl

3400/88-Eng. 642
8¾" 2 Compartment Relish

3400/90-Eng. 611
2 Compartment Relish

3400/1192-Eng. 642
6" Candlestick .

3400/89-Eng. 642
11" 2 Compartment Relish

3400/34-Eng. 641
9½" Bowl

3400/1-Eng. 640
13" Bowl

3400/21-Eng. 640
9" Bowl

Rock Crystal Engraved "Laurel Wreath"

1304-11" Urn

3400/102 5" Globe Jar

993
12½" Bowl

647
5½" Candelabrum

531
7¼" Comport

922
Cream Soup and Saucer

556
8" Plate

324
6 Pc. Relish Set

3400/100
14 oz. Tumbler

3400/100
76 oz. Jug

3400/79
6 oz. Oil

3400/77
Shaker Glass Top

3400/8
11½" Sandwich Plate

1066
11 oz. Goblet

1066
7 oz. Tall Sherbet

1066
3½ oz. Tall Cocktail

1066
12 oz. Ftd. Tumbler

1066
9 oz. Ftd. Tumbler

1066
5 oz. Ftd. Tumbler

Rock Crystal Engraved

3400/101-Eng. 639
76 oz. Jug

3400/100-Eng. 639
13 oz. Tumbler

3400/38-Eng. 639
80 oz. Ball Jug

3400/38-Eng. 639
12 oz. Tumbler

1070-Eng. 639
36 oz. Pinch Decanter

1070-Eng. 639
2 oz. Pinch
Tumbler

1205-Eng. 560
64 oz. Jug

3135-Eng. 560
12 oz. Ftd.
Tumbler

3400/92-Eng. 639
32 oz. Ball Decanter

8161-Eng. 639
2 oz. Tumbler

3011-Eng. 639
9' Luster Cut
Prism
Candlestick

660-Tray Eng. 639
3400/94-Puff Box Eng. 639
3400/97-Cologne Eng. 639

3011-Eng. 639
9' Candlestick

3400/96-Eng. 639
3 Pc. Vinegar and
Oil Set

3400/78-Eng. 611
Cocktail Shaker

3130-Eng. 611
2½ oz. Ftd.
Tumbler

3400/98-Eng. 639
Ball Sugar and Cream

3400/99-Eng. 639
6 oz. Oil

3400/106-Eng. 639
Marmalade Jar and Cover

3400/54-Eng. 642
Cup and Saucer

3400/55-Eng. 615
Cream Soup and Saucer

3400/39-Eng. 611
Cream

3400/40-Eng. 611
Sugar Shaker
Glass Top

968/698-Eng. 639
3 Pc. Sea Food or Fruit
Cocktail Set

556-Eng. 628
8" Salad Plate

3400/1176-Eng. 638
8½" Salad Plate

3400/62-Eng. 640
8½" Salad Plate

3400/68-Eng. 621 Sugar and Cream
1071-9" Eng. 621 Tray

"Martha Washington" Stemware

1400
10 oz. Goblet

1400
7 oz. Tall Sherbet

1400
7 oz. Low Sherbet

1400
3½ oz. Cocktail

1400
2 oz. Wine

1400
1 oz. Cordial

1400
5½ oz. Sherbet

1401
3 oz. Wine

1401
3 oz. Cocktail

1401
6 oz. Tall Sherbet

1401
10 oz. Goblet

1400
Finger Bowl & Plate

1400
5 oz. Ftd. Tumbler

1400
12 oz. Ftd. Tumbler

1401
10 oz. Ftd. Tumbler

1401
4½ oz. Claret

1401
5 oz. Ftd. Tumbler

1401
1 oz. Cordial

1401
Finger Bowl

1204
14 oz. Tumbler

1404
6 oz. Hollow Stem Ginger Ale

1203
2½ oz. Tumbler

1203
5 oz. Tumbler

1203
7 oz. Old Fashioned Cocktail

1203
8 oz. Tumbler

1203
10 oz. Tumbler

1203
12 oz. Tumbler

1203
14 oz. Tumbler

"Martha Washington"

50 12 oz. Ftd. Tumbler Plate Etched "Grape"

49 10 oz. Ftd. Tumbler

48 8 oz. Ftd. Tumbler

46 5 oz. Ftd. Tumbler

47 7 oz. Fruit Salad

45 7 oz. Tall Sherbet

51 10 oz. Goblet

35 10 oz. Ftd. Tumbler

34 9 oz. Goblet

36 6 oz. Sherbet

54 8 oz. Stein

55 10 oz. Stein

56 12 oz. Stein

15 5½" Comport

19 Sugar

19 Cream

14 Sugar

14 Cream

1 Sugar

1 Cream

1400 6" Comport

57 5¼" Fruit Saucer

42 Cup and Saucer

10 5½" Comport

20 6⅜" Bread and Butter Plate

21 8⅜" Salad Plate Plate Etched "Grape"

52 Finger Bowl
53 Finger Bowl Plate

16
10″ Vase

40
14½″ Urn

3
9″ Candlestick

41
9½″ Urn

2
4″ Candlestick

17
7½″ Fan Vase

1269
10″ Lustre Cut Prism
Candlestick, No. 2 Prism

39
10″ Urn

9
10″ Comport

18
11″ Vase

58
6½″ Ice Tub

7
12½″ Bowl
11
13″ Bowl

12
9½″ Bowl

13
7½″ Bowl

27
8½″ Bow

4-9″ Bowl
5-10½″ Bowl
6-10″ Bowl

44
11½″ Sandwich Plate

28
10″ Bowl

25-10½″ Bowl
8-12½″ Bowl
26-13½″ Bowl
Etched Grape

43
7½″-3 Compartment
Candy Box

23
12½″ Plate
Etched Grape

MISCELLANEOUS

Mount Vernon
91. 86 oz. Jug

Mount Vernon
84. 14 oz. Stein

Martha Washington
56. 12 oz. Stein

Martha Washington
30. 80 oz. Jug

Martha Washington
60. 4½ oz. Oyster Cocktail

Mount Vernon
72. 7½ in. Coupe Salad or Jug Coaster

Martha Washington
22. 7½ in. Coupe Salad or Jug Coaster

Martha Washington
59. 5 oz. Ftd. Sherbet

Martha Washington
66. 11 in. Cheese and Cracker

Martha Washington
61. 3½ oz. Cocktail

"Mount Vernon"

1
9 oz. Goblet

2
6½ oz. Tall Sherbet

22
3 oz. Ftd. Tumbler

21
5 oz. Ftd. Tumbler

3
10 oz. Ftd. Tumbler

20
12 oz. Ftd. Tumbler

13
12 oz. Tumbler

14
14 oz. Tumbler

84
14 oz. Stein

13
3 pint Jug

52
40 oz. Decanter

7
Cup and Saucer

8
Sugar

8
Cream

102
Ind. Salt Oval

24
Ind. Salt

28
Shaker Glass Top

29
2½ oz. Mustard

74
Honey Jar & Cover

40
10½" Dinner Plate

5
8½" Salad Plate

19
6⅜" Bread & Butter Plate

"Mount Vernon"

105
8½"-4 compt. Sweetmeat

104
12" Celery & Relish

103
8" Relish

1340
2½ oz. Cologne

15
4½" Toilet Box

23
Finger Bowl and Plate

6
5¼" Fruit Saucer

16
3" Toilet Box

76
6" Preserve

18
7 oz. Toilet Bottle

78
6" Hdl. Pickle

31
4½" Fruit Saucer

32
6" Cereal

17
4" Toilet Box

79
12" Celery Tray

80
12"-2 part Relish

101
6" Hdl. Relish

30
Sauce Boat
and Ladle

10
7" Bon Bon

33
4½" Comport

34
6" Comport

50
6" Vase

97
6½" Comport

99
9½" Comport

96
6½" Comport

77
6" Comport

46
10" Vase
54
7" Vase

12
4½" Rose Bowl
or Ivy Ball

9
8" Urn

11
7½" Comport

"Mount Vernon"

38
13½" Candelabrum
No. 1 Prism

36
8½" Lustre Cut Prism
Candlestick, No. 2 Prism

35
8" Candlestick

130
4" Candlestick

135
11" Oval Bowl

39
10" Bowl

45
12½" Bowl
129
12" Bowl

100
9" Oval Comport

37
11½" Plate

43
10½" Bowl

44
12½" Bowl

9403-14 oz. Tumblers

Varsity Sport Glassware

3400/38 Jug

3000
3 oz. Ftd. Tumbler

1321 Decanter

1021-2½ oz.
Ftd. Tumbler

1020
Cocktail Shaker

1322 Decanter

9403-12 oz.
Tumbler
601 Coaster

1070
Pinch Decanter

3135-12 oz.
Ftd. Tumbler

3400/91
Relish

851
Ice Pail

499-20 oz.
Tumbler Cut Flute

8161-2½ oz.
Tumbler

3400/92
Decanter

320-7 oz.
Old Fashioned
Cocktail

8151-2½ oz.
Tumbler

1324
Decanter

973/8701-10 oz.
5 Pc. Bridge Set

693/3000-3 oz.
Canape Set

3400/8-11½" Plate

3000-3 oz. Ftd. Tumbler
1198 Tray

623/8701-8 oz.
5 Pc. Bridge Set

1025
Cigar Humidor

882
Tobacco Humidor

617
Cigarette Jar

885
Cigarette Jar

616
Cigarette Box

390
6" Ash Tray

1402/1. 18 oz. Goblet
Etched Imperial Hunt

1402/2. 14 oz. Goblet
Etched Catawba

1402/3. 10 oz. Goblet
R.C. Engraved 690

1402/4. 10 oz. Lunch Goblet

1402/7. 6 oz. Tall Stem
Tomato or Orange Juice

1402/9. 4½ oz. Claret

1402/10. 3 oz. Cocktail

1402/13.
1 oz. Cordial

1402/8. 5 oz. Low Stem
Tomato or Orange Juice

1402/6. 6½ oz. Low Sherbet

1402/14. Fingerbowl.
1402/15. Fingerbowl Plate.

1402/12. 2½ oz. Wine

1402/11. 4 oz. Low Stem
Cocktail or Oyster Cocktail

1402/5. 7½ oz. Tall Sherbet

1402. TALLY-HO LINE

1402/17. Sauce Boat, Plate, and Ladle

1402/34. 11½ in. 2 Handled Sandwich Plate

1402/24. 9½ in. Dinner Plate

1402/22. 7 in. Tea Plate D/1007

1402/32. 6½ in. Grape Fruit

1402/30. 4½ in. Ftd. Fruit Saucer
Also: 1402/31. 6½ in. Ftd. Cereal

1402/33. Sugar and Cream

1402/23. 8 in. Salad Plate.
Also: 1402/21. 6 in. Bread and Butter Plate.
1402/25. 10½ in. Service Plate.
1402/28. 18 in. Buffet Lunch Plate.

1402/19. Cup and Saucer.

1402/65. 4½ in. Tall Comport

1402/61. Low Footed Mint D/1008

1402/60. 4½ in. Low Footed Comport

1402/66. 6 in. High Footed Mint

1402/62. 7 in. Low Footed Comport
Also: 1402/63. 8 in.

1402/67. 6½ in. Tall Comport

1402/54. 5 in. Frappe Cocktail and Liner

1402/55. 6 in. Iced Fruit or Salad Service
Also 1402/56 7 in.

1402/52. Ice Pail with Chromium Plated Handle

1402/53. Tall Frappe Cocktail and Liner

Also: 1402/59. 7 in.

1402. TALLY-HO LINE

1402/77. 13 in. Footed Punch Bowl

1402/70. 10½ in. Bowl

1402/64. 10½ in. Low. Footed Bowl

1402/78. Footed Punch Cup

1402/76. 5 in. Candlestick

1402/72. 9 in. Pan Bowl
Also:
1402/73. 10 in.
1402/74. 12½ in.
1402/75. 17 in.

1402/71. 10½ in. 2 Handled Bowl

1402/68. 8 in. Bowl
Also:
1402/69. 9 in.

1402/79. 12 in. Footed Vase

1402/34. 11½ in.
Sandwich Plate
E: Valencia

1402/100. Goblet
E: Valencia

1402/100. Goblet
E: Minerva

1402/100. Goblet
E: Elaine

1402/100. Claret
E: Minerva

1402/100. Tall Sherbet
E: Elaine

1420/100. Tall Sherbet
E: Valencia

1402/100. Oyster Cocktail
E: Valencia

1402/100. Wine
E: Elaine

1402/100. Low Sherbet
E: Elaine

1402/100. Cocktail
E: Minerva

1402/34. 11½ in.
Sandwich Plate
E: Elaine

1402/34. 11½ in.
Sandwich Plate
E: Minerva

1402/100. TALLY-HO STEMWARE

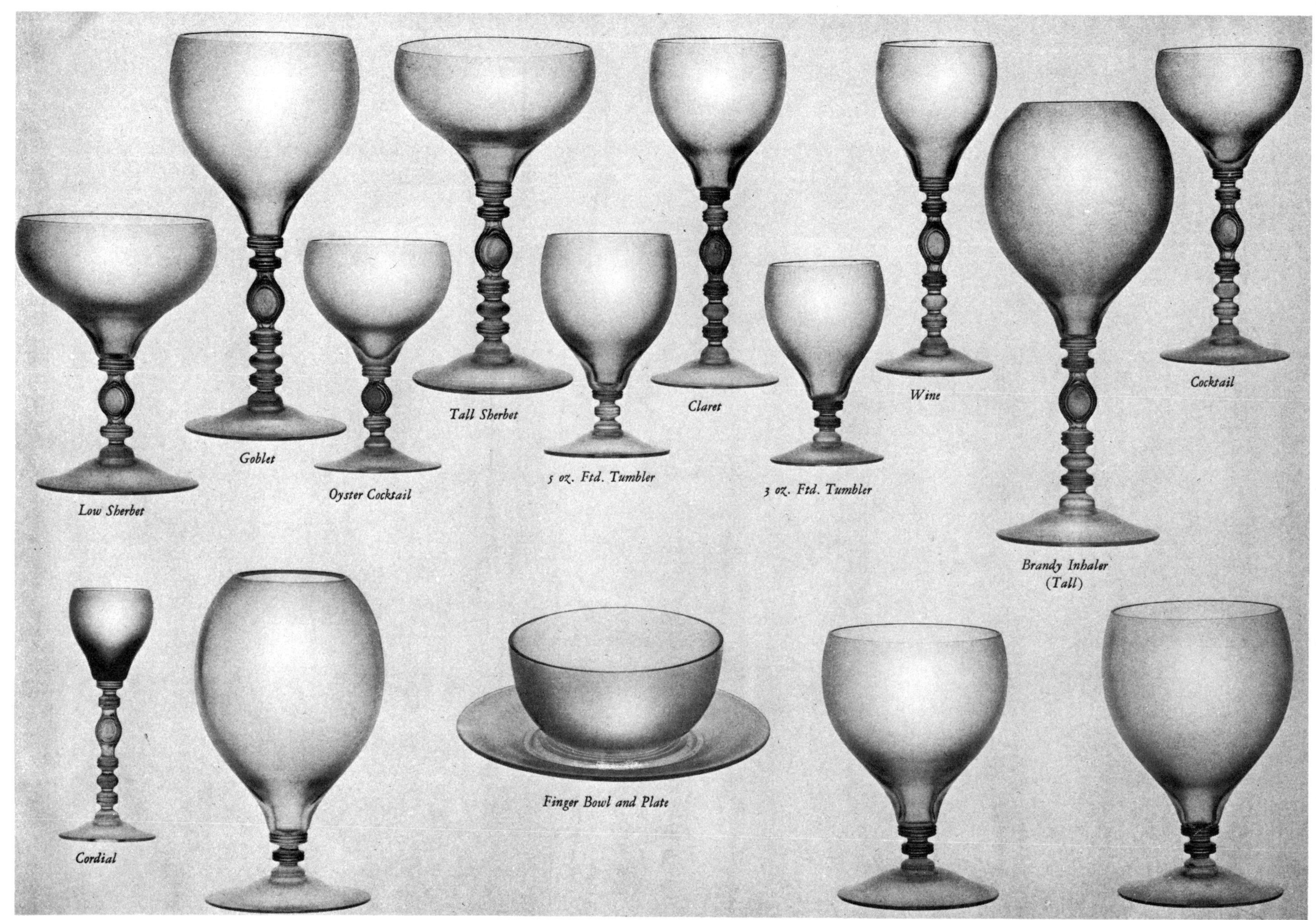

Low Sherbet · *Goblet* · *Oyster Cocktail* · *Tall Sherbet* · *5 oz. Ftd. Tumbler* · *Claret* · *3 oz. Ftd. Tumbler* · *Wine* · *Brandy Inhaler (Tall)* · *Cocktail*

Cordial · *Brandy Inhaler (Low)* · *Finger Bowl and Plate* · *12 oz. Ftd. Tumbler* · *16 oz. Ftd. Tumbler*

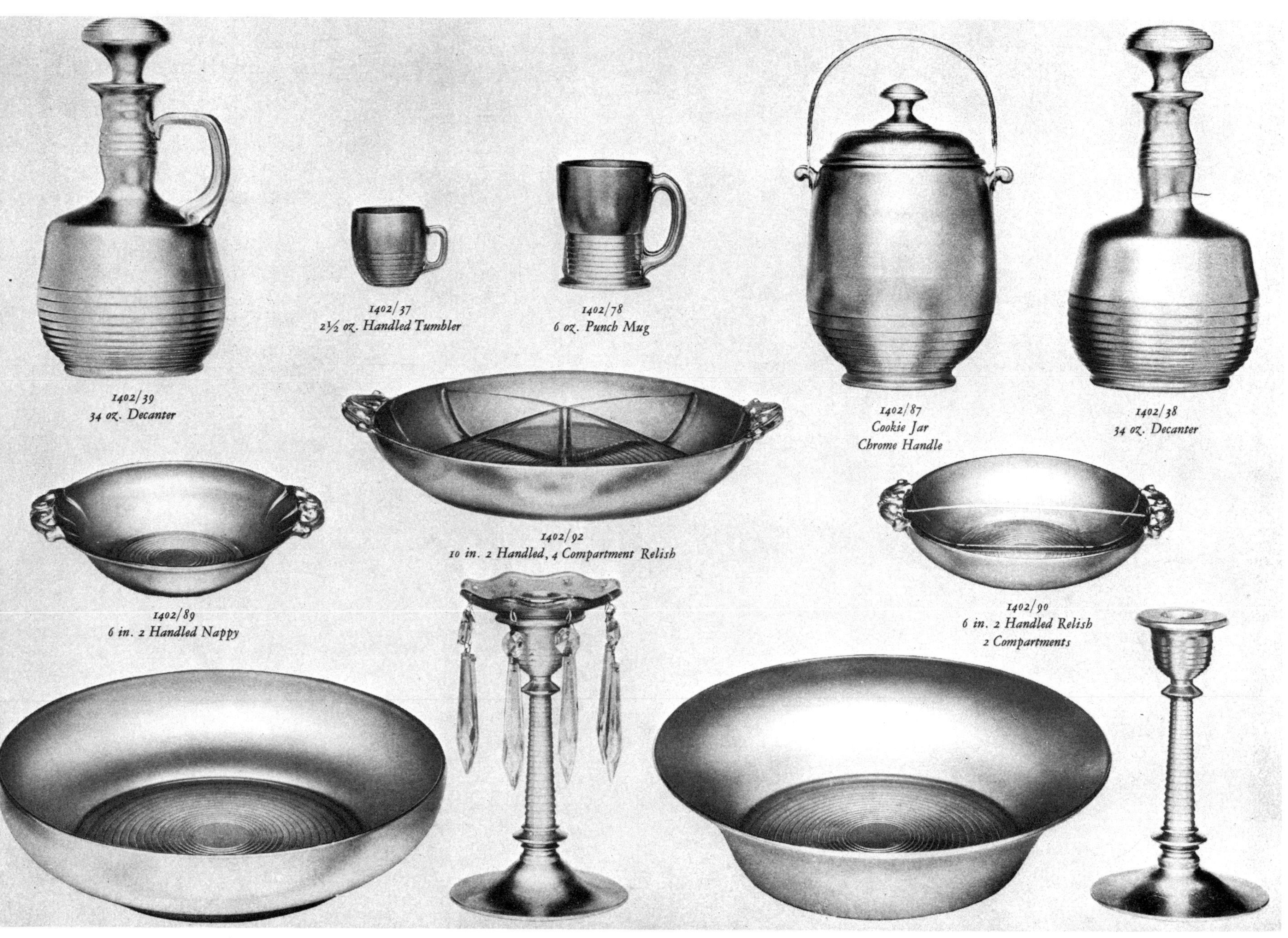

1402/39
34 oz. Decanter

1402/37
2½ oz. Handled Tumbler

1402/78
6 oz. Punch Mug

1402/87
Cookie Jar
Chrome Handle

1402/38
34 oz. Decanter

1402/92
10 in. 2 Handled, 4 Compartment Relish

1402/89
6 in. 2 Handled Nappy

1402/90
6 in. 2 Handled Relish
2 Compartments

1402/82
10 in. Bowl

1402/81
6½ in. Candelabrum
Bobeche and Prisms

1402/88
11 in. Bowl

1402/80
6½ in. Candlestick

1402. TALLY-HO LINE

1402/94. 12 in. Celery

1402/85. 4 in. Ash Tray

1402/91. 8 in. Relish, 3 Compt.

1402/104. 14 in. Cheese and Cracker
1402/101. 18 in. Cheese and Cracker

1402/99. 7 in. Hdl. Plate

1402/98. 6½ in. 2 Hdl. Nappy

1402/86. 4 in. Ash Tray

1402/86. 2 Pc. Ash Well

1402/95. 4 Pc. Twin Salad Dressing Set

1066. Cigarette Holder (Oval)

1402/96. 3 Pc. Twin Salad Dressing Set

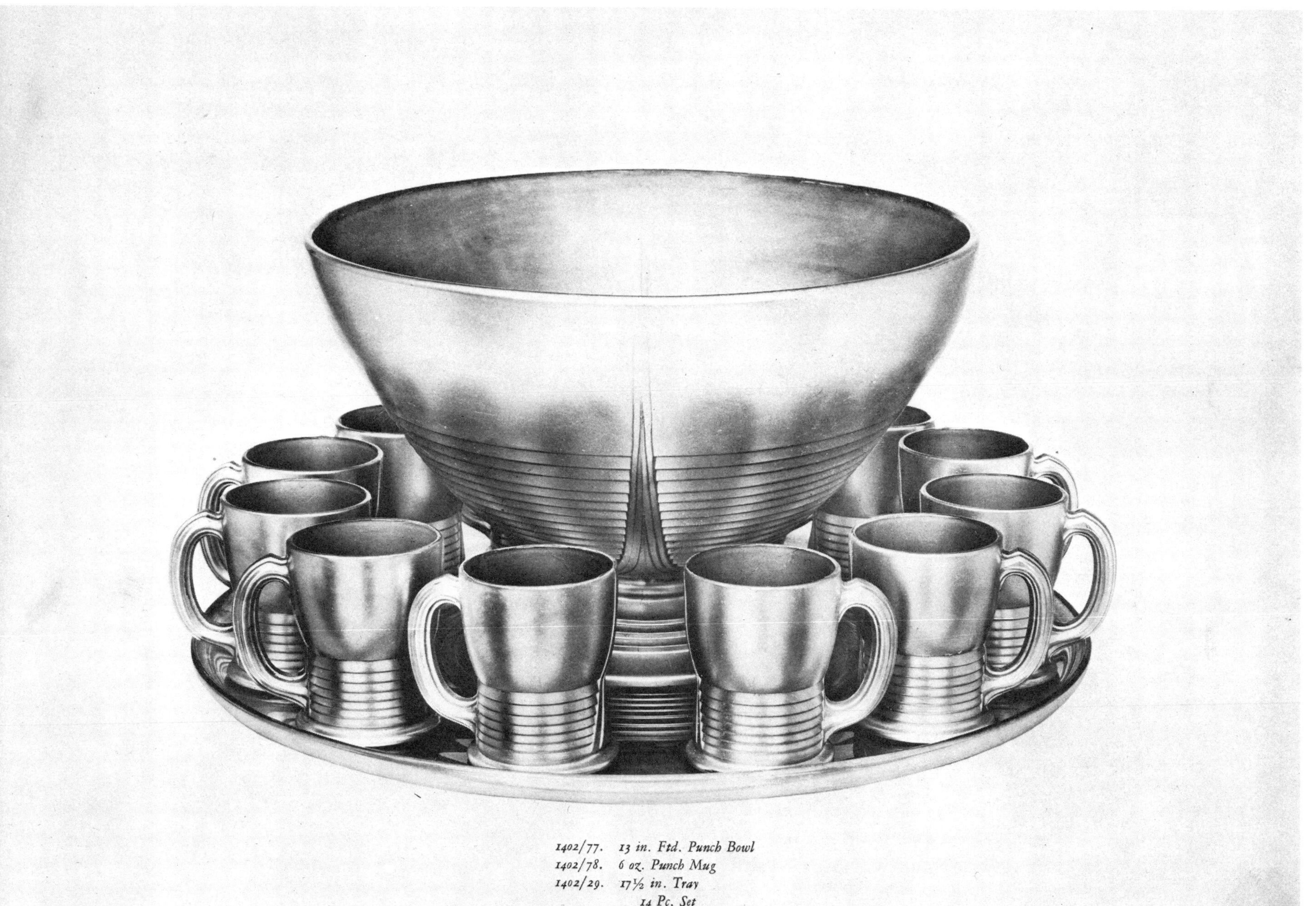

1402/77. 13 in. Ftd. Punch Bowl
1402/78. 6 oz. Punch Mug
1402/29. 17½ in. Tray
14 Pc. Set

1402. TALLY-HO LINE

1402/28. 18 in. Buffet Plate

1402/29. 17½ in. Cabaret Plate

1402/101/102. 17½ in. Cheese and Cracker

1402/97. 4-Piece Salad Set, 18 in.

1402/96/102. 4-Piece Salad Set, 17½ in.

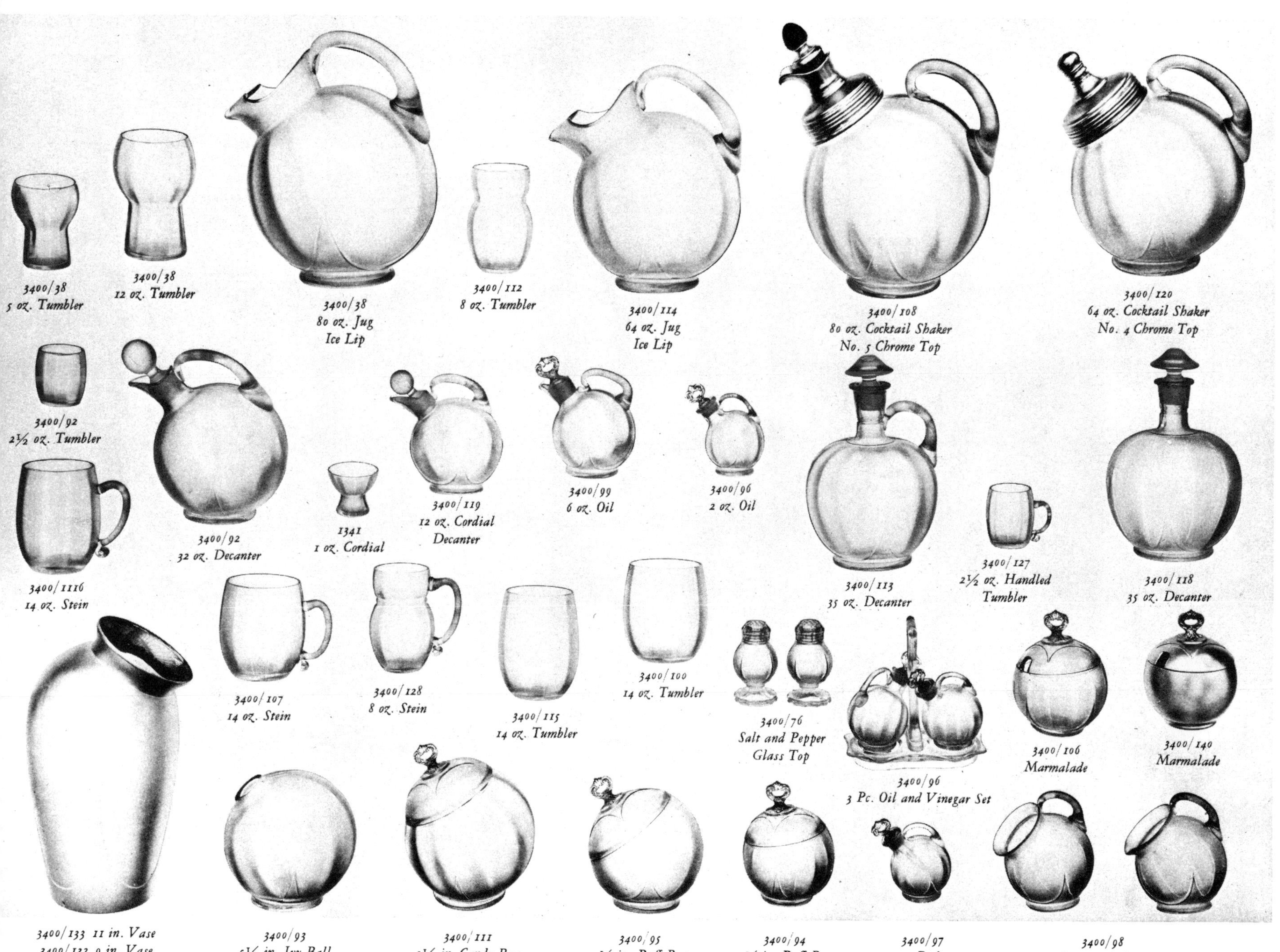

3400/38
5 oz. Tumbler

3400/38
12 oz. Tumbler

3400/38
80 oz. Jug
Ice Lip

3400/112
8 oz. Tumbler

3400/114
64 oz. Jug
Ice Lip

3400/108
80 oz. Cocktail Shaker
No. 5 Chrome Top

3400/120
64 oz. Cocktail Shaker
No. 4 Chrome Top

3400/92
2½ oz. Tumbler

3400/92
32 oz. Decanter

1341
1 oz. Cordial

3400/119
12 oz. Cordial
Decanter

3400/99
6 oz. Oil

3400/96
2 oz. Oil

3400/113
35 oz. Decanter

3400/127
2½ oz. Handled
Tumbler

3400/118
35 oz. Decanter

3400/1116
14 oz. Stein

3400/107
14 oz. Stein

3400/128
8 oz. Stein

3400/115
14 oz. Tumbler

3400/100
14 oz. Tumbler

3400/76
Salt and Pepper
Glass Top

3400/96
3 Pc. Oil and Vinegar Set

3400/106
Marmalade

3400/140
Marmalade

3400/133 11 in. Vase
3400/132 9 in. Vase
3400/134 13 in. Vase

3400/93
5½ in. Ivy Ball

3400/111
5½ in. Candy Box

3400/95
4½ in. Puff Box

3400/94
3½ in. Puff Box

3400/97
2 oz. Perfume
Dropper Stopper

3400/98
Sugar and Cream

3500. "GADROON" LINE

Low Sherbet
E: Valencia

Goblet, Long Bowl
E: Valencia

3500/39. 12 in. Ftd.
Sandwich Plate, E: Valencia

Tall Sherbet
E: Valencia

Ftd. Tumbler, 5 oz.
E: Minerva

Goblet, Long Bowl
E: Elaine

Ftd. Tumbler, 2½ oz.
E: Elaine

Cocktail
E: Elaine

Goblet, Short Bowl
E: Minerva

Wine
E: Minerva

Ftd. Tumbler, 10 oz.
E: Minerva

3500/39. 12 in. Ftd.
Sandwich Plate
E: Elaine

3500/39. 12 in Ftd.
Sandwich Plate
E: Minerva

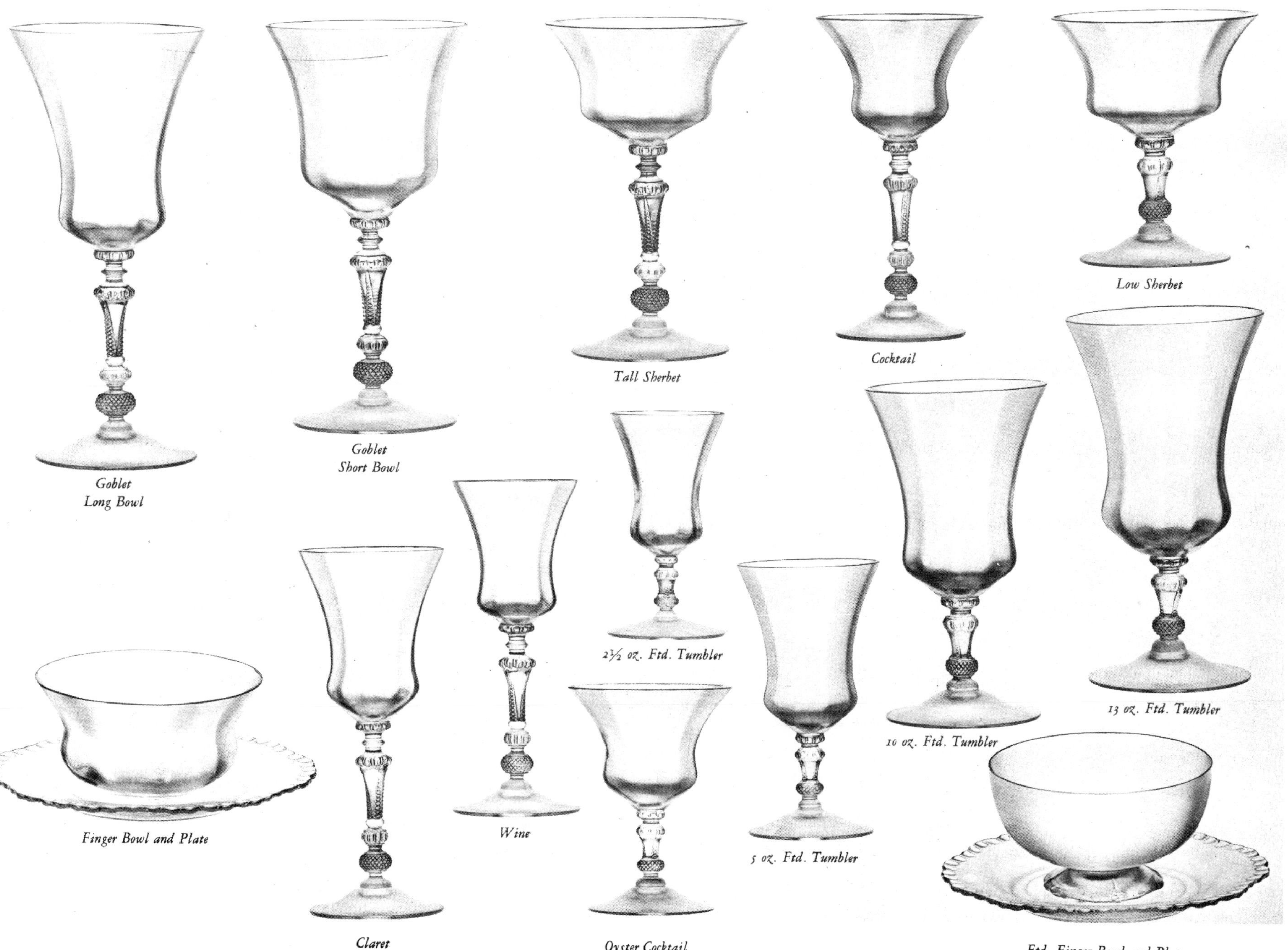

Goblet Long Bowl

Goblet Short Bowl

Tall Sherbet

Cocktail

Low Sherbet

Finger Bowl and Plate

Claret

Wine

2½ oz. Ftd. Tumbler

Oyster Cocktail

5 oz. Ftd. Tumbler

10 oz. Ftd. Tumbler

13 oz. Ftd. Tumbler

Ftd. Finger Bowl and Plate

3500. "GADROON" LINE

3500/5. 8½ in. Salad Plate

3500/4.
7½ in. Dessert Plate

3500/3.
6 in. Bread and Butter Plate

3500/10. 5 in. Fruit Saucer

3500/39.
12 in. Ftd. Sandwich Plate

3500/11. 6 in. Cereal

3500/2.
Cream Soup and Saucer

3500/1.
Cup and Saucer

3500/36. 6 in. Tall Comport

3500/37. 7 in. Tall Comport

3500/17. 12 in. Bowl

3500/28. 10 in. Bowl

3500/21. 12 in. Oval Bowl

3500/25. 9 in. Bowl

3500/16. 11 in. Bowl

3500. "GADROON" LINE

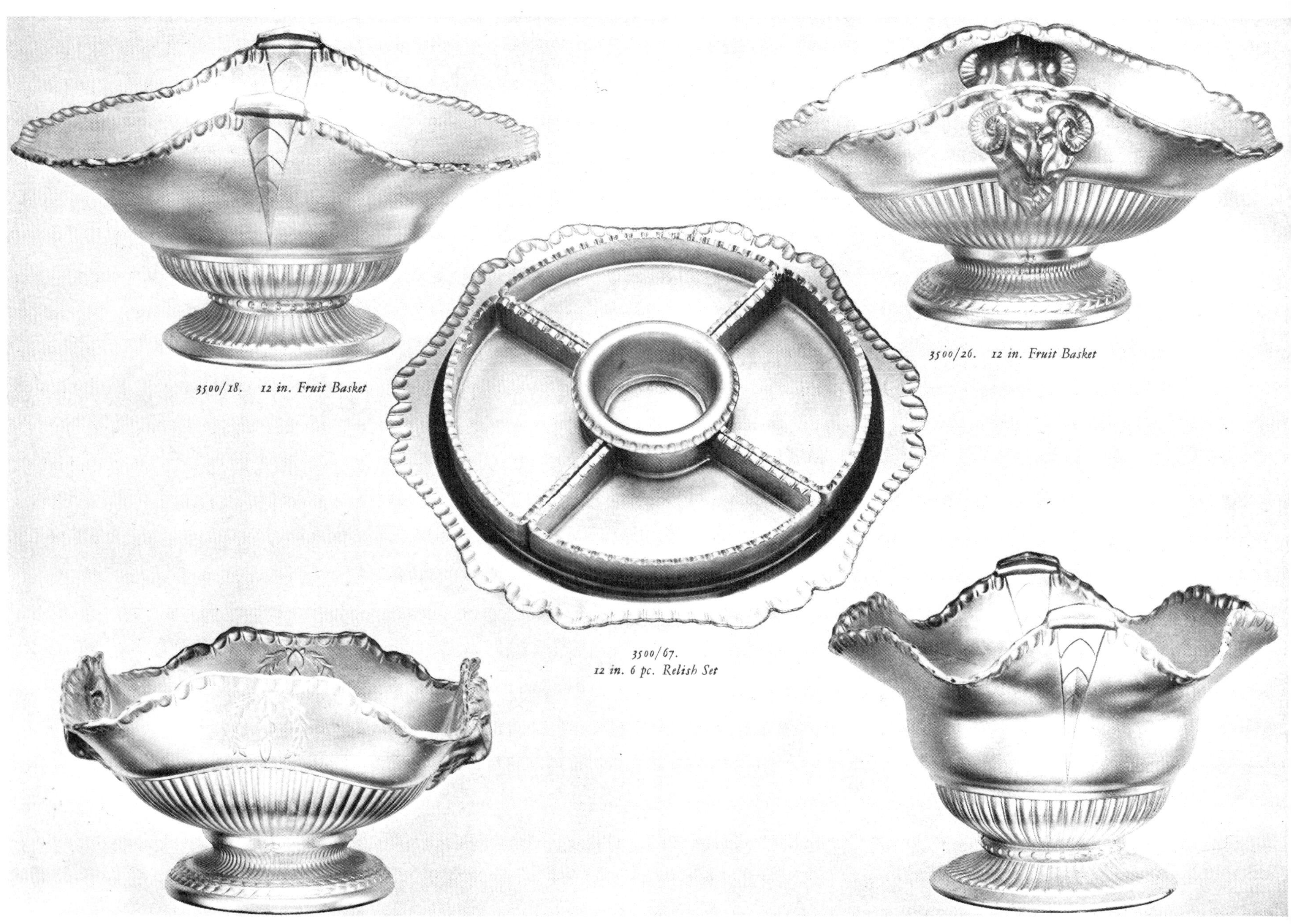

3500/18. 12 in. Fruit Basket

3500/26. 12 in. Fruit Basket

3500/67. 12 in. 6 pc. Relish Set

3500/27. 8 in. Bowl

3500/19. 11 in. Bowl

3500. "GADROON" LINE

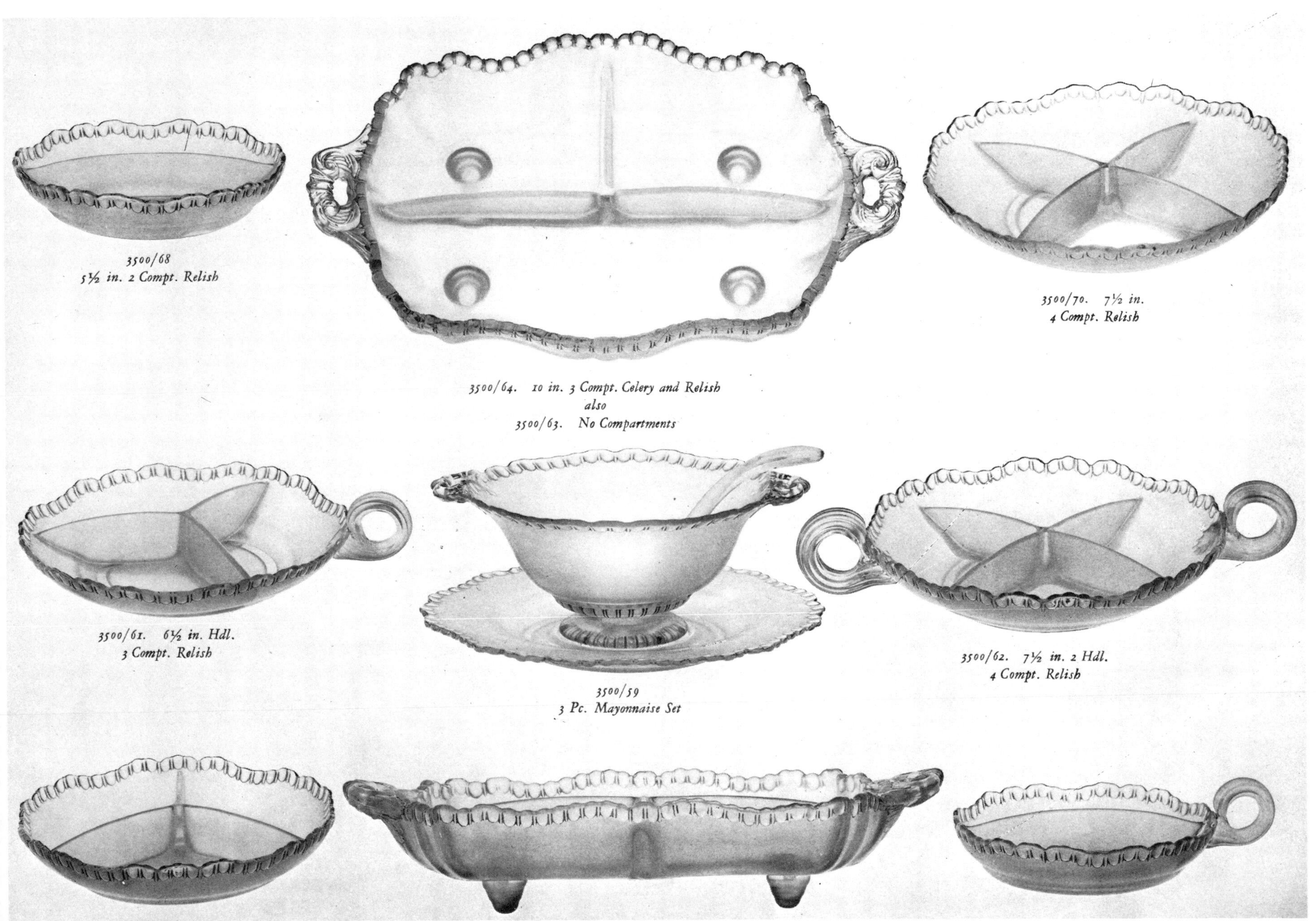

3500/68
5½ in. 2 Compt. Relish

3500/64. 10 in. 3 Compt. Celery and Relish
also
3500/63. No Compartments

3500/70. 7½ in.
4 Compt. Relish

3500/61. 6½ in. Hdl.
3 Compt. Relish

3500/59
3 Pc. Mayonnaise Set

3500/62. 7½ in. 2 Hdl.
4 Compt. Relish

3500/69. 6½ in. 3 Compt. Relish

3500/65. 10 in. 4 Compt. Relish

3500/60. 5½ in. Hdl. 2 Compt. Relish

Page 33-14

3500. "GADROON" LINE

3500/56. 7 in. Basket

3500/55. 6 in. Basket

3500/47. 5 in. Bon Bon

3500/54. 6½ in. Low Comport

3500/52. 6 in. Hdl. Basket

3500/49. 5 in. Hdl. Nappy

3500/50. 6 in. Hdl. Nappy

3500/51. 5 in. Hdl. Basket

3500/14. Sugar and Cream
Also 3500/15. Sugar and Cream, (Ind.)

3500/67. 12 in. Tray

3500/13. Sugar Basket
Chrome Hdl. and Tongs

3500/38. 13 in. Tort Plate

1338. Candelabrum

3500/31. 6½ in. Candlestick

3500/32. 6½ in. Candelabrum Bobeche and Prisms

3500/44. 8 in. Ftd. Vase

3500/41. 10 in. Urn or Candy Jar

3500/45. 10 in. Ftd. Vase

3500/42. 12 in. Urn

3078. STEMWARE

Goblet

Tall Sherbet

Low Sherbet

Oyster Cocktail

Cocktail

Wine

15 oz. Tumbler

3 oz. Ftd. Tumbler

5 oz. Ftd. Tumbler

9 oz. Ftd. Tumbler

12 oz. Ftd. Tumbler

Claret

5 oz. Tumbler

Finger Bowl and Plate

84 oz. Jug

12 oz. Tumbler

2½ oz. Tumbler

32 oz. Decanter

1336. 18 in. Vase
Rock Crystal Eng. 698

1336. 18 in. Vase
E/Diane

CONSOLE SETS

3400/135. 9 in. Bowl

3500/32. 6½ in. Candelabrum With Bobeche and Prisms

993. 12½ in. Bowl E/Lorna

3400/136. 6 in. Bowl or Vase

3500/31. 6 in. Candlestick

1348. 11 in. Bowl E/758

1307. Candelabrum E/764

1349. 12 in. Bowl E/764

628. 3½ in. Candlestick E/758

3122
5½ in. Tall Comport

1066
5½ in. Low Comport

3126
5½ in. Tall Comport

308. 4½ in. Vase

309. 4½ in. Vase

306. 3 in. Vase

1352
Hld. Frog Vase

6004
6 in. Vase

6004
5 in. Vase

0379
3 in. Vase

3400/129
6 in. Lemon Tray

1362
8 in. Coupe Salad
or
Large Coaster

1361
7 in. Coupe Salad
or
Large Coaster

1332
6 in. Plate

1333
7½ in. Plate

1334
8½ in. Plate

BEVERAGE ACCESSORIES

1321. 32 oz.
Decanter
Jigger Stopper

3400/122. 38 oz.
Tomato or Orange Juice
Jug

3400/122. 5 oz.
Tomato or Orange Juice
Tumbler

3400/121. 38 oz.
Cocktail Shaker
No. 5 Chrome Top

1070. 36 oz.
Pinch Decanter
No. 1 Jigger Stopper

1322. 26 oz.
Decanter
No. 1 Jigger Stopper

1324. 22 oz.
Decanter
No. 1 Jigger Stopper

Height
17 in.
Diameter
3 in.
Chrome
Churner

1217. 4 oz.
Bitter Bottle

1344. 1 oz.
Cordial

270. 1 oz.
Cordial

1408. 60 oz.
Cocktail Mixer

1329. 4½ oz.
Mustard,
Notched Cover

3400/46. 12 oz.
Cabinet Flask

1323. 28 oz.
Decanter
No. 1 Jigger Stopper

1327. 1 oz.
Cordial

1213. 8 oz.
Bitter Bottle

3187. 4 oz.
Cocktail

1070. 14 oz.
Pinch Tumbler

1405. 16 oz.
Stein

1066. 6 oz.
Cafe Parfait

1069. 11 oz.
Goblet

3400/130. 11 oz.
Tumbler

1406. 6 oz.
Old Fashion
Cocktail

1407. 9 oz.
Old Fashion Cocktail
No. 1 Muddler

1337
Cigarette Holder

1216. Flower Holder

1207. 11 in. Bowl

1210. Flower Holder

Vases are removable and can be used as Candlesticks, as shown below

1209. Candlestick

1211. Candelabrum

NOVELTY SETS IN DISPLAY BOXES

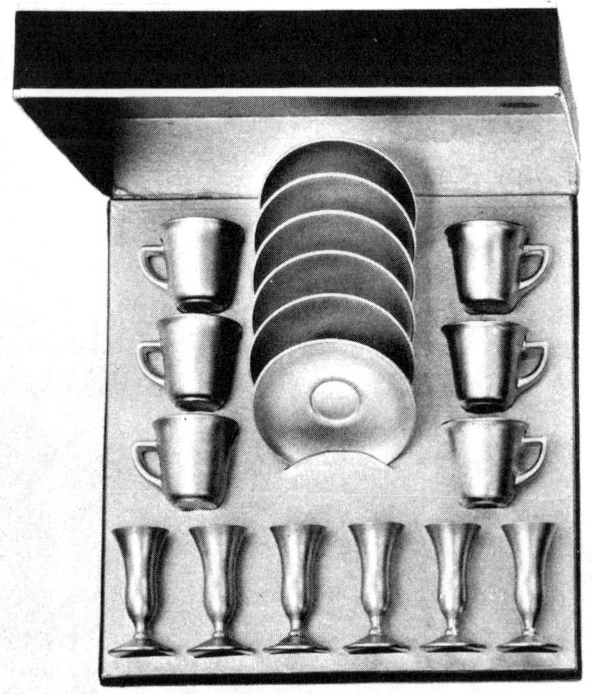

925/1327. 18 pc. After Dinner Coffee and Cordial Set

3500/15. Individual Sugar and Cream Set

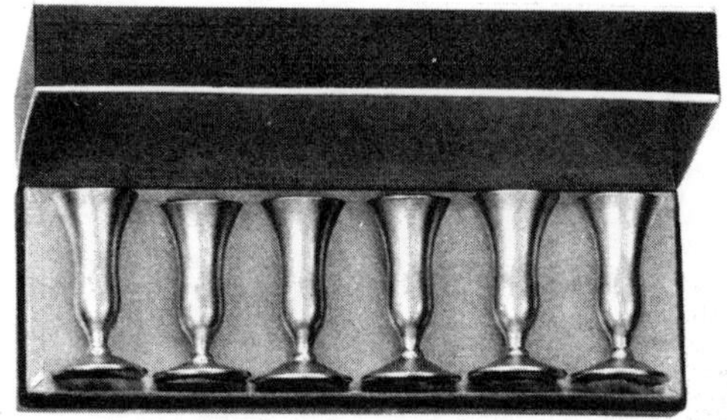

1327. 6 pc. Cordial Set

3011. 6 pc. Cocktail Set

3400/107. 6 pc. Stein Set

1402/39/37. 7 pc. Decanter Set

3400/92. 7 pc. Decanter Set

925. 12 pc. After Dinner Coffee Set

3011. 3 pc. Smoker Set

"EVERGLADE"

26
Sugar and Cream

24
Sherbet

25
8 inch Plate

27
7½ inch Bowl

23
5 inch Vase

20
10½ inch Vase

21
7½ inch Vase

22
6 inch Vase

3
Candelabrum

1
10 inch Bowl

3
Candelabrum

2
Candlestick

19
12 inch Oval Bowl

2
Candlestick

"EVERGLADE"

10
4 inch Candlestick

8
12 inch Bowl

7
11 inch Bowl

10
4 inch Candlestick

6
3 Pc. Flower Holder

28
16 inch Bowl

5
2 Pc. Flower Holder

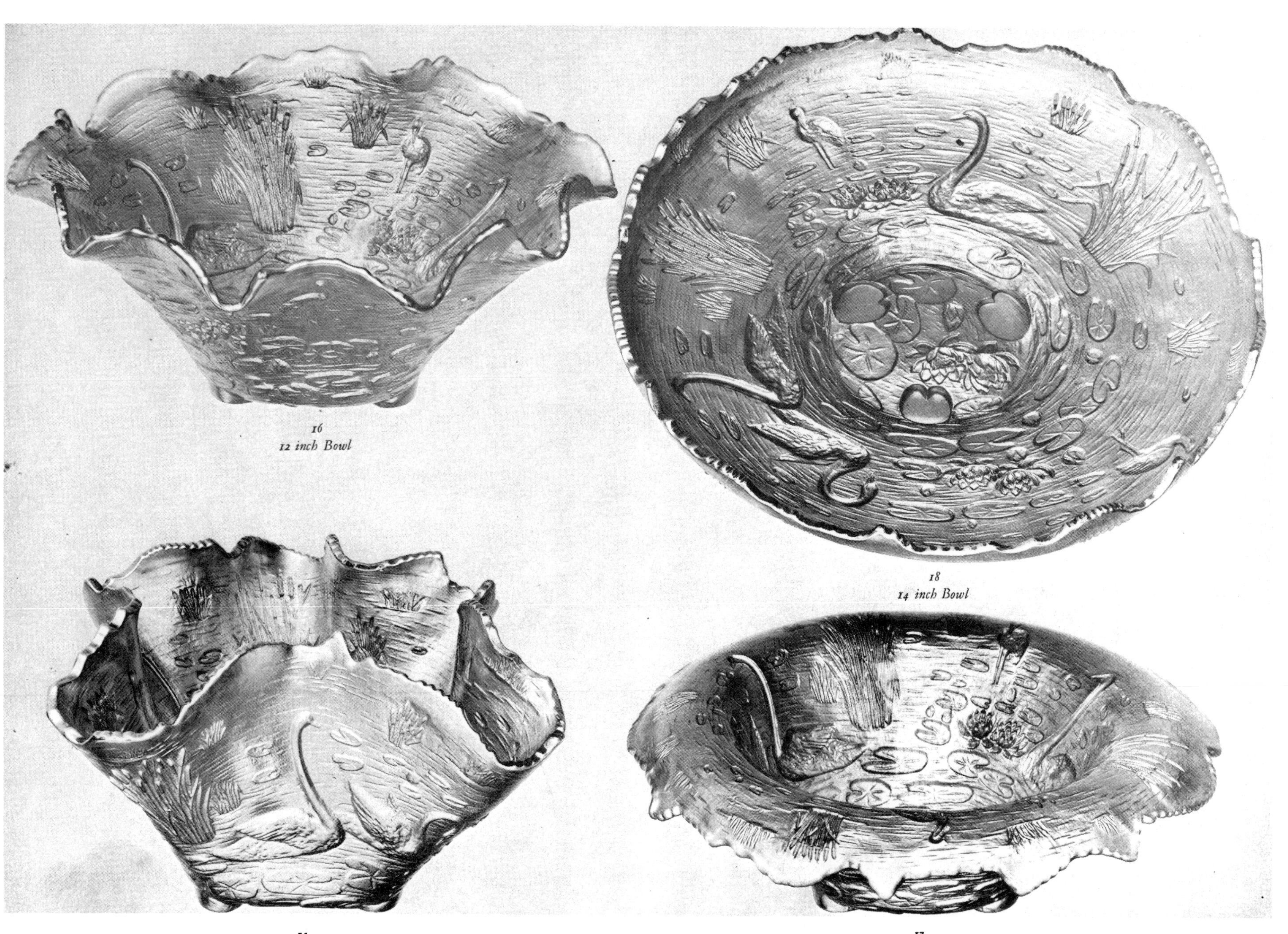

16
12 inch Bowl

18
14 inch Bowl

15
11 inch Bowl

17
13 inch Bowl

"EVERGLADE"

11
10½ inch Bowl

14
14 inch Bowl

13
13 inch Bowl

12
12 inch Bowl

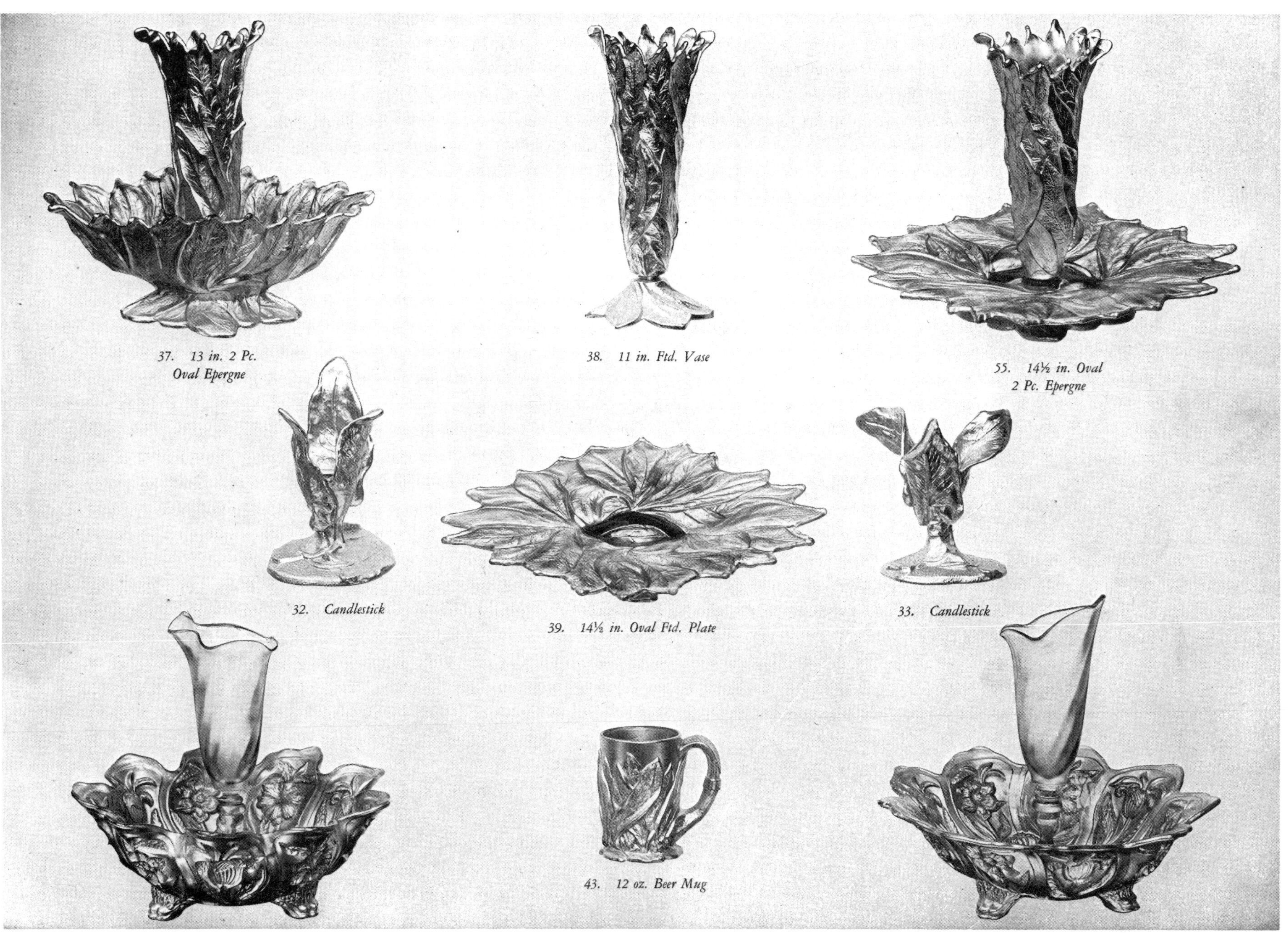

37. 13 in. 2 Pc. Oval Epergne

38. 11 in. Ftd. Vase

55. 14½ in. Oval 2 Pc. Epergne

32. Candlestick

39. 14½ in. Oval Ftd. Plate

33. Candlestick

43. 12 oz. Beer Mug

53. 2 Pc. Epergne

51. 2 Pc. Epergne

"EVERGLADE"

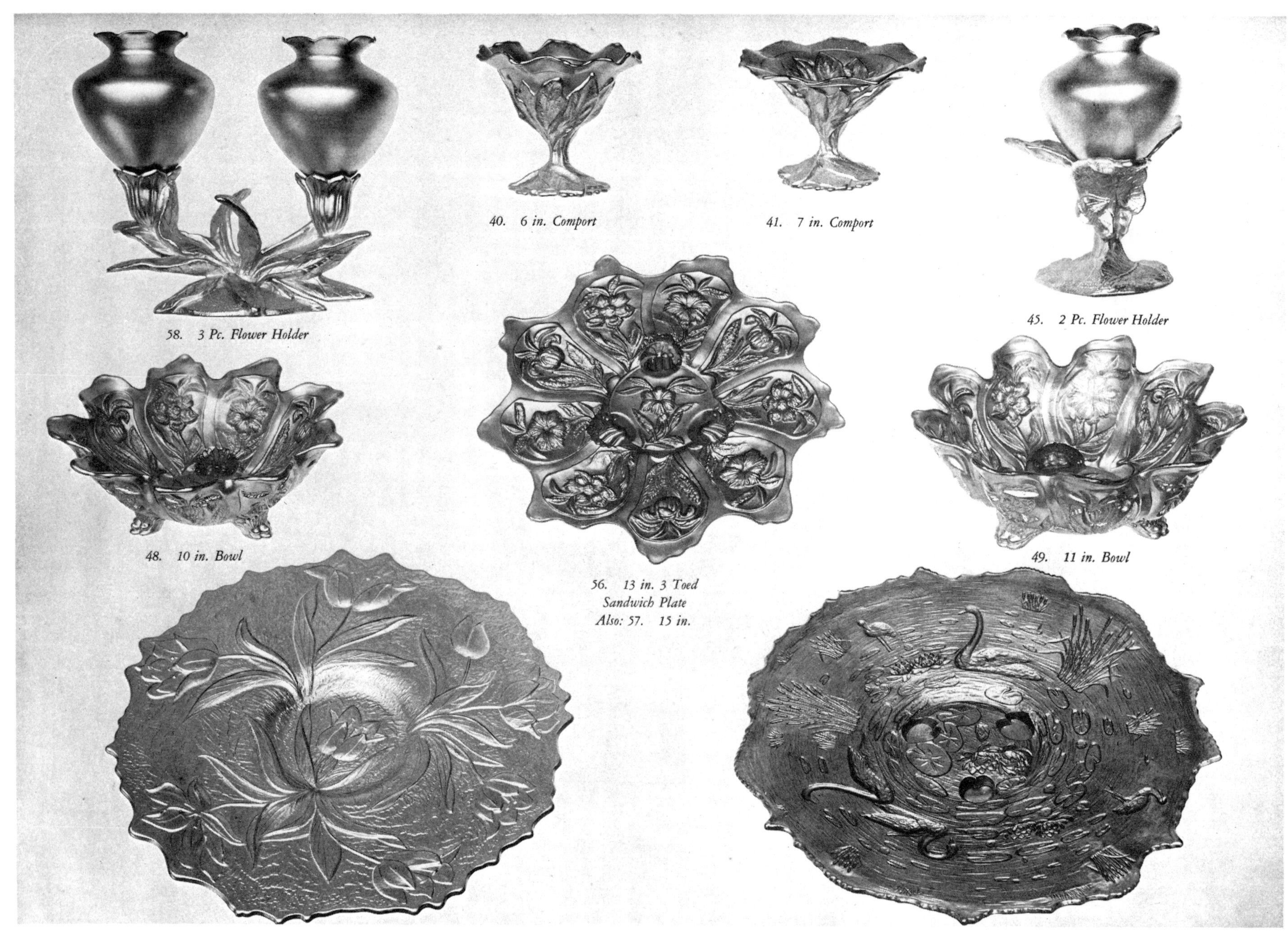

58. *3 Pc. Flower Holder*

40. *6 in. Comport*

41. *7 in. Comport*

45. *2 Pc. Flower Holder*

48. *10 in. Bowl*

56. *13 in. 3 Toed Sandwich Plate*
Also: 57. *15 in.*

49. *11 in. Bowl*

31. *16 in. Plate*

30. *16 in. Plate*

3500/42. 12 in. Urn
D/1007-8

3400/45. 11 in. Bowl
D/1001
518. Figure
Flower Holder

3500/41. 10 in. Urn
D/995

1040½. 3 in. Swan

1043. 8½ in. Swan

1307. Candelabrum
D-1001

1240. 12 inch Bowl
D/1012

3400/114. 64 oz. Jug
D/995

3011. Candlestick
with Prisms
D/1007-8

3011. Ash Tray
D/1007-8

3011. Cigarette Box
D/1007-8

3011. Comport
D/1007-8

Plate 33-31

1298. 13 in. Vase
D/995

1130. 11 in. Vase
D/1007-8

1297. 11 in. Vase
D/1001

1301. 10 in. Vase
D/995

1299. 11 in. Vase
D/1012

1300. 8 in. Vase
D/1012

1238. 12 in. Vase
D/1007-8

1228. 9 in. Vase
D/1001

3400/103. 6 in. Vase
D/1001

3400/102. 5 in. Vase
D/995

1309. 5 in. Vase
D/1012

1302. 9 in. Vase
D/1007-8

NEW BUFFET OR SUNDAY EVENING SUPPER SETS

Set
Consists of

1402/101. 18 in. Buffet Plate Flat Rim, with seat
1402/101. 9 in. Comport with seat
1402/3. 5 oz. Cocktail, for catsup, mustard or other cocktail sauces

1402/101/101/8. 3-PC. BUFFET OR SUNDAY EVENING SUPPER SET

The 1402/101 Flat Rim, Buffet Shape Plate or the 1402/102 Turned-up Edge, Cabaret Shape Plate may be used in either combination.

Set
Consists of

1402/102. 17½ in. Cabaret Plate, Turned-up edge with seat
1402/101. 9 in. Comport with seat
1402/33. Whipped Cream or Small Mayonnaise

1402/102/101/33. 3-PC. BUFFET OR SUNDAY EVENING SUPPER SET

7801 LINE STEMWARE

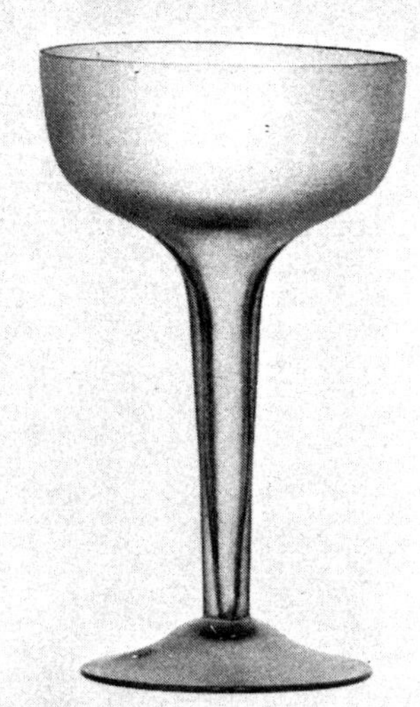

7801. 6 oz. Hollow Stem Champagne, saucer shape

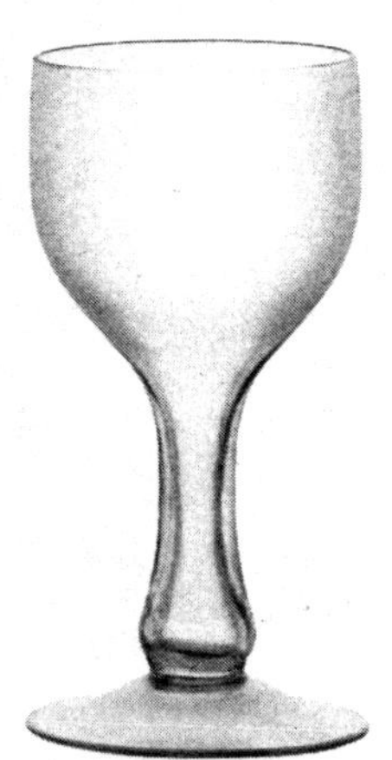

7801. 4 oz. Hollow Stem Champagne (7927)

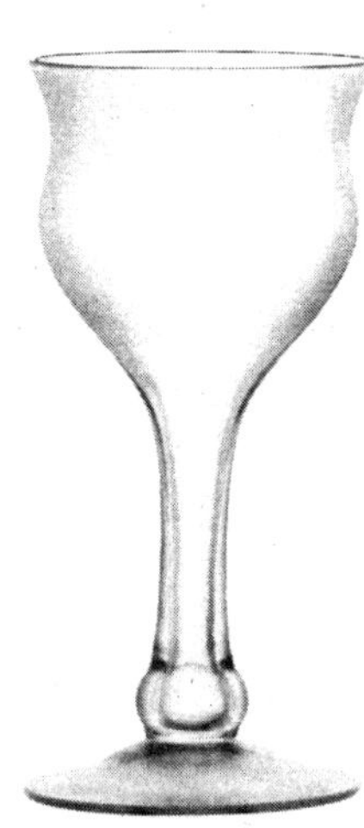

7801. 5 oz. Hollow Stem Champagne (7927½)

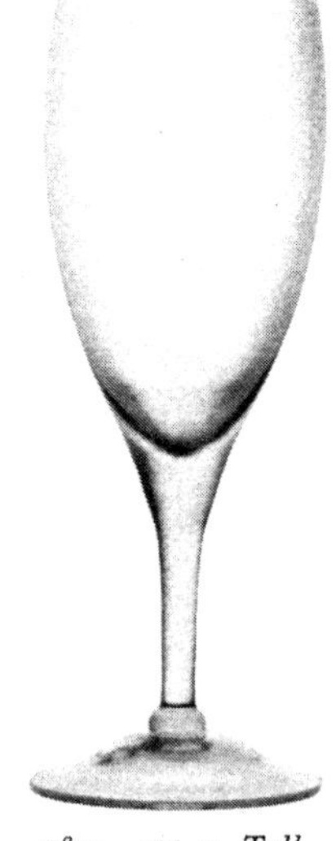

7801. 5½ oz. Tall Champagne (7516)

7801. 6 oz. Low Sherbet

7801. 6 oz. Hollow Stem Champagne (saucer shape) Cut stem

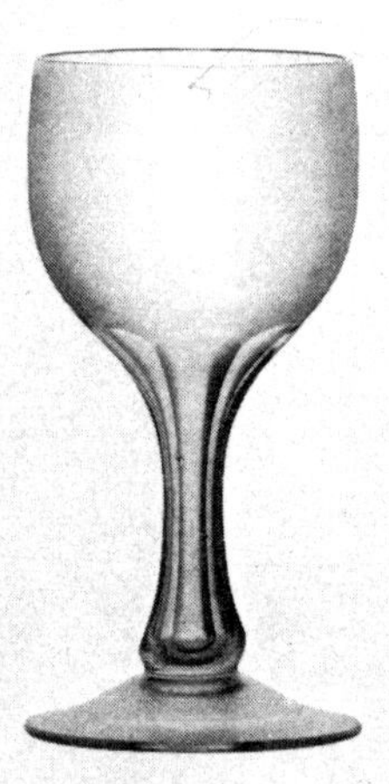

7801. 4 oz. Hollow Stem Champagne (7927) Cut stem

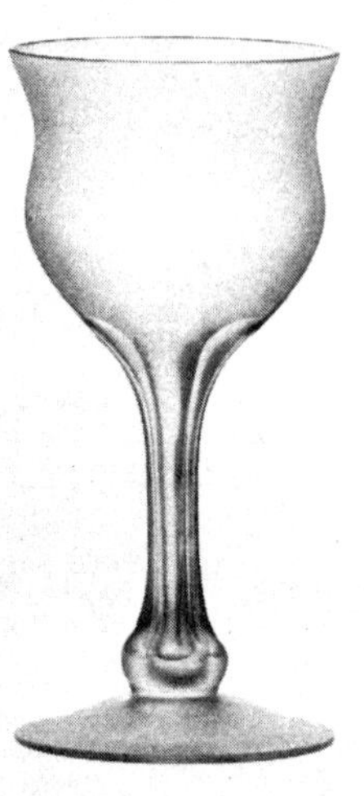

7801. 5 oz. Hollow Stem Champagne (7927½) Cut stem

7801. 6 oz. Low Stem Saucer Champagne

7801. 6 oz. Tall Stem Saucer Champagne

(Illustrations Half Size)

7801. 9 oz. Tall Stem Goblet

7801. 9 oz. Low Stem Goblet

7801. 4 oz. Claret

7801. 2 oz. Wine

(Illustrations Half Size)

7801 LINE STEMWARE

7801. 3½ oz. Cocktail

7801. 2 oz. Sherry (7966)

7801. 1½ oz. Sherry (7966)

7801. 1 oz. Cordial (7966)

7801. 4½ oz. Claret (7901)

7801. 4½ oz. Claret (3280)

7801. 4½ oz. Oyster Cocktail (7608)

7801. 2½ oz. Creme de menthe (7967)

7801. 3½ oz. Cocktail (7966)

7801. 3 oz. Cocktail (7911)

7801. 4 oz. Side Car Cocktail (7911)

7801. 4½ oz. Side Car Cocktail (7911)

2900. 5 oz. Punch Cup

(Illustrations Half Size)

BEER AND BAR GLASSWARE

(Mugs and Steins, Pressed)

550. 10 oz.

611. 8 oz.

593. 8 oz.

595. 12 oz.

1405. 16 oz.

1402/36. 14 oz.

54. 8 oz. M. W.

55. 10 oz. M. W.

56. 12 oz. M. W.

1402/35. 12 oz.

3400/149. 13 oz.

3400/151. 13 oz.

3400/150. 12 oz.

84. 14 oz. Mt. V.

BEER AND BAR GLASSWARE

(Mugs and Pilsners, Blown)

7857. 12 oz. Pilsner

7857. 10 oz. Pilsner

7857. 6½ oz. Pilsner

7857. 8 oz. Pilsner

7857½. 12 oz. Pilsner, Low Foot

7857½. 10 oz. Pilsner, Low Foot

1206. 12 oz. Ftd. Tumbler, Spiral

7857½. 8 oz. Pilsner, Low Foot

7857½. 6½ oz. Pilsner, Low Foot

3400/128. 8 oz. Mug

3400/116. 14 oz. Mug

3400/107. 14 oz. Mug

1402/113. 16 oz.

3135. 10 oz. Ftd. Tumbler

BEER AND BAR GLASSWARE

(Pilsners and Weiss Beer Goblets, Pressed)

971. 8 oz. Goblet

972. 9 oz. Goblet

1403. 10 oz. Pilsner

1403. 8 oz. Pilsner

973. 11 oz. Goblet

1057½. 14 oz. Weiss Beer

1403½. 8 oz. Pilsner, Low Foot

575. 34 oz. Weiss Beer

1041½. 12 oz. Weiss Beer

1055. 32 oz. Weiss Beer

BEER AND BAR GLASSWARE

(Goblets, Pressed)

BEER AND BAR GLASSWARE

(Goblets, Blown)

1066. 11 oz.
Low Foot

7974. 8½ oz.

301. 9 oz.
Low Foot

1402/100. 12 oz.
Low Foot, Also 16 oz.

3078. 9 oz.
Low Foot, Also 12 oz.

3078. 10 oz.

BEER AND BAR GLASSWARE

(Miscellaneous, Pressed)

690½. 4 oz. Claret, optic

764½. 3½ oz. Cocktail

765. 4 oz. Cocktail

764. 3 oz. Cocktail

903. 4½ oz. Rhine Wine

827. 5 oz. Hot Whiskey

901. 4½ oz. Rhine Wine

828. 4½ oz. Hot Whiskey

1404. 6 oz. Hollow Stem Champagne

848. 2 oz. Wine

769. 2½ oz. Creme de Menthe

922½. 2½ oz. Sherry

924. 1½ oz. Sherry

935. 1 oz. Pousse Cafe

695. 3 oz. Wine Optic

599. 5¼ in. Coaster

603. 4 in. Coaster

1402/47. 4 in. Coaster

601. 3 in. Coaster

602. 5¼ in. Coaster

BEER AND BAR GLASSWARE
(Miscellaneous, Blown)

BEER AND BAR GLASSWARE

(Tumblers, Pressed)

BEER AND BAR GLASSWARE

(Tumblers, Blown)

1066. 14 oz. Light, also Sham

1402/112. 16 oz.

1066. 12 oz. Light also Sham

1066. 10 oz. Light also Sham

1066. 7 oz. Light also Sham

1066. 5 oz. Light also Sham

1066. 2½ oz. Light also Sham

9024. 2½ oz.

9024. 8 oz.

9024. 10 oz.

9024. 14 oz.

9024. 16 oz.

3400/115. 14 oz.

3400/100. 13 oz.

3078. 2½ oz.

3078. 5 oz. Half Sham

3078. 12 oz. Half Sham

3078. 15 oz. Half Sham

499. 20 oz. Sham Cut Flute

493. 14 oz. Sham Cut Flute

498. 12 oz. Sham Cut Flute

497. 8 oz. Sham Cut Flute

321. 9 oz. Sham Cut Flute

320. 7 oz. Old Fashioned Cocktail Sham, Cut Flute

318. 4 oz. Sham Cut Flute

496. 2½ oz. Sham Cut Flute

BEER AND GLASSWARE
(Tumblers, Blown)

8701. 14 oz. 8701. 12 oz. 8701. 10 oz. 8701. 8 oz. 1306. 20 oz.

BEER AND BAR GLASSWARE

(Jugs, Pretzel Jars, etc.)

96. 69 oz. Tankard Jug
Also: 59 oz., 32 oz. 40 oz., 18 oz.

1402/49. 88 oz. Jug

1402/50. 74 oz. Tankard Jug

1402/93. Covered Pretzel Jar

3400/101. 76 oz. Jug

3400/38. 80 oz. Ball Shape Jug

3400/141. 80 oz. Jug

402/87. Covered Pretzel Jar W/Chromium Plated Handle

67. Covered Pretzel Jar M. W.

1229. Shaker C. N. Top

396. Shaker Chromium Plated Top

3400/76. Shaker W/glass top

1212. 11 oz. Bitter Bottle W/Tube

1213. 8 oz. Bitter Bottle W/Tube

1217. 4 oz. BitterBottle W/Tube

395. Shaker Chromium Plated Top

3400/77. Shaker W/glass top

3450. NAUTILUS

(Design Patents 84482 and 89828)

84 oz. Jug

40 oz. Decanter G. S.

28 oz. Decanter G. S.

Sugar and Cream

9 in. Ftd. Vase

2 oz. Wine

1 oz. Cordial

1 oz.

2 oz.

2½ oz.

5 oz.

12 oz.

15 oz.

7 in. Ftd. Vase

14 oz. Decanter G. S.

1½ oz. Perfume G. S.

3 Pc. Oil and Vinegar Set

3 Pc. Salt and Pepper Shaker Set

3011. FIGURE STEM LINE

3011/1
Banquet Goblet

3011/2
Table Goblet

3011/3
Saucer Champagne

3011/5
6 oz. Hoch

3011/7
4½ oz. Claret

3011/6
5 oz. Roemer

3011/11
3 oz. Cocktail

3011/8
4½ oz. Sauterne

3011/10
3 oz. Cocktail

3011/9
3 oz. Cocktail

3011/12
3 oz. Wine

3011/13
1 oz. Brandy

3011/14
1 oz. Cordial

3011. 7 in.
Comport, Flared

3011
9 in. Candlestick

3011. 9 in.
Lustre Cut Prism
Candlestick with
Bobeche and Prisms

3011. 7 in.
Comport, Cupped

3011
Covered Sweetmeat

3011
Cigarette Holder

3011
Covered Cigarette Box
(Short Stem)

3011
Covered Cigarette Box
(Tall Stem)

3011. Ash Tray

7966. STEMWARE PLATE ETCHED "BACCHUS"

6 oz. Hollow Stem Champagne Cut Flute Stem

6 oz. Saucer Champagne

1402/150. STEMWARE PLATE ETCHED "ELAINE"
1402/200. STEMWARE PLATE ETCHED "766 CHINTZ"

Plate 34-4

1402/150. 12 oz. Tall Ftd. Tumbler

1402/150. 12 oz. Ftd. Tumbler

1402/150
9 oz. Ftd. Tumbler

1402/150
5 oz. Claret

1402/150
3 oz. Wine

1402/150. Fingerbowl and Plate

1402/150. Low Sherbet

1402/150. 3½ oz. Cocktail

1402/150
1 oz. Cordial

1402/200
Fingerbowl and Plate

1402/200
10 oz. Ftd. Tumbler

1402/200
5 oz. Ftd. Tumbler

1402/200
6 oz. Low Sherbet

1402/200
3 oz. Ftd. Tumbler

1402/200
3½ oz. Cocktail

1402/200
1 oz. Pousse-Café

ROUND DINNERWARE PLATE ETCHED "766 CHINTZ"

531
7 in. Comport

533. 3 Pc.
Mayonnaise Set

103. 6 in. 3 Compt.
Covered Candy Box

851. Ice Pail, Chrom. Hdl.

441. 10½ in. Low Ftd. Comport or Bowl

628. 3½ in. Candlestick

993. 12½ in. Bowl

628. 3½ in. Candlestick

135. 10 in. Cheese and Cracker

168. 10 in. Hdl. Sandwich Tray

668. 6 in. Plate

556. 8 in. Plate

242. 13½ in. Plate

652. 12 in. Celery

3129. STEMWARE PLATE ETCHED "VICHY" (765)

Plate 34-6

10 oz. Goblet

5 oz. Tall Champagne

5 oz. Roemer

6 oz. Tall Hoch

4 oz. Claret

6 oz. Saucer Champagne

3½ oz. Cocktail

6 oz. Hollow Stem Champagne

4 oz. Hollow Stem Sparkling Burgundy

6 oz. Hollow Stem Champagne Cut Flute Stem

4 oz. Hollow Stem Sparkling Burgundy Cut Flute Stem

1 oz. Cordial

1 oz. Pousse-Café

¾ oz. Brandy

6 oz. Low Sherbet

2 oz. Sherry (7966)

2 oz. Burgundy Wine

2 oz. Sherry Cut Flute Stem (7966)

2 oz. Wine

1½ oz. Sherry (7966)

1½ oz. Sherry Cut Flute Stem (7966)

Fingerbowl and Plate

3109. STEMWARE, PLATE ETCHED "VINTAGE"

9 oz. Goblet

6 oz. Hollow Stem Champagne

6 oz. Hollow Stem Champagne Cut Flute Stem

6 oz. Saucer Champagne

6 oz. Low Sherbet

5 oz. Sherbet Tall Bowl

6 oz. Tall Ale

5 oz. Hollow Stem Sparkling Burgundy

5 oz. Hollow Stem Sparkling Burgundy Cut Flute Stem

5½ oz. Tall Champagne

5 oz. Tall Champagne

4 oz. Claret

2½ oz. Creme de Menthe

3 oz. Wine

2 oz. Wine

4 oz. Cocktail

3½ oz. Cocktail

3 oz. Cocktail

1 oz. Cordial

1 oz. Pousse-Cafe

3109. STEMWARE, PLATE ETCHED "VINTAGE"

14 oz. Tumbler

12 oz. Tumbler

10 oz. Tumbler

8 oz. Tumbler

9 oz. Tumbler

5 oz. Tumbler

Fingerbowl and Plate

6 oz. Fruit Salad

4½ oz. Oyster Cocktail

1 oz. Tumbler

2 oz. Tumbler

3 oz. Tumbler

5 oz. Cafe Parfait

3 oz. Ftd. Tumbler

5 oz. Ftd. Tumbler

10 oz. Ftd. Tumbler

12 oz. Ftd. Tumbler

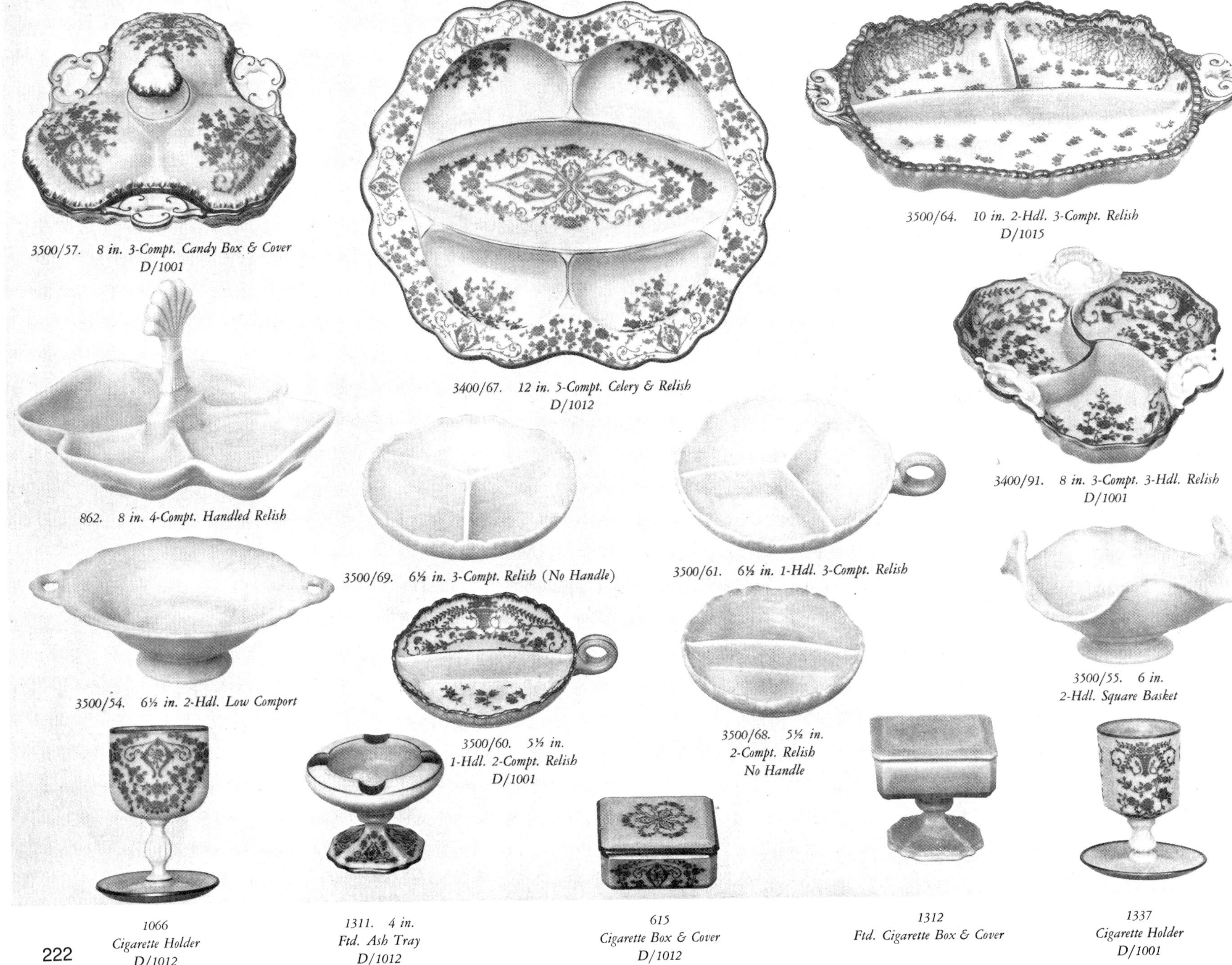

3500/57. 8 in. 3-Compt. Candy Box & Cover D/1001

3400/67. 12 in. 5-Compt. Celery & Relish D/1012

3500/64. 10 in. 2-Hdl. 3-Compt. Relish D/1015

862. 8 in. 4-Compt. Handled Relish

3400/91. 8 in. 3-Compt. 3-Hdl. Relish D/1001

3500/69. 6½ in. 3-Compt. Relish (No Handle)

3500/61. 6½ in. 1-Hdl. 3-Compt. Relish

3500/54. 6½ in. 2-Hdl. Low Comport

3500/55. 6 in. 2-Hdl. Square Basket

3500/60. 5½ in. 1-Hdl. 2-Compt. Relish D/1001

3500/68. 5½ in. 2-Compt. Relish No Handle

1066 Cigarette Holder D/1012

1311. 4 in. Ftd. Ash Tray D/1012

615 Cigarette Box & Cover D/1012

1312 Ftd. Cigarette Box & Cover

1337 Cigarette Holder D/1001

3500/16. 11 in. Footed Bowl

3400/4. 12 in. 4-Toed Bowl

3500/110. 13 in. Torte Plate

3500/26. 12 in. Fruit Basket (Ram's Head)

3400/32. 11½ in. Bowl, Flared

3500/39. 11 in. Footed Cake Plate

3500/21. 12 in. Handled & Footed Bowl, Oval D/1015

3500/28. 10 in. 2-Hdl. Bowl

3400/136 6 in. 4-Toed Bowl Fancy

526. 3½ in. Candlestick

3011. 9 in. Candlestick

647. 2-Holder Candelabrum

3500/74. 4 in. Candlestick

CROWN TUSCAN

83. *12 in. Vase* D/1001

82. *10 in. Vase*

80. *10 in. Vase*

79. *8 in. Vase*

274. *10 in. Vase* D/1007/8

1430. *8 in. Vase*

1418. *5½ in. Vase*

1236. *Ivy Ball*

119. *7 in. Hdl. Basket* D/1001

1321. *28 oz. Ftd. Decanter, G. S.* D/1015

7966. *2 oz. Sherry* D/1015

3400/152. *76 oz. Jug*

1402/52. *Ice Pail Chrom. Hdl.*

3500/36. *6 in. Tall Comport*

1066. *5⅜ in. Comport*

3011. Cigarette Box & Cover

274. 10 in. Vase

1283. 8 in. Vase

3011. Ash Tray

1066. 5⅜ in. Comport

6004. 6 in. Vase

1300. 8 in. Vase

3011. 7 in. Comport

1312. Ftd. Cigarette Box & Cover

1337 Cigarette Holder

1311. 4 in. Ftd. Ash Tray

1314. 3 in. Ftd. Ash Tray

1066 Cigarette Holder

DECANTERS

1379. 26 oz.

1383. 24 oz.

1378. 26 oz.

1402/39. 34 oz.

1402/38. 34 oz.

1388. 28 oz.
Cut Neck

1380. 26 oz.
Square
Etched Scotch

1387. 14 oz.

1380. 26 oz.
Square. Etched Rye

1321. 28 oz.

1380. 26 oz.
Square
Etched Gin

1320. 14 oz.
Cut Neck

1382. 14 oz.
Square

1324. 22 oz.

1385. 28 oz.

3450. 40 oz.
Nautilus

3450. 28 oz.
Nautilus

3450. 14 oz.
Nautilus

3400/46. 12 oz.
Flask

3400/156. 12 oz.

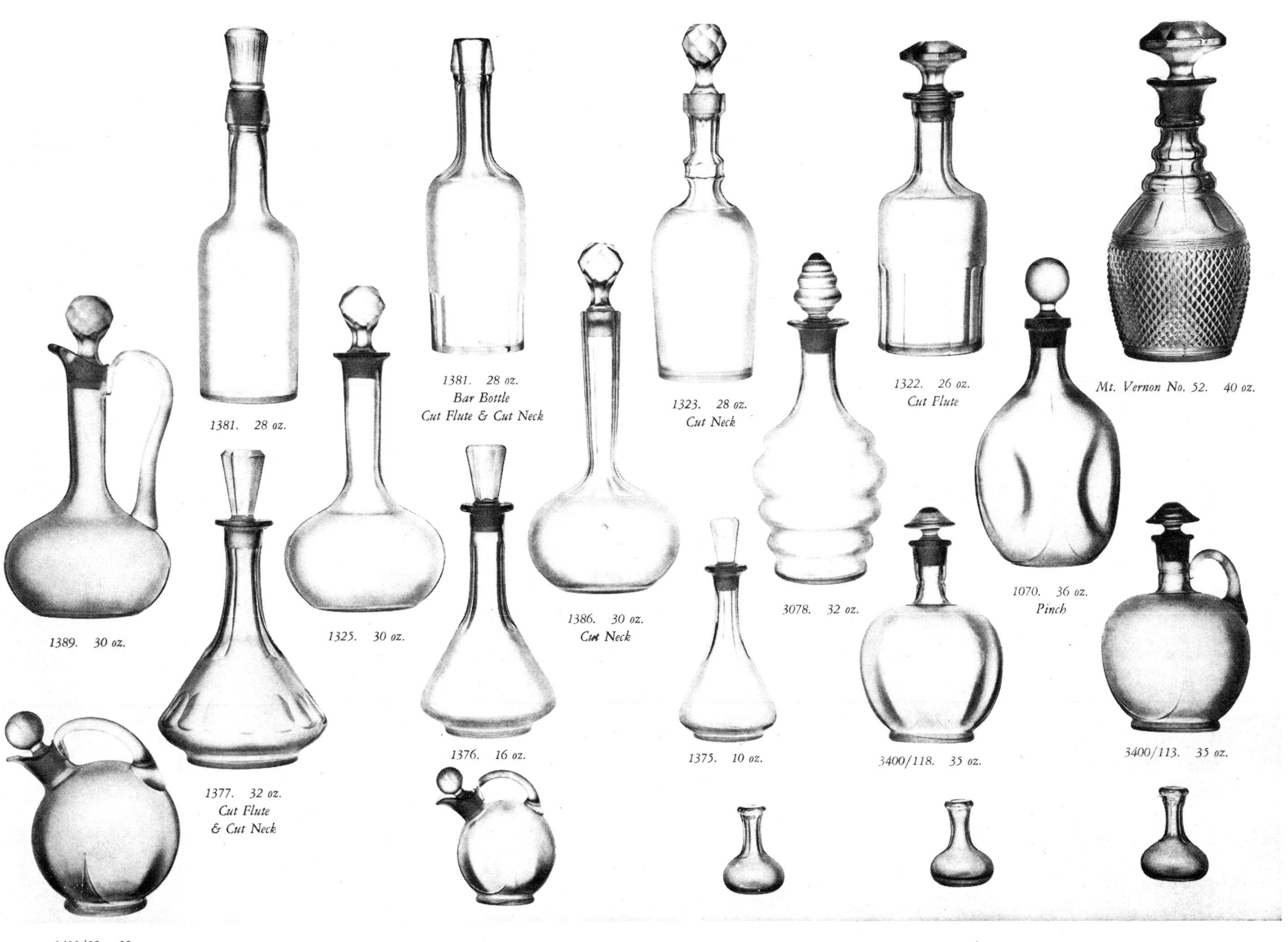

1381. 28 oz.

1381. 28 oz.
Bar Bottle
Cut Flute & Cut Neck

1323. 28 oz.
Cut Neck

1322. 26 oz.
Cut Flute

Mt. Vernon No. 52. 40 oz.

1389. 30 oz.

1325. 30 oz.

1386. 30 oz.
Cut Neck

3078. 32 oz.

1070. 36 oz.
Pinch

1377. 32 oz.
Cut Flute
& Cut Neck

1376. 16 oz.

1375. 10 oz.

3400/118. 35 oz.

3400/113. 35 oz.

3400/92. 32 oz.
Ball Shape

3400/119. 12 oz.
Ball Shape

2764. 1½ oz.

1121. 1¼ oz.

1121. 2 oz.

CANDELABRA

1358. 3 Holder
with Bobèches and Prisms

3500/94. 2 Holder

1355. 2 Holder

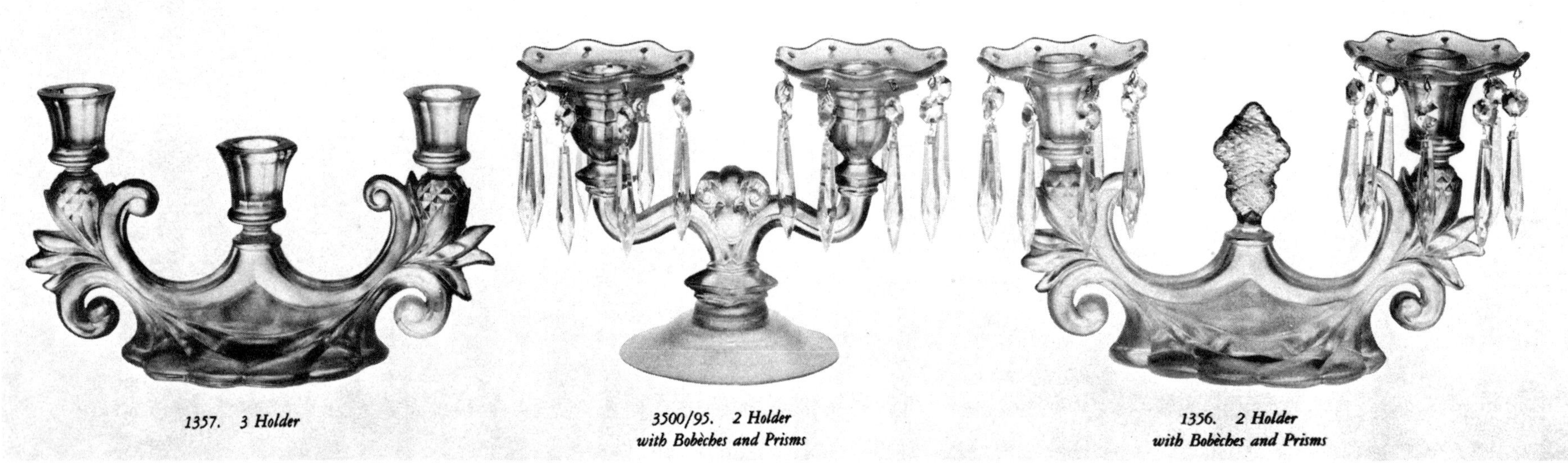

1357. 3 Holder

3500/95. 2 Holder
with Bobèches and Prisms

1356. 2 Holder
with Bobèches and Prisms

14 Piece Set
3500/112 Tray 3400/119 Decanter 3109 1-oz. Tumbler

8 Piece Set
3500/112 Tray 3400/156 Decanter
1327 1-oz. Cordial

10 Piece Set
3500/112 Tray 3450 14-oz. Decanter 3450 1-oz. Tumbler

11 Piece Set
3500/113 Tray 1382 14-oz. Decanter
3109 1-oz. Tumbler

9 Piece Set
3500/113 Tray No. 1 Muddler
1203 7-oz. O. F. Cocktail

10 Piece Set
3500/72 Tray 52 Decanter
57 7-oz. O. F. Cocktail
62 Bitter Bottle No. 1 Muddler

9 Piece Set
3500/100 Tray 1393 Mixer with No. 1 Spoon
1402/200 3½-oz. Cocktail

5 Piece Set
3500/113 Tray 1382 14-oz. Decanter

MISCELLANEOUS BLOWN WARE

7801. 5 in. Grape Fruit and Liner

7801. 5 in. Low Comport

7801. 6 in. Low Comport

7801. 7 in. Low Comport

7801. 8 in. Low Comport

7801. 6 in. Tall Comport

7801. 8 in. Bowl

7801. 5½ in. Fruit

7801. 5 in. Fruit

7801. 4 in. Fruit

0431. 2½ oz. Tumbler

0431. 9 oz. Tumbler

0431. 15 oz. Tumbler

0431. 18 oz Tumbler

7801. 5 oz. Ftd. Tumbler

7801. 8 oz. Ftd. Tumbler

7801. 10 oz. Ftd. Tumbler

7801. 12 oz. Ftd. Tumbler

3129. 10 oz. Ftd. Tumbler

3129. 12 oz. Ftd. Tumbler

1402/100. 12 oz. Ftd. Tumbler Tall Bowl

3126. 12 oz. Ftd. Tumbler Tall Bowl

3500. 12 oz. Ftd. Tumbler Tall Bowl

7966. 12 oz. Ftd. Tumbler

7966. 10 oz. Ftd. Tumbler

7966. 8 oz. Ftd. Tumbler

7966. 5 oz. Ftd. Tumbler

7966. 2½ oz. Ftd. Tumbler

1066. 2 oz. Sherry

7801. 2 oz. London Dock

3101. ¾ oz. Pousse Café

1066. 1 oz. Pousse Café

1066. ¾ oz. Brandy

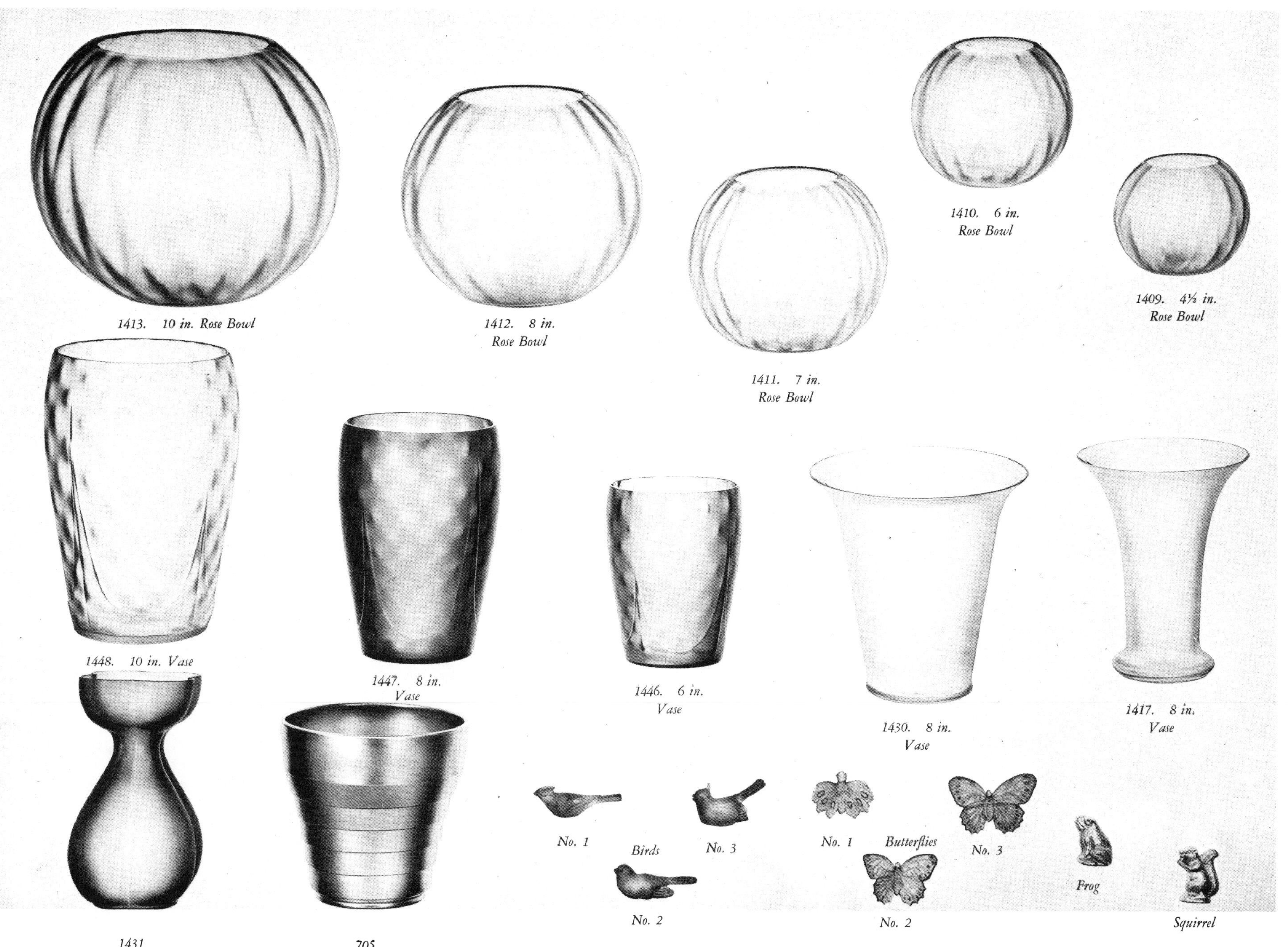

1413. 10 in. Rose Bowl

1412. 8 in. Rose Bowl

1411. 7 in. Rose Bowl

1410. 6 in. Rose Bowl

1409. 4½ in. Rose Bowl

1448. 10 in. Vase

1447. 8 in. Vase

1446. 6 in. Vase

1430. 8 in. Vase

1417. 8 in. Vase

Birds: No. 1, No. 2, No. 3

Butterflies: No. 1, No. 2, No. 3

Frog

Squirrel

1431 Bulb Vase

705 Flower Pot

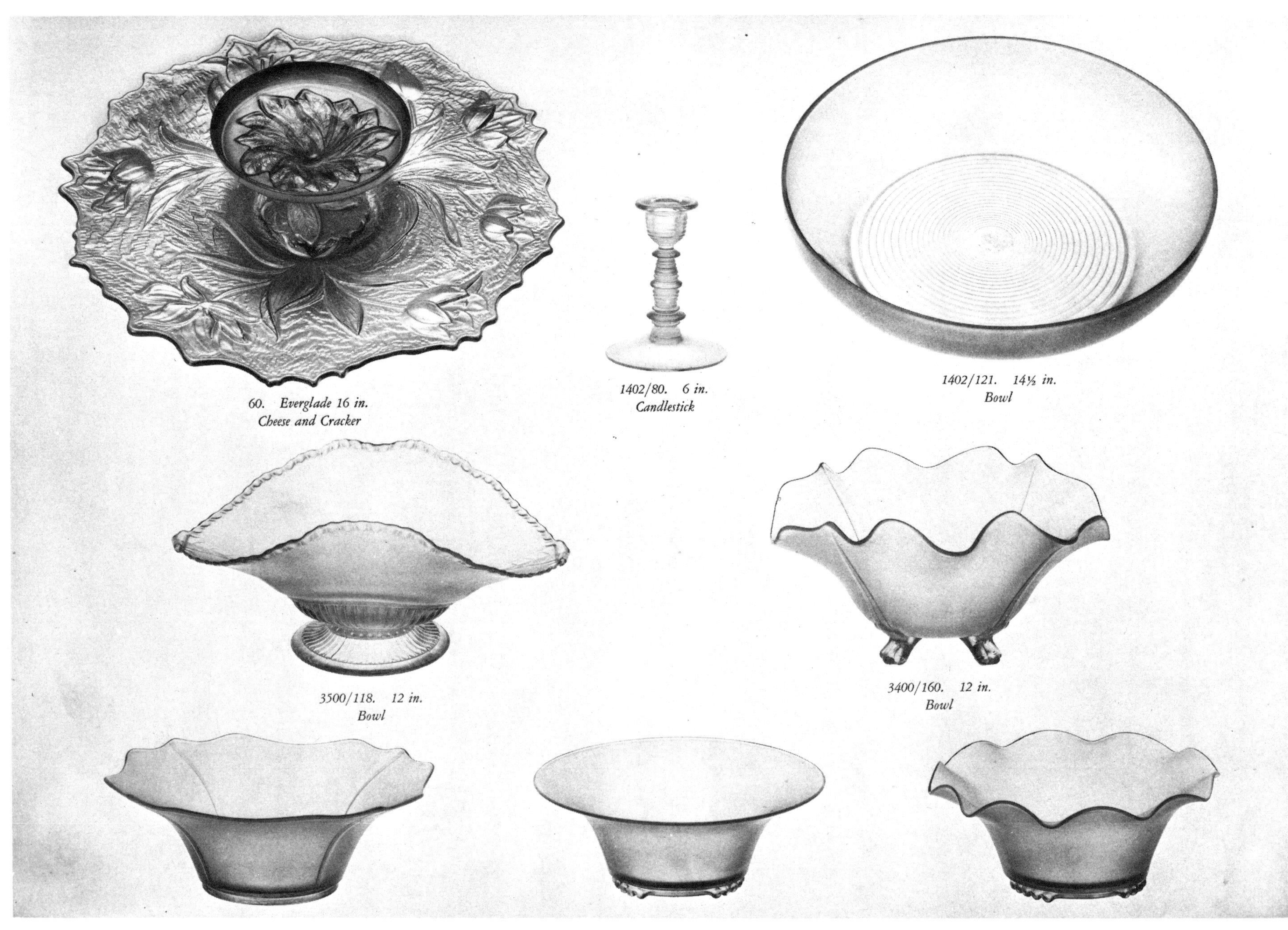

60. Everglade 16 in.
Cheese and Cracker

1402/80. 6 in.
Candlestick

1402/121. 14½ in.
Bowl

3500/118. 12 in.
Bowl

3400/160. 12 in.
Bowl

3400/168. 10½ in.
Bowl

1359. 10½ in.
Bowl

1351. 10 in.
Bowl

3500/119. 13 in. Punch Bowl
1439 Ladle

1402/122. 11 in.
3-Compt. Bowl

2750. 16 in.
Punch Bowl and Foot

79. Martha Washington
15 in. 2 Piece Buffet Set

1402/119. 18 in. Ftd. Plate

MISCELLANEOUS

3400/158
Cocktail Shaker
No. 6 Top

3400/157
Cocktail Shaker
No. 5 Top

3400/159
Cocktail Shaker
No. 4 Top

1395 Cocktail Mixer
with Top
and No. 2 Spoon

1394 Cocktail Mixer
with Top
and No. 1 Spoon

1393 Cocktail Mixer
with No. 1 Spoon

Mt. V. 90
50 oz. Jug

1374. 10 oz. Bitter Bottle
with Chrome Tube

Mt. V. 62. Bitter Bottle
with Chrome Tube

1121. 2 oz.
Bitter Bottle
with Chrome Tube

3400/161
6 oz. Oil
g. s.

M. W. 76
Salt and Pepper
Shaker
Glass Top

1378. 2½ oz.
Tumbler

1371
Bridge
Hound

No. 1
Muddler

No. 2
Muddler

1425. 4 in. Ash Receiver with Lugs
Etched "Minerva"

3500/139
Honey Jar and Cover

394. 10 in. 5-Compt.
Relish

393. 10 in. 5-Compt.
Relish

1365. 6 in.
Ash Tray

9 oz. Goblet

6 oz. Tall Sherbet

4½ oz. Claret

3 oz. Wine

2 oz. Sherry

5 oz. Oyster Cocktail

6 oz. Low Sherbet

2½ oz. Crème de Menthe

3 oz. Cocktail

12 oz. Ftd. Tumbler

1 oz. Cordial

¾ oz. Brandy

1 oz. Pousse-Café

Finger Bowl and Plate

3103 STEMWARE ETCHED "MARLENE"

9 oz. Goblet

6 oz. Low Sherbet

4½ oz. Claret

2 oz. Sherry

3 oz. Wine

2½ oz. Crème de Menthe

3 oz. Cocktail

5 oz. Oyster Cocktail

12 oz. Ftd. Tumbler

1 oz. Pousse-Café

¾ oz. Brandy

1 oz. Cordial

Finger Bowl and Plate

9 oz. Goblet

7 oz. Tall Sherbet

5 oz. Tall Hock

4½ oz. Claret

5 oz. Roemer

2 oz. Sherry

3 oz. Wine

2½ oz. Crème de Menthe

3½ oz. Cocktail

1 oz. Cordial

¾ oz. Brandy

1 oz. Pousse-Café

Finger Bowl and Plate

3106 STEMWARE ETCHED "DIANE"

10 oz. Goblet Low Bowl

7 oz. Low Sherbet

9 oz. Goblet Tall Bowl

1 oz. Cordial

7 oz. Tall Sherbet

¾ oz. Brandy

4½ oz. Claret

1 oz. Pousse-Café

2½ oz. Wine

2½ oz. Crème de Menthe

2 oz. Sherry

3 oz. Cocktail

12 oz. Ftd. Tumbler

9 oz. Ftd. Tumbler

5 oz. Ftd. Tumbler

3 oz. Ftd. Tumbler

5 oz. Oyster Cocktail

Finger Bowl and Plate

VALUE GUIDE*

Page 1 – 3400 Line Etched Apple Blossom		Crystal	Pastel
3400/1	13" Bowl	80.00	100.00
3400/2	12½" Bowl	75.00	95.00
3400/6	Cheese and Cracker	65.00	95.00
3400/10	Handled Tray	60.00	85.00
3400/647	Candlesticks ....pr.	75.00	100.00

Page 2 – 3400 Line Etched Apple Blossom		Crystal	Pastel
3400/3	11" Bowl	55.00	95.00
3400/9	7" Candy	70.00	140.00
3400/11	3-Piece Mayonnaise	55.00	90.00
3400/14	7" Compote	50.00	85.00
3400/15	4" Compote	20.00	35.00
3400/1186	12½" Plate	35.00	55.00

Page 3 – 3400 Line Etched Apple Blossom		Crystal	Pastel
3400/4	12" Bowl	70.00	100.00
3400/638	Candlesticks ....pr.	75.00	145.00
3400/646	Candlesticks ....pr.	60.00	80.00
3400/1185	10" Bowl	45.00	100.00
3400/1240	12" Oval Bowl	65.00	115.00

Page 4 – 3400 Line Etched Apple Blossom		Crystal	Pastel
3400/18	Salt and Pepper	60.00	115.00
3400/51	10" Baker	45.00	100.00
3400/53	6" Cereal	20.00	35.00
3400/54	Cup and Saucer	30.00	40.00
3400/55	Cream Soup and Saucer	30.00	45.00
3400/62	8½" Plate	18.00	25.00
3400/67	12" Celery	65.00	95.00
3400/68	Cream and Sugar	45.00	70.00
3400/1174	Bread and Butter Plate	12.00	18.00
3400/1176	Salad Plate	19.00	32.00
3400/1177	Dinner Plate	35.00	65.00
3400/1177	10½" Service Plate	75.00	115.00

Page 5 – 3400 Line Etched Apple Blossom		Crystal	Pastel
3400/8	11½" Sandwich Plate	45.00	80.00
3400/16	Cream and Sugar	45.00	80.00
3400/52	5½" Butter	140.00	375.00
3400/56	5½" Fruit Saucer	15.00	35.00
3400/57	11½" Platter	35.00	65.00
3400/59	9" Pickle	30.00	65.00
3400/60	Bread and Butter Plate	12.00	18.00

Page 6 – 3400 Line Etched Apple Blossom		Crystal	Pastel
3400/58	13½" Platter	55.00	110.00
3400/61	7½" Tea Plate	20.00	35.00
3400/63	9½" Dinner Plate	60.00	90.00
3400/66	10" Club Plate	50.00	80.00
3400/1177	Dinner Plate	60.00	90.00
3400/1188	11" Fruit Bowl	50.00	90.00

Page 7 – 3135 Line Etched Apple Blossom		Crystal	Pastel
711	76 oz. Jug	200.00	500.00
3135	12 oz. Footed Tumbler	20.00	45.00
3135	10 oz. Footed Tumbler	15.00	35.00
3135	8 oz. Footed Tumbler	15.00	35.00
3135	5 oz. Footed Tumbler	12.00	30.00
3135	8 oz. Goblet	18.00	35.00
3135	6 oz. Tall Sherbet	15.00	25.00
3135	6 oz. Low Sherbet	15.00	25.00
3135	3 oz. Cocktail	18.00	30.00
3135	Finger Bowl and Plate	35.00	50.00

Page 8 – 3130 Line Etched Apple Blossom		Crystal	Pastel
1205	64 oz. Jug	155.00	295.00
3130	Finger Bowl and Plate	35.00	50.00
3130	12 oz. Footed Tumbler	20.00	45.00
3130	10 oz. Footed Tumbler	20.00	35.00
3130	8 oz. Footed Tumbler	18.00	35.00
3130	5 oz. Footed Tumbler	15.00	30.00
3130	8 oz. Goblet	20.00	40.00
3130	6 oz. Low Sherbet	14.00	20.00
3130	6 oz. Tall Sherbet	15.00	25.00
3130	3 oz. Cocktail	20.00	35.00

Page 9 – 3400 Line Etched Apple Blossom		Crystal	Pastel
3400	50 oz. Footed Jug	155.00	295.00
3400	12 oz. Footed Tumbler	20.00	45.00
3400	9 oz. Footed Tumbler	15.00	35.00
3400	2½ oz. Footed Tumbler	15.00	35.00
3400	6 oz. Footed Sherbet	15.00	25.00
3400	9 oz. Lunch Goblet	18.00	35.00
3400/1179	5½" Bon Bon	15.00	30.00
3400/1180	5¼" Bon Bon	15.00	30.00
3400/1181	6" Plate	12.00	16.00
3400/1182	6" Basket	15.00	20.00

Page 10 – Decagon Etched Cleo		Crystal	Pastel
811	9½" Dinner Plate	30.00	75.00
865	Cup and Saucer	15.00	25.00
867	Cream and Sugar	28.00	50.00
1011	6" Cereal	12.00	30.00
1075	Cream Soup and Saucer	20.00	45.00
1078	12" Oval Tray	25.00	55.00
1082	9" Pickle	10.00	20.00

Page 11 – Decagon Etched Cleo		Crystal	Pastel
193	6 oz. Oil	50.00	110.00
749	6½" Bon Bon	10.00	20.00
758	5½" Bon Bon	10.00	20.00
759	7" Plate	11.00	18.00
760	7" 2-Handled Basket	10.00	20.00
866	Bouillon and Saucer	12.00	20.00
983	3-Piece Mayonnaise	30.00	60.00
1087	9½" Vegetable Oval	25.00	65.00
1091	Sauce Boat	50.00	145.00

Page 12 – 3077 Stemware Etched Cleo		Crystal	Pastel
3077	12 oz. Footed Tumbler	18.00	25.00
3077	10 oz. Footed Tumbler	18.00	25.00
3077	8 oz. Footed Tumbler	15.00	22.00
3077	5 oz. Footed Tumbler	15.00	22.00
3077	9 oz. Goblet	18.00	35.00
3077	6 oz. Tall Sherbet	16.00	28.00
3077	6 oz. Low Sherbet	14.00	25.00
3077	2½ oz. Cocktail	20.00	35.00
3077	Finger Bowl and Plate	22.00	48.00
3077/10	63 oz. Jug	125.00	195.00

Page 13 – 3115 Stemware Etched Cleo		Crystal	Pastel
1090	7" Tall Compote	30.00	55.00
3115	12 oz. Footed Tumbler	15.00	20.00
3115	10 oz. Footed Tumbler	15.00	20.00
3115	8 oz. Footed Tumbler	14.00	20.00
3115	5 oz. Footed Tumbler	14.00	22.00
3115	9 oz. Goblet	20.00	30.00
3115	6 oz. Tall Sherbet	15.00	20.00
3115	6 oz. Fruit Salad	12.00	18.00
3115	3½ oz. Cocktail	20.00	25.00
3115	Finger Bowl and Plate	24.00	45.00

Page 14 – Decagon Etched Cleo		Crystal	Pastel
971	8½" Bowl	25.00	50.00
972	11" Plate	25.00	50.00
977	11" Basket	30.00	55.00
984	10" Bowl	25.00	45.00

Page 15 – Plate Etched 739		Crystal	Pastel
627	Candlesticks ....pr.	25.00	35.00
638	Candelabra ....pr.	40.00	55.00
855	11" Bowl	25.00	35.00
1240	12" Refectory Bowl	30.00	50.00

Page 16 – Decagon Etched 739		Crystal	Pastel
809	6¼" Plate	10.00	12.00
865	Cup and Saucer	18.00	25.00
917/1167	Gravy Boat and Stand	50.00	85.00
1068	11" Relish	20.00	35.00
1075	Cream Soup and Saucer	20.00	30.00
1085	9" Vegetable Dish	25.00	45.00
1200	10" Club Plate	20.00	35.00
1263	French Dressing Bottle	35.00	45.00

Page 17 – 3130 Stemware Etched 739		Crystal	Pastel
935	64 oz. Jug	65.00	120.00
3130	12 oz. Footed Tumbler	12.00	18.00
3130	10 oz. Footed Tumbler	10.00	15.00
3130	8 oz. Footed Tumbler	10.00	15.00
3130	5 oz. Footed Tumbler	10.00	15.00
3130	8 oz. Goblet	20.00	25.00
3130	6 oz. Tall Sherbet	15.00	18.00
3130	6 oz. Low Sherbet	12.00	16.00
3130	3 oz. Cocktail	18.00	20.00
3130	Finger Bowl and Plate	18.00	28.00

Page 18 – 3120 Stemware Etched 739		Crystal	Pastel
1090	7" Tall Compote	25.00	40.00
3120	12 oz. Footed Tumbler	15.00	20.00
3120	10 oz. Footed Tumbler	15.00	20.00
3120	8 oz. Footed Tumbler	15.00	20.00
3120	5 oz. Footed Tumbler	12.00	18.00
3120	9 oz. Goblet	18.00	25.00
3120	6 oz. Tall Sherbet	15.00	20.00
3120	4½ oz. Oyster Cocktail	12.00	18.00
3120	3 oz. Cocktail	18.00	25.00
3120	Finger Bowl and Plate	18.00	26.00

Page 19 – Decagon Etched 738		Crystal	Pastel
627	4" Candlesticks ....pr.	25.00	40.00
842	12" Bowl	22.00	35.00
855	11" Bowl	20.00	30.00
856	11" Bowl	20.00	30.00
867	Sugar and Cream	20.00	40.00
868	Cheese and Crackers	25.00	45.00
870	11" Handled Tray	20.00	30.00
873	3-Piece Mayonnaise Set	25.00	45.00
877	11½" Compote	25.00	40.00
878	4" Candlesticks ....pr.	25.00	35.00
971	8½" Bowl	25.00	35.00
972	11" Plate	20.00	30.00
977	11" Basket	25.00	40.00
984	10" Bowl	20.00	30.00
1090	7" Tall Compote	25.00	45.00

Page 20 – Decagon Dinnerware		Crystal	Pastel
807	6" Cereal, Flat Rim	10.00	12.00
865	Cup and Saucer	10.00	14.00
866	Bouillon Cup and Saucer	10.00	15.00
1011	6" Cereal	10.00	12.00
1075	Cream Soup and Saucer	12.00	17.00
1096	Sugar and Cream	18.00	27.00
1098	5½" Fruit, Belled	10.00	14.00
1099	5¾" Fruit, Flat Rim	10.00	14.00
1101	3½" Cranberry, Belled	10.00	18.00
1102	3¾" Cranberry, Flat Rim	10.00	18.00

Page 21 – Decagon Dinnerware		Crystal	Pastel
808	8½" Soup, Flat Rim	10.00	18.00
809	6¼" Bread and Butter	6.00	10.00
811	9½" Dinner Plate	15.00	20.00
815	7½" Plate	6.00	10.00
1012	8½" Soup Plate	8.00	17.00
1077	11" Oval Tray	12.00	25.00
1078	12" Oval Tray	12.00	28.00
1079	15" Oval Tray	15.00	30.00

Page 22 – Decagon Dinnerware		Crystal	Pastel
597	8⅜" Salad Plate	10.00	15.00
598	12½" Plate	15.00	20.00
812	10½" Service Plate	12.00	26.00
1013	10" Berry Bowl	12.00	25.00

Page 23 – Decagon Dinnerware		Crystal	Pastel
1067	9" 2-Part Relish	10.00	20.00
1068	11" 2-Part Relish	12.00	22.00
1082	9" Pickle Tray	10.00	20.00

CR — Carmen RB — Royal Blue Crown — Crown Tuscan P — Pink Gr — Green

No.	Item		
1083	11" Celery Tray	12.00	20.00
1087	9½" Vegetable Dish	15.00	25.00
1088	10½" Vegetable Dish	18.00	30.00

Page 24 – Decagon Dinnerware		Crystal	Pastel
867	Sugar and Cream	20.00	30.00
873	3-Piece Mayonnaise Set	25.00	40.00
979	Sugar and Cream	18.00	28.00
983	3-Piece Mayonnaise Set	25.00	40.00
1094	Sugar and Cream	18.00	30.00

Page 25 – Decagon Dinnerware		Crystal	Pastel
193	6 oz. Oil	25.00	45.00
197	6 oz. Oil	25.00	45.00
758/759/445	Mayonnaise	35.00	45.00
917/1167	Gravy Boat and Stand	35.00	55.00
1091	Sauce Boat and Stand	35.00	55.00
1261	French Dress. (Eng. Oil & Vin.)	35.00	50.00
1263	French Dress. (Eng. Oil & Vin.)	35.00	50.00

Page 26 – Decagon Dinnerware		Crystal	Pastel
1084	13" Service Tray	25.00	40.00
1085	9" Vegetable Dish	15.00	24.00
1167	8" Pickle Tray	12.00	18.00
1200	10" Club Plate	15.00	25.00

Page 27 – Decagon Dinnerware		Crystal	Pastel
608	6½" Compote	15.00	20.00
611	2½" Individual Almond	15.00	26.00
612	6" Footed Almond	20.00	35.00
613	1½" Salt Dip	20.00	35.00
749	6¼" Bon Bon	12.00	15.00
758	5½" Bon Bon	12.00	15.00
759	7" Plate	10.00	15.00
760	7" Basket	12.00	15.00
869	5¾" Compote	12.00	20.00
1090	7" Tall Compote	18.00	30.00

Page 28 – Round Dinnerware Etched 732		Crystal	Pastel
193	6 oz. Oil	35.00	55.00
381	8½" Soup Plate	15.00	20.00
810	9½" Dinner Plate	18.00	24.00
907	9" Pickle Tray	12.00	18.00
914	12" Open Dish, Oval	15.00	35.00
922	Cream Soup and Saucer	18.00	22.00
933	Cup and Saucer	12.00	18.00
944	Sugar and Cream	20.00	30.00

Page 29 – 3130 Stemware Etched 732		Crystal	Pastel
955	62 oz. Jug	85.00	135.00
3130	12 oz. Footed Tumbler	12.00	18.00
3130	10 oz. Footed Tumbler	12.00	18.00
3130	8 oz. Footed Tumbler	12.00	18.00
3130	5 oz. Footed Tumbler	10.00	15.00
3130	8 oz. Goblet	18.00	25.00
3130	6 oz. Tall Sherbet	14.00	18.00
3130	6 oz. Low Sherbet	12.00	15.00
3130	3 oz. Cocktail (Note No. 3120 Cocktail Shown in Catalog)	16.00	22.00
3130	Finger Bowl and Plate	18.00	28.00

Page 30 – 3120 Stemware Etched 732		Crystal	Pastel
712	76 oz. Jug	85.00	135.00
3120	12 oz. Footed Tumbler	12.00	18.00
3120	8 oz. Footed Tumbler	12.00	18.00
3120	2½ oz. Footed Tumbler	12.00	18.00
3120	9 oz. Goblet	18.00	25.00
3120	6 oz. Tall Sherbet	14.00	18.00
3120	6 oz. Fruit Salad	12.00	18.00
3120	3 oz. Cocktail (Note No. 3130 Cocktail Shown in Catalog)	16.00	22.00
3120	1 oz. Cordial	50.00	75.00
3120	Finger Bowl and Plate	15.00	25.00

Page 31 – Round Dinnerware Etched 732		Crystal	Pastel
135	10" Cheese and Cracker	25.00	45.00
168	10" Handle Sandwich Tray	20.00	30.00
173	12" Oval Sandwich Tray	20.00	30.00
300	6" Candy Box	45.00	65.00
441	10½" Compote	25.00	35.00
487	12" Oval Cheese and Cracker	30.00	45.00
531	7¼" Tall Compote	28.00	35.00
533	3-Piece Mayonnaise Set	30.00	45.00
628	Candlesticks pr.	40.00	55.00
674	13" Bowl	25.00	30.00
676	11½" Bowl	25.00	35.00

Page 32 – Round Dinnerware Etched 520		Crystal	Pastel
138	Sugar and Cream	20.00	30.00
197	6 oz. Oil	45.00	70.00
466	6½" Cereal or Fruit	10.00	18.00
810	9½" Dinner Plate	18.00	30.00
928	5¼" Fruit Saucer	12.00	16.00
933	Cup and Saucer	15.00	18.00
934	Bouillon and Saucer	16.00	20.00

Page 33 – 3060 Stemware Etched 520		Crystal	Pastel
531	7¼" Tall Compote	20.00	35.00
3060	10 oz. Footed Tumbler	12.00	15.00
3060	5 oz. Footed Tumbler	12.00	15.00
3060	3 oz. Footed Tumbler	12.00	15.00
3060	9 oz. Goblet	18.00	24.00
3060	7 oz. Fruit Salad	12.00	15.00
3060	6 oz. Tall Sherbet	15.00	18.00
3060	2½ oz. Cocktail	16.00	20.00
3060	2½ oz. Wine	18.00	24.00
3060	Finger Bowl and Plate	15.00	25.00

Page 34 – Round Dinnerware		Crystal	Pastel
3½	Cup and Saucer, Ovide	12.00	15.00
138	Sugar and Cream	18.00	30.00
494	Footed Cup and Saucer	12.00	15.00
495	Footed Bouillon Cup & Saucer	15.00	18.00
920	Butter and Cover with Drainer	35.00	65.00
922	Cream Soup and Saucer	12.00	18.00
933	Cup and Saucer	12.00	15.00
934	Bouillon Cup and Saucer	12.00	18.00

		Crystal	CR-RB
925	After Dinner Cup and Saucer	20.00	50.00

Page 35 – Round Dinnerware		Crystal	Pastel
381	8½" Soup Plate	10.00	15.00
466	Cereal or Grapefruit	10.00	15.00
554	7" Plate	8.00	10.00
556	8" Plate	8.00	10.00
559	8½" Plate	8.00	12.00
668	6" Bread and Butter Plate	6.00	8.00
928	5¼" Fruit Saucer	6.00	8.00

Page 36 – Round Dinnerware		Crystal	Pastel
242	13½" Plate	12.00	18.00
244	10½" Service Plate	15.00	20.00
810	9½" Dinner Plate	12.00	15.00
899	9¼" Service Tray, Oval	12.00	15.00
901	12½" Service Tray, Oval	12.00	15.00
903	14½" Service Tray, Oval	15.00	20.00
904	16" Service Tray, Oval	18.00	25.00

Page 37 – Round Dinnerware		Crystal	Pastel
606	Celery Dip	5.00	10.00
652	11" Celery	15.00	20.00
907	9" Pickle Tray, Oval	10.00	15.00
908	11" Celery Tray, Oval	10.00	15.00
909	Open Service Dish, Oval	15.00	22.00
914	12" Open Service Dish, Oval	15.00	22.00
915	12" Service Dish and Cover	25.00	45.00

Page 38 – Round Dinnerware		Crystal	Pastel
378	11" Club Plate	10.00	15.00
380	10" Club Plate	10.00	15.00
911	10½" Open Service Dish	15.00	20.00
912	10½" Casserole and Cover	25.00	40.00
931	Individual Cake Tray	10.00	12.00
932	10½" Cake Tray	15.00	20.00

Page 39 – Round Dinnerware		Crystal	Pastel
193	6 oz. Oil	25.00	45.00
197	6 oz. Oil	25.00	45.00
752	Egg Cup	10.00	18.00
941	Sugar	10.00	15.00
942	Sugar and Cover	15.00	20.00
943	Cream	10.00	15.00
944	Sugar and Cream	20.00	30.00
961	Sugar and Cream	20.00	30.00
1261	French Dress. (Eng. Oil & Vin.)	35.00	50.00
1263	French Dress. (Eng. Oil & Vin.)	35.00	50.00

Page 40 – Round Dinnerware		Crystal	Pastel
137	Sugar and Cream	15.00	30.00
158	Marmalade and Cover	20.00	30.00
170	9 oz. Syrup, Metal Top	25.00	60.00
174	9 oz. Syrup, Metal Top	25.00	60.00
175	8 oz. Syrup and Cover	25.00	60.00
395	Shaker	10.00	15.00
396	Shaker	10.00	15.00
397	Shaker	10.00	15.00
398	Shaker	10.00	15.00
400	Individual Salt	8.00	15.00
940	Individual Sugar and Cream	10.00	20.00
960	Sugar and Cream	10.00	15.00
602	5¼" Plate	5.00	10.00

Page 41 – Round Dinnerware		Crystal	Pastel
254	5½" Compote	12.00	18.00
531	7½" Compote	15.00	20.00
532	6½" Compote	12.00	18.00
533	3-Piece Mayonnaise Set	20.00	35.00
837	3-Piece Shaker Set	30.00	45.00
917	Double Gravy Boat and Stand	35.00	55.00
953	Sauce Boat and Stand	35.00	55.00

Page 42 – Miscellaneous Items		Crystal	Pastel
102	Individual Salt	18.00	25.00
396	Shaker	10.00	15.00
703	Flower Holder with 3" Block	25.00	45.00
813	Sugar Sifter	35.00	65.00
816	Tall Cream	20.00	25.00
829	7-Piece Condiment Set	50.00	95.00
830	5-Piece Condiment Set	45.00	75.00
833	Oil Bottle	35.00	55.00
1095	3-Piece Sugar and Cream Set	20.00	30.00
1110	Dessert Mold	10.00	15.00
1215/619	3-Pc. Oil and Vinegar Set	30.00	50.00
1215/1094	3-Piece Sugar and Cream Set	25.00	40.00
1220	Individual Shaker	10.00	15.00
3077	Cheese Dish and Cover	25.00	45.00

Page 43 – Relishes and Cake Trays		Crystal	Pastel
324	12" 6-Piece Relish Set	20.00	30.00
385	8½" Relish	15.00	20.00
392	11" Tray	15.00	20.00
397	Celery and Relish Tray	15.00	22.00
707	11" Cake Plate	25.00	45.00
862	4-Part Relish	12.00	20.00
1031	13" Cake Plate	12.00	15.00
1093	2-Part Relish	12.00	18.00
1169	Sugar Basket	15.00	22.00
3400/67	12" Celery	15.00	20.00

Page 44 – Tumblers and Coasters Sea Food or Fruit Cocktails Hotel & Tea Room Glassware		Crystal	CR-RB
316	Georgian Sundae	12.00	20.00
319	9 oz. Georgian Tumbler	16.00	20.00
320	7 oz. Tumbler, Cut Flute	10.00	
496	2½ oz. Tumbler, Cut Flute	10.00	
497	8 oz. Tumbler, Cut Flute	10.00	
498	12 oz. Tumbler, Cut Flute	12.00	
601	Coaster	5.00	10.00
602	5¼" Coaster Plate	8.00	10.00
603	4" Coaster Plate	8.00	10.00
800	9 oz. Goblet	16.00	
968	Sea Food Cocktail and Liner	20.00	
969	Sea Food Cocktail and Liner	20.00	
1070	12 oz. Pinch Tumbler	10.00	16.00

No.	Item		
1070	10 oz. Pinch Tumbler	10.00	16.00
1070	8 oz. Pinch Tumbler	10.00	16.00
1070	5 oz. Pinch Tumbler	8.00	14.00
1070	2 oz. Pinch Tumbler	8.00	14.00
1201	2½ oz. Georgian Tumbler	15.00	18.00
1202	12 oz. Georgian Tumbler	15.00	25.00
1630	12 oz. Tumbler	10.00	
1630	10 oz. Tall Tumbler	10.00	
1630	12 oz. Tumbler	8.00	
3145	14 oz. Tumbler	10.00	20.00
3145	10 oz. Tumbler	10.00	20.00
8701	10 oz. Tumbler	10.00	
8701	8 oz. Tumbler	10.00	
8858	2 oz. Tumbler	8.00	
9403	12 oz. Tumbler	10.00	

Page 45 – Beverage Set		**Crystal**	**Pastel**
1	Keg Set	155.00	250.00
693	2-Piece Canape Set	16.00	20.00
820	Serving Tray	12.00	18.00
1020	34 oz. Cocktail Shaker	35.00	55.00
1021	2½ oz. Tumbler	10.00	12.00
1105	34 oz. Cocktail Shaker	45.00	65.00
1106	2½ oz. Tumbler	10.00	12.00
		Crystal	**CR-RB**
315	28 oz. Decanter	30.00	
315	16 oz. Decanter	25.00	
1070	36 oz. Pinch Decanter	35.00	95.00
3145	84 oz. Jug, Ice Lip	45.00	135.00
3145	32 oz. Decanter	30.00	95.00
3145	14 oz. Tumbler	10.00	18.00
3145	2½ oz. Tumbler	10.00	15.00

Page 46 – Ice Pails, Candy Boxes & Bridge Set		**Crystal**	**Pastel**
103	Candy Box, E 725	30.00	50.00
300	Candy Box, E 520	35.00	55.00
730	½ lb. Candy Jar, E 732	35.00	50.00
845	Ice Bucket	25.00	40.00
847	Ice Tub, E 718	45.00	75.00
851	Ice Pail, E Cleo	40.00	70.00
864	Candy Box, E Cleo	40.00	85.00
880/881	5-Pc. Bridge Set E Golf Scene	85.00	140.00
957	Ice Pail, E 732	25.00	50.00
973/8701	5-Piece Bridge Set, E 726	75.00	95.00
1121	Ice Pail, E Chrys	35.00	55.00
1122	Ice Pail, E Tulip	25.00	55.00
1147	Ice Tub, E 739	25.00	55.00
1215/8701	3-Piece Set	20.00	25.00

Page 47 – Ice Teas and Water Sets		**Crystal**	**Pastel**
107	76 oz. Jug, E Chrys	75.00	135.00
119	83 oz. Jug, E Tulip	65.00	120.00
124	68 oz. Jug, E Cleo	125.00	195.00
935	64 oz. Jug, E 739	65.00	120.00
937	68 oz. Jug, E 695	65.00	120.00
937	68 oz. Jug, E 520	65.00	120.00
955	62 oz. Jug, E 732	85.00	135.00
1630	12 oz. Tumbler, E Chrys	15.00	18.00
1630	12 oz. Tumbler, E Tulip	15.00	18.00
1630	12 oz. Tumbler, E 695	15.00	18.00
1630	10 oz. Tumbler, E 732	15.00	18.00
1630	10 oz. Tumbler, E 739	15.00	18.00
3077	12 oz. Footed Tumbler, E 718	18.00	25.00
3077/10	63 oz. Jug, E 718	125.00	210.00
9403	12 oz. Tumbler, E Cleo	18.00	25.00
9403	12 oz. Tumbler, E 520	15.00	18.00

Page 48 – Swans (Swans Shown Have Complete Feather Detail and Are Signed)		**Crystal**	**P-Gr***
1040	3" Individual Nut or Mint	30.00	55.00
1041	Candy Dish	40.00	60.00
1041/1050	Candle Holder	50.00	70.00
1042	6½" Swan	55.00	75.00
1043	8½" Swan	65.00	150.00
1044	10" Swan	175.00	325.00
1045	13" Swan	400.00	500.00

Page 49 – Flower Blocks and Holders		**Crystal**	**P-Gr***
509	8¾" Figure Flower Holder	175.00	250.00
513	13" Figure Flower Holder	165.00	250.00
518	8½" Figure Flower Holder	95.00	180.00
836	5" Oval Flower Block	11.00	15.00
849	Flower Holder, Oval Base	125.00	185.00
1114	6" Figure Flower Holder	75.00	175.00
1115	11" Figure Flower Holder	185.00	275.00
2899	2¼" Flower Block	5.00	8.00
2899	2¾" Flower Block	5.00	8.00
2899	3" Flower Block	6.00	10.00
2899	3½" Flower Block	7.00	12.00
2899	4" Flower Block	8.00	12.00
2899	5" Flower Block	8.00	12.00
2899	6" Flower Block	10.00	14.00
2900	5½" Flower Circle	20.00	30.00
2900	7" Flower Circle	25.00	40.00

*Pastel refers to Pink & Green

Page 50 – Vase		**Crystal**	**Pastel**
277	9" Vase, E 737	40.00	65.00
779	14" Vase, E Dragon	175.00	225.00
797	8" Vase, E Martha	45.00	65.00
1002	1½ Gallon Aquarium, E 736	175.00	225.00
1023	9½" Vase, E 741	35.00	60.00
1130	11" Vase	35.00	55.00

Page 51 – Vases		**Crystal**	**Pastel**
84	12" Vase, E 724	45.00	65.00
272	10" Vase, E 743	35.00	50.00
274	10" Vase, E 743	35.00	50.00
275	10" Vase, E 724	35.00	55.00
276	10" Vase, E 724	35.00	55.00
278	11" Vase, E 724	45.00	70.00
280	12" Vase, E 724	45.00	70.00
281	12" Vase, E 724	45.00	70.00

Page 52 – Vase		**Crystal**	**Pastel**
279	13" Vase, E 742	50.00	75.00
402	12" Vase, E 741	50.00	75.00
782	8" Vase, E 717	65.00	120.00
1005	6" Vase, E 732	45.00	65.00
1037	10" Vase, E725/737	45.00	75.00

Page 53 – Candlesticks		**Crystal**	**Pastel**
227½	Candlestick ea.	10.00	15.00
624	Candlestick ea.	20.00	25.00
625	Candlestick ea.	10.00	15.00
627	Candlestick ea.	15.00	20.00
628	Candlestick ea.	15.00	20.00
630	Candlestick ea.	15.00	20.00
636	9½" Candlestick ea.	20.00	30.00
638	Candlestick ea.	22.00	30.00
639	Candlestick ea.	15.00	20.00
646	Candlestick ea.	16.00	22.00
647	Candlestick ea.	20.00	27.00
687	Candlestick ea.	12.00	18.00
747	Candlestick ea.	12.00	18.00
878	Candlestick ea.	15.00	20.00

Page 54 – Smokers Articles		**Crystal**	**Pastel**
112	Ash Tray	10.00	12.00
117	Ash Tray, Oval	10.00	12.00
130	Individual Ash Tray	10.00	12.00
212	Match Holder	15.00	20.00
387	2½" Ash Tray	6.00	8.00
388	4" Ash Tray	9.00	12.00
390	6" Ash Tray	12.00	14.00
391	8" Ash Tray	15.00	18.00
430	Cigarette Box	12.00	20.00
605	Cigarette Box	25.00	35.00
615	Cigarette Box	15.00	20.00
616	Cigarette Box	15.00	22.00
617	Cigarette Jar	20.00	30.00
882	Tobacco Humidor, Ash Tray Cover	50.00	75.00
883	Ash Tray, Set of 4	65.00	75.00
885	Cigarette Jar, Ash Tray Cover	25.00	40.00
1025	Cigar Humidor and Moistener, Ash Tray Cover	55.00	90.00
1208	Cigarette Box	20.00	30.00
607	Cigarette Box	50.00	80.00

Page 55 – Bathroom Bottles		**Crystal**	**Pastel**
894	Bottle, E Boric Acid	25.00	45.00
895	Bottle, E Toilet Water	25.00	45.00
896	Bottle, E Bath Salts	25.00	45.00
897	Bottle, E Epsom Salts	25.00	45.00
1194	Bottle, E Bicarb. Soda	25.00	45.00
1195	Bottle, E Witch Hazel	25.00	45.00
1196	Bottle, E Cotton	25.00	45.00
1197	15" x 3½" Tray	25.00	45.00
1198	6" x 6" Tray	25.00	45.00
896/1194 1195/1197	6-Piece Set	150.00	270.00
896/1195 1198	5-Piece Set	125.00	225.00
897/1196 1198	5-Piece Set	125.00	225.00
895/897 1196/1197	6-Piece Set	150.00	270.00

Page 56 – 3120 Stemware Crystal "Majestic" (Etched & Eng.)		**Crystal**
556	8" Plate	12.00
628	3½" Candlesticks pr.	20.00
676	11½" Bowl	20.00
3120	12 oz. Footed Tumbler	12.00
3120	10 oz. Footed Tumbler	12.00
3120	8 oz. Footed Tumbler	12.00
3120	5 oz. Footed Tumbler	12.00
3120	9 oz. Goblet	22.00
3120	6 oz. Tall Sherbet	15.00
3120	6 oz. Low Sherbet	12.00
3120	6 oz. Fruit Salad	15.00
3120	4½ oz. Oyster Cocktail	15.00
3120	3 oz. Cocktail	18.00

Page 57 – 3400 Line Engraved 541		**Crystal**
3400/1	13" Bowl	27.00
3400/2	12½" Bowl	27.00
3400/3	11" Low Footed Bowl	27.00
3400/4	12" Bowl	28.00
3400/6	11½" Cheese and Cracker	28.00
3400/9	7" Candy Box	50.00
3400/10	11" Handled Sandwich Tray	24.00
3400/11	3-Piece Mayonnaise Set	30.00
3400/13	6" Compote	20.00
3400/14	7" Tall Compote	35.00
3400/16	Sugar and Cream	27.00
3400/17	12" Vase	40.00
3400/627	Candlesticks pr.	45.00
3400/851	Ice Pail	45.00
3400/1179	5½" Mint	14.00
3400/1180	5¼" Jelly	14.00
3400/1181	6" Plate	12.00
3400/1182	6" Basket	15.00

Page 58 – 3400 Line Engraved 542		**Crystal**
3400/1	13" Bowl	24.00
3400/2	12½" Bowl	24.00
3400/3	11" Low Footed Bowl	24.00
3400/4	12" Bowl	25.00
3400/6	11½" Cheese and Crackers	25.00
3400/8	11½" Sandwich Plate	22.00
3400/9	7" Candy Box	40.00
3400/10	11" Handled Sandwich Tray	22.00
3400/11	3-Piece Mayonnaise Set	25.00
3400/4	7" Tall Compote	40.00
3400/16	Sugar and Cream	24.00
3400/627	Candlesticks pr.	30.00
3400/1185	10" Bowl	25.00
3400/1186	12½" Plate	22.00
3400/1188	11" Bowl	25.00

Page 59 – 3130 Stemware Engraved 538		**Crystal**
597	8" Plate	15.00
3130	12 oz. Footed Tumbler	15.00

3130	10 oz. Footed Tumbler	15.00
3130	8 oz. Footed Tumbler	12.00
3130	5 oz. Footed Tumbler	10.00
3130	2½ oz. Footed Tumbler	10.00
3130	8 oz. Goblet	20.00
3130	6 oz. Tall Sherbet	15.00
3130	6 oz. Low Sherbet	12.00
3130	3 oz. Cocktail	18.00
3130	Finger Bowl and Plate	20.00

Page 60 – Engraved 538 Crystal		**Crystal**
104	6" Candy Box and Cover	30.00
135	10" Cheese and Cracker	28.00
168	10" Handled Sandwich Tray	24.00
173	12" Handled Tray, Oval	24.00
278	11" Vase	40.00
441	10½" Compote	35.00
532	6½" Tall Compote	35.00
533	3-Piece Mayonnaise Set	40.00
628	3½" Candlesticks pr.	28.00
674	13" Bowl	25.00
676	11½" Bowl	20.00
944	Sugar and Cream	30.00

Page 61 – Rock Crystal Composition Engraved 479		**Crystal**
64	5¼" Compote	15.00
158	Marmalade and Cover	25.00
272	10" Vase	15.00
533	6¼" Compote	15.00
749	6¼" Bon Bon	12.00
758	5½" Bon Bon	12.00
759	7" Plate	12.00
760	7" Basket	12.00
869	5½" Compote	15.00
1075	5" Bon Bon	12.00
1096	Sugar and Cream5	20.00
1917/92	3-Toed Card Tra5	15.00
1917/255	3-Toed Mayonnaise	15.00
	Rock Crystal Engraving 497	**Crystal**
1179	5½" Bon Bon	15.00
1180	5¼" Bon Bon	15.00
1181	6" Bon Bon	15.00
1182	6" Bon Bon	15.00

Page 62 – Engraved 515		**Crystal**
278	11" Vase	35.00
627	4" Candlesticks pr.	30.00
842	12" Bowl	26.00
851	Ice Pail	45.00
856	11" Bowl	25.00
867	Sugar and Cream	30.00
868	11" Cheese and Cracker	25.00
870	11" Handled Sandwich Tray	25.00
873	3-Piece Mayonnaise Set	35.00
877	11½" Compote	28.00
971	8½" Bowl	22.00
972	11" Plate	20.00
977	11" Basket	30.00
984	10" Bowl	22.00
1090	7" Tall Compote	32.00

Page 63 – Engraved 540 Composition		**Crystal**
135	10" Cheese and Cracker	18.00
168	10" Handled Sandwich Tray	15.00
173	12" Handled Tray, Oval	15.00
300	6" Candy Box and Cover	25.00
441	10½" Compote	20.00
487	12" Cheese & Cracker, Oval	18.00
533	3-Piece Mayonnaise Set	25.00
628	3½" Candlesticks pr.	20.00
674	13" Bowl	16.00
676	11½" Bowl	16.00

Page 64 – Springtime Line, Frosted		**Crystal**	**Pastel**
646	5" Candlesticks pr.	32.00	44.00
849	Figure Flower Holder, Oval	130.00	175.00
1008	12" Vase	75.00	95.00
1009	6" Vase	45.00	65.00
1250	6" Vase	45.00	65.00
1251	8" Vase	55.00	75.00
1252	10" Vase	65.00	85.00
1253	12" Vase	75.00	95.00
1256	11" Oval Bowl	50.00	65.00

Page 65 – Table Centers, Frosted		**Crystal**	**Pastel**
638	Candlesticks pr.	44.00	60.00
646	5" Candlesticks pr.	32.00	44.00
647	Candelabra pr.	40.00	54.00
1115	11" Figure Flower Holder	185.00	275.00
1139	14" Bowl	55.00	85.00
1140	15" Bowl	60.00	95.00
1254	14" Bowl	55.00	85.00
1255	15" Bowl	60.00	85.00

Page 66 – Table Centers		**Crystal**	**Pastel**
518	8½" Figure Flower Holder	95.00	180.00
638	5" Candelabra pr.	44.00	60.00
646	5" Candlesticks pr.	32.00	44.00
647	Candelabra pr.	40.00	54.00
1114	6" Figure Flower Holder	75.00	175.00
1150	12½" Bowl	50.00	95.00
1151	12¾" Bowl	50.00	95.00
1152	10" Bowl	50.00	95.00
1153	10½" Bowl	50.00	95.00
1155	Candlesticks pr.	40.00	60.00

Page 67 – Table Centers		**Crystal**	**Pastel**
513	13" Figure Flower Holder	165.00	250.00
638	Candelabra pr.	44.00	60.00
647	Candelabra pr.	40.00	54.00
1115	11" Figure Flower Holder	185.00	275.00
1125	15½" Bowl	85.00	150.00
1126	16" Bowl	85.00	150.00

Page 68 – Table Centers		**Crystal**	**Pastel**
518	8½" Figure Flower Holder	95.00	180.00
849	Figure Flower Holder, Oval	130.00	175.00
2899	3½" Flower Block	7.00	12.00
3400/1	13" Bowl, Eng 541	27.00	
3400/2	12½" Bowl, Eng 542	24.00	
3400/4	12" Bowl, E Apple Blossom	70.00	100.00
3400/5	12" Bowl, E Apple Blossom	75.00	100.00
3400/627	4" Candlesticks, Eng 541 pr.	40.00	
3400/638	Candelabra, E Apple Blossom	75.00	145.00
3400/646	Candlesticks, E Apple Blossom	60.00	80.00
3400/647	Candelabra, Eng 542 pr.	60.00	
3400/1240	12" Oval Bowl, E Apple Blossom	65.00	115.00

Page 69 – Table Centers		**Crystal**	**Pastel**
518	8½" Figure Flower Holder	95.00	180.00
628	3½" Candlesticks, E 520 pr.	40.00	50.00
628	3½" Candlesticks, E 704 pr.	40.00	50.00
628	3½" Candlesticks, E 732 pr.	40.00	50.00
673	15" Bowl, E 704	35.00	60.00
674	13" Bowl, E 520	30.00	50.00
676	11" Bowl, E 732	25.00	35.00
732	Refectory Bowl, E 741	45.00	75.00
747	Candlesticks pr.	35.00	45.00
836	5½" Oval Flower Block	12.00	18.00
1115	11" Figure Flower Holder	185.00	275.00
2899	3½" Flower Block	7.00	12.00

Page 70 – Table Centers		**Crystal**	**Pastel**
518	8" Figure Flower Holder	95.00	180.00
627	4" Candlesticks, E Cleo pr.	35.00	50.00
638	Candelabra, E 739 pr.	50.00	65.00
646	5" Candlesticks, E 731 pr.	35.00	55.00
647	Candelabra, E Cleo pr.	45.00	65.00
841	15½" Oval Bowl, E Cleo	25.00	50.00
842	12" Bowl, E 731	25.00	35.00
849	Figure Flower Holder, Oval	125.00	185.00
855	11" Bowl, E 739	25.00	35.00
856	11" Bowl, E Cleo	30.00	50.00
857	14" Bowl, E 739	25.00	40.00
878	4" Candlesticks, E 739 pr.	25.00	35.00
1115	11" Figure Flower Holder	185.00	275.00
2899	3½" Flower Block	7.00	12.00

Page 71 – Flower Centers		**Crystal**	**Pastel**
518	8½" Figure Flower Holders	95.00	180.00
627	4" Candlesticks pr.	30.00	40.00
630	4" Candlesticks pr.	30.00	40.00
637	3½" Candlesticks pr.	24.00	36.00
639	4" Candlesticks pr.	30.00	40.00
675	9½" Bowl	17.00	30.00
842	12" Bowl	18.00	35.00
987	11" Bowl	17.00	30.00
993	12½" Bowl	17.00	30.00
1114	6" Figure Flower Holder	75.00	175.00
1235	9½" Bowl	20.00	40.00
2899	2¾" Flower Block	7.00	12.00
2899	3½" Flower Block	8.00	14.00
1192	6" Candlesticks pr.	35.00	45.00

Page 72 – 3400 Line Etched 746 Gloria		**Crystal**	**Pastel**
3400/1	13" Bowl	35.00	65.00
3400/5	12" Bowl, 4-Toed	35.00	65.00
3400/6	11½" Cheese and Cracker	40.00	65.00
3400/10	11" Handled Sandwich Tray	25.00	45.00
3400/627	Candlesticks pr.	35.00	65.00

Page 73 – 3400 Line Etched 746 Gloria		**Crystal**	**Pastel**
3400/9	7" Candy Box and Cover	70.00	135.00
3400/11	3-Piece Mayonnaise Set	40.00	75.00
3400/15	4" Compote	15.00	25.00
3400/65	14" Chop or Salad Plate	40.00	75.00
3400/707	11" Footed Cake Plate	75.00	145.00
3400/851	Ice Pail	50.00	85.00

Page 74 – 3400 Line Etched 746 Gloria		**Crystal**	**Pastel**
3400/4	12" Bowl	35.00	65.00
3400/17	12" Vase	70.00	145.00
3400/23	10" Vase	60.00	125.00
3400/1185	10" Bowl	35.00	75.00
3400/1192	6" Candlesticks pr.	40.00	70.00
3400/1240	12" Oval Bowl	30.00	65.00

Page 75 – 3400 Line Etched 746 Gloria		**Crystal**	**Pastel**
3400/18	Salt and Pepper	35.00	70.00
3400/51	10" Baker	40.00	75.00
3400/53	6" Cereal	15.00	27.00
3400/54	Cup and Saucer	20.00	30.00
3400/55	Cream Soup and Saucer	25.00	40.00
3400/62	8½" Salad Plate	12.00	18.00
3400/67	12" Celery & Relish Service	45.00	65.00
3400/68	Sugar and Cream	25.00	40.00
3400/69	After Dinner Cup and Saucer	75.00	125.00
3400/1174	Bread and Butter Plate	10.00	15.00
3400/1176	Salad Plate	12.00	20.00
3400/1177	Dinner Plate	55.00	75.00
3400/1178	Service Plate	65.00	115.00

Page 76 – 3400 Line Etched 746 Gloria		**Crystal**	**Pastel**
3400/8	11½" Sandwich Plate	20.00	45.00
3400/16	Sugar and Cream	25.00	40.00
3400/52	5½" Butter and Cover	125.00	275.00
3400/56	5½" Fruit Saucer	12.00	20.00
3400/57	11½" Platter	55.00	115.00
3400/59	9" Pickle Tray	20.00	30.00
3400/60	6" Bread and Butter Plate	10.00	12.00

Page 77 – 3400 Line Etched 746 Gloria		**Crystal**	**Pastel**
3400/21	9" Salad Bowl	25.00	65.00
3400/22	10" Salad Bowl	20.00	35.00
3400/61	7½" Tea Plate	12.00	15.00
3400/63	9½" Dinner Plate	55.00	75.00
3400/1177	Dinner Plate	55.00	75.00
3400/1188	11" Fruit Bowl	30.00	55.00

Page 78 – 3400 Line Etched 746 Gloria		**Crystal**	**Pastel**
3400/25	5" Footed Bon Bon	15.00	25.00
3400/26	5½" Footed Bon Bon	15.00	25.00
3400/862	Relish Tray	35.00	65.00
3400/1093	Relish Tray	30.00	45.00
3400/1179	5½" Bon Bon	15.00	20.00
3400/1180	5¼" Bon Bon	15.00	22.00

		Crystal	Pastel
3400/1181	6" Plate	12.00	15.00
3400/1182	6" Basket	16.00	30.00

Page 79 – 3135 Stemware Etched Gloria		Crystal	Pastel
3135	12 oz. Footed Tumbler	18.00	30.00
3135	10 oz. Footed Tumbler	15.00	22.00
3135	5 oz. Footed Tumbler	15.00	20.00
3135	8 oz. Goblet	22.00	30.00
3135	6 oz. Tall Sherbet	16.00	22.00
3135	6 oz. Low Sherbet	12.00	18.00
3135	6 oz. Fruit Salad	12.00	18.00
3135	4½ oz. Oyster Cocktail	15.00	18.00
3135	1 oz. Cordial	65.00	125.00
3135	Finger Bowl and Plate	20.00	35.00
3400/14	7" Tall Compote	35.00	70.00

Page 80 – 3130 Stemware Etched Gloria		Crystal	Pastel
3130	12 oz. Footed Tumbler	18.00	25.00
3130	10 oz. Footed Tumbler	15.00	22.00
3130	5 oz. Footed Tumbler	15.00	20.00
3130	2½ oz. Footed Tumbler	18.00	35.00
3130	8 oz. Goblet	22.00	30.00
3130	6 oz. Tall Sherbet	16.00	22.00
3130	6 oz. Low Sherbet	12.00	18.00
3130	6 oz. Fruit Salad	12.00	18.00
3130	2½ oz. Wine	22.00	45.00
3400/78	Cocktail Shaker	125.00	210.00

Page 81 – 3120 Stemware Etched Gloria		Crystal	Pastel
1205	64 oz. Jug and Cover	165.00	295.00
3120	12 oz. Footed Tumbler	18.00	25.00
3120	10 oz. Footed Tumbler	15.00	22.00
3120	5 oz. Footed Tumbler	15.00	20.00
3120	9 oz. Goblet	22.00	30.00
3120	6 oz. Tall Sherbet	16.00	33.00
3120	6 oz. Low Sherbet	12.00	18.00
3120	4½ oz. Claret	35.00	50.00
3120	1 oz. Cordial	65.00	130.00
3120	Finger Bowl and Plate	20.00	35.00

Page 82 – 3115 Stemware Etched 742		Crystal	Pastel
597	8⅜" Salad Plate	10.00	15.00
1205	64 oz. Jug	75.00	140.00
3115	12 oz. Footed Tumbler	12.00	16.00
3115	10 oz. Footed Tumbler	12.00	15.00
3115	8 oz. Footed Tumbler	12.00	15.00
3115	9 oz. Goblet	20.00	25.00
3115	6 oz. Tall Sherbet	15.00	18.00
3115	6 oz. Low Sherbet	12.00	15.00
3115	6 oz. Fruit Salad	12.00	15.00
3115	3½ oz. Cocktail	18.00	20.00

Page A – Round Dinnerware Etched 734		Crystal	Pastel
556	8" Plate	10.00	14.00
652	11" Celery Tray	15.00	25.00
901	12½" Service Tray, Oval	17.00	31.00
922	Cream Soup and Saucer	14.00	26.00
925	After Dinner Cup and Saucer	24.00	48.00
933	Cup and Saucer	11.00	19.00
944	Sugar and Cream	24.00	34.00

Page B – 3060 Stemware Etched 704		Crystal	Pastel
955	62 oz. Jug	75.00	100.00
3060	12 oz. Footed Tumbler	10.00	18.00
3060	12 oz. Tumbler	12.00	20.00
3060	10 oz. Tumbler	10.00	16.00
3060	9 oz. Goblet	16.00	23.00
3060	6 oz. Tall Sherbet	12.00	15.00
3060	5 oz. Parfait	14.00	19.00
3060	4½ oz. Oyster Cocktail	10.00	14.00
3060	2 oz. Tumbler	10.00	12.00
3060	Finger Bowl and Plate	16.00	22.00

Page C – Decagon Dinnerware Etched 731		Crystal	Pastel
597	8⅜" Plate	10.00	12.00
865	Cup and Saucer	14.00	18.00
1012	8½" Soup Plate	12.00	15.00
1083	11" Celery Tray	18.00	22.00
1096	Sugar and Cream	25.00	45.00
1098	5½" Fruit	10.00	14.00
1101	3½" Cranberry Dish	18.00	36.00

Page D – 3115 Stemware Etched 731		Crystal	Pastel
955	62 oz. Jug	65.00	125.00
3115	12 oz. Footed Tumbler	12.00	16.00
3115	10 oz. Footed Tumbler	10.00	16.00
3115	8 oz. Footed Tumbler	9.00	15.00
3115	2½ oz. Footed Tumbler	10.00	18.00
3115	9 oz. Goblet	20.00	25.00
3115	6 oz. Tall Sherbet	14.00	18.00
3115	6 oz. Low Sherbet	10.00	12.00
3115	3½ oz. Cocktail	18.00	22.00
3115	Finger Bowl and Plate	20.00	26.00

Page E – Rock Crystal Engraved 539		Crystal
135	10" Cheese and Cracker	23.00
168	10" Handled Sandwich Tray	20.00
173	12" Hdl. Sandwich Tray, Oval	20.00
278	11" Vase	30.00
441	10½" Compote	23.00
532	6½" Tall Compote	26.00
533	3-Piece Mayonnaise Set	22.00
628	3½" Candlesticks ...pr.	23.00
674	13" Bowl	22.00
676	11½" Bowl	20.00

Page F – 3135 Stemware Engraved 539		Crystal
556	8" Plate	10.00
3135	12 oz. Footed Tumbler	12.00
3135	10 oz. Footed Tumbler	12.00
3135	5 oz. Footed Tumbler	10.00
3135	2½ oz. Footed Tumbler	12.00
3135	8 oz. Goblet	20.00
3135	6 oz. Tall Sherbet	14.00
3135	6 oz. Low Sherbet	12.00
3135	3 oz. Cocktail	20.00
3135	Finger Bowl and Plate	15.00

Page G – Engraved 530 Crystal		Crystal
278	11" Vase	45.00
627	4" Candlesticks ...pr.	35.00
842	12" Bowl	25.00
851	Ice Pail	43.00
856	11" Bowl	22.00
867	Sugar and Cream	30.00
868	11" Cheese and Cracker	24.00
870	11" Handled Sandwich Tray	23.00
873	3-Piece Mayonnaise Set	29.00
877	11½" Compote	28.00
971	8½" Bowl	20.00
972	11" Plate	19.00
977	11" Basket	28.00
984	10" Bowl	20.00
1090	7" Tall Compote	40.00

Page H – Engraved 534 Assortment		Crystal
627	Candlesticks ...pr.	24.00
842	12" Bowl	17.00
856	11" Bowl	17.00
867	Sugar and Cream	22.00
868	11" Cheese and Cracker	22.00
870	11" Handled Sandwich Tray	17.00
873	3-Piece Mayonnaise Set	22.00
877	11" Compote	23.00
971	8½" Bowl	14.00
972	11" Plate	17.00
977	11" Basket	22.00
984	10" Bowl	17.00

Page I – Lustre Cut Prism Candlesticks		Crystal	CR-RB
1269	11" Candlestick ...ea.	60.00	
1270	6½" Candlestick ...ea.	55.00	
1271	7" Candlestick ...ea.	55.00	
1272	10½" Candlestick ...ea.	60.00	
1273	10½" Candlestick ...ea.	60.00	

Page J – Miscellaneous		Crystal	CR
30	Base for Bowls	50.00	
609	Salad Fork and Spoon	25.00	
1111	12" Figure Flower Holder	165.00	
1222	8" Turkey and Cover	*	*
1257	Shaker, Glass Top	10.00	
1260	Shaker, Glass Top	10.00	
1262	Shaker, Glass Top	10.00	
1265	Shaker, Glass Top	10.00	
1266	Shaker, Glass Top	10.00	
3200	Punch Bowl and Foot	350.00	*
3200	Punch Cup	20.00	*

*No suggested values due to lack of trading

Page K – Miscellaneous		Crystal	Pastel
214	10" Handled Tray	15.00	22.00
321	9 oz. Tumbler, E Gloria	20.00	40.00
499	20 oz. Tumbler, E Gloria	30.00	55.00
1074	17" Handled Tray	20.00	40.00
1225	9" 2-Handled Plate, E Lorna	20.00	35.00
1266	10½" 2-Handled Plate, E Lorna	20.00	34.00
3077	8" Salad Plate	5.00	10.00
3140	10 oz. Footed Tumbler	12.00	18.00
3140	Footed Sherbet	10.00	15.00
3140	Hot Coffee Glass	15.00	25.00
3400/32	11½" Bowl, E Apple Blossom	50.00	70.00
3400/33	11¼" Bowl, E Apple Blossom	50.00	70.00

		Crystal	CR-RB
1243	10" Vase, Aero Optic	35.00	95.00

Page 31-1 – 3015 Stemware Plate Etched 748 Lorna		Crystal	Pastel
935	64 oz. Jug	75.00	120.00
3015	Fingerbowl and Plate	15.00	24.00
3015	10 oz. Footed Tumbler	12.00	20.00
3015	6 oz. Fruit Salad	12.00	15.00
3015	6 oz. Low Sherbet	12.00	16.00
3015	12 oz. Footed Tumbler	12.00	20.00
3015	5 oz. Footed Tumbler	10.00	20.00
3015	2½ oz. Cocktail	16.00	22.00
3015	9 oz. Goblet	16.00	25.00
3015	2½ oz. Wine	20.00	25.00
3015	6 oz. Tall Sherbet	15.00	20.00

Page 31-2 – Decagon Dinnerware Plate Etched 748 Lorna		Crystal	Pastel
597	Salad Plate	12.00	15.00
749	6" Handled Bon Bon	12.00	15.00
865	Cup and Saucer	16.00	22.00
867	Sugar and Cream	40.00	50.00
968/698	Fruit Cocktail	40.00	65.00
1068	2-Part Relish	20.00	25.00
1075	Cream Soup and Saucer	18.00	25.00
1087	Oval Vegetable	20.00	30.00
1098	5½" Fruit	10.00	15.00

Page 31-3 – 3035 Stemware Plate Etched 746 Gloria		Crystal	Pastel
3035	6 oz. Fruit Salad	15.00	22.00
3035	9 oz. Goblet	22.00	38.00
3035	2½ oz. Wine	25.00	45.00
3035	4½ oz. Oyster Cocktail	14.00	22.00
3035	6 oz. Low Sherbet	11.00	22.00
3035	12 oz. Footed Tumbler	20.00	30.00
3035	6 oz. Tall Sherbet	17.00	22.00
3035	3 oz. Cocktail	22.00	34.00
3035	4½ oz. Claret	24.00	55.00
3035	5 oz. Footed Tumbler	14.00	24.00
3035	10 oz. Footed Tumbler	14.00	25.00

Page 31-4 – Plate Etching 746 Gloria		Crystal	Pastel
1228	9" Oval Vase	90.00	175.00
1242	11" Vase	60.00	115.00
3400/13	6" Compote	22.00	42.00
3400/70	3½" Cranberry	30.00	55.00
3400/71	3" Individual Nut	54.00	72.00
3400/74	5" Compote	22.00	42.00
3400/75	Square Cup and Saucer	22.00	45.00
3400/76	Shaker, Glass Top	18.00	35.00
3400/77	Shaker, Glass Top	18.00	35.00

3400/81	5" Square Fruit Saucer	12.00	18.00
3400/82	6" Square Cereal	14.00	25.00
3400/83	Square A.D. Cup and Saucer	78.00	110.00
3400/85	Square Cream Soup & Saucer	24.00	50.00
3400/90	8" 2-Handled Relish	19.00	30.00
3400/91	8" 3- Handled Relish	28.00	45.00

Page 31-5 – 3025 Stemware Plate Etched 744	Apple Blossom	Crystal	Pastel
935	64 oz. Jug	145.00	250.00
3025	Finger Bowl and Plate	25.00	35.00
3025	12 oz. Footed Tumbler	20.00	32.00
3025	4 oz. Footed Tumbler	20.00	25.00
3025	10 oz. Footed Tumbler	16.00	20.00
3025	4½ oz. Oyster Cocktail	15.00	20.00
3025	7 oz. Low Sherbet	15.00	20.00
3025	10 oz. Goblet	22.00	35.00
3025	7 oz. Tall Sherbet	15.00	20.00

Page 31-6 – 1066 Stemware		Crystal	CR-RB
1066	11 oz. Goblet	16.00	27.00
1066	5 oz. Claret	18.00	27.00
1066	3 oz. Cocktail	16.00	25.00
1066	7 oz. Tall Sherbet	12.00	22.00
1066	6 oz. Fruit Salad	10.00	15.00
3135	12 oz. Footed Tumbler	15.00	22.00
3135	10 oz. Footed Tumbler	15.00	22.00
3135	8 oz. Footed Tumbler	15.00	22.00
3135	5 oz. Footed Tumbler	12.00	22.00
3135	3 oz. Footed Tumbler	10.00	17.00

Page 31-7 – Victorian Period Glassware		Crystal	CR
M.W.1	Sugar and Cream	25.00	65.00
M.W.2	4" Candlestick ea.	14.00	30.00
M.W.3	10" Candlesticks pr.	65.00	140.00
M.W.4	9" Bowl	17.00	45.00
M.W.5	10½" Bowl	20.00	50.00
M.W.9	10" Compote	28.00	65.00
M.W.17	7½" Fan Vase	20.00	55.00
M.W.18	12" Footed Vase	40.00	95.00
M.W.21	8" Salad Plate	10.00	18.00
M.W.23	12½" Plate	20.00	45.00
M.W.25	10½" Bowl	20.00	40.00
M.W.26	13½" Bowl	25.00	42.00
M.W.34	8 oz. Goblet	15.00	30.00
M.W.35	10 oz. Footed Ice Tea	15.00	30.00
M.W.36	6 oz. Footed Sherbet	12.00	25.00
M.W.41	1 lb. Candy Jar and Cover	45.00	95.00

Page 31-7 – Victorian Line		Crystal	CR
M.W.6	10" Bowl, Cupped	20.00	50.00
M.W.10	5½" Compote	14.00	25.00
M.W.16	10" Sweet Pea Vase	40.00	95.00
M.W.19	Sugar and Cream	25.00	65.00
M.W.20	6⅜" Bread and Butter Plate	8.00	15.00
M.W.46	5 oz. Footed Juice	10.00	15.00
M.W. 47	7 oz. Fruit Salad	10.00	15.00
M.W.48	8 oz. Footed Tumbler	10.00	18.00
M.W.49	10 oz. Footed Tumbler	10.00	18.00
M.W.50	12 oz. Footed Tumbler	10.00	18.00
M.W.52/53	Finger Bowl and Plate	15.00	35.00
M.W.54	8 oz. Stein Footed & Handled	18.00	40.00
M.W.55	10 oz. Stein Footed & Handled.	18.00	45.00
M.W.56	12 oz. Stein Footed & Handled.	18.00	50.00
M.W.57	5" Fruit Saucer	5.00	10.00

Page 31-8 – Miscellaneous		Crystal
1191	Candlestick ea.	175.00
1192	6" Candlestick ea.	25.00
1193	12" Vase	240.00
1209	Candlestick ea.	25.00
1210	10" Vase	50.00
1211	Candelabra ea.	50.00
1214	12" Vase	60.00
1236	Ivy Ball	45.00

Page 31-9 – Vases		Crystal
1285	6" Vase	18.00
1286	8" Vase	20.00
1287	10" Vase	22.00
1288	12" Vase	30.00
1289	6" Vase	18.00
1290	8" Vase	20.00
1291	10" Vase	22.00
1292	12" Vase	30.00

Page 31-10 – Ebony Silver Decorated		Ebony
851	Ice Pail D/971-S	160.00
862	4-Comp. Relish D/973-S	110.00
867	Sugar and Cream D/973-S	120.00
870	11" Sandwich Tray D/975-S	90.00
935	64 oz. Jug D/973-S	325.00
1020	Cocktail Shaker D/970-S	240.00
1070	36 oz. Pinch Bottle D/970-S	240.00
1084	13" 2-Handled Tray D/975-S	140.00
1090	7" Compote D/971-S	130.00
1093	2-Comp. Relish D/970-S	90.00
3400/67	Celery and Relish D/970-S	110.00
3400/68	Sugar and Cream D/970-S	110.00

Page 31-11 – Ebony Silver Decorated		Ebony
274	10" Vase D/971-S	100.00
402	12" Vase D/970-S	150.00
638	3-Hldr Candelabra D/971-S ea.	80.00
646	4" Candlestick D/970-S ea.	50.00
779	14" Vase D/971-S	240.00
782	8" Vase D/975-S	150.00
1130	11" Vase D/972-S	330.00
1228	9" Vase D/970-S	240.00
1240	12" Oval Bowl D/971-S	175.00
1242	10" Vase D/973-S	150.00
3400/17	12" Vase D/972-S	375.00

Page 31-12 – Ebony Silver Decorated		Ebony
842	12¼" Bowl, Belled D/975-S	90.00
856	11" R.E. Bowl D/973-S	75.00
972	11" 2-Handled Plate D/975-S	85.00
984	10" 2-Handled Bowl D/973-S	85.00
1185	10" 2-Handled Bowl D/970-S	100.00
1186	12½" 2-Hdl. Plate D/971-S	90.00
3400/4	12" 4-Toed Bowl D/970-S	130.00
3400/5	12" 4-Toed Bowl D/971-S	100.00
3400/10	11" Sandwich Tray D/971-S	90.00

Page 31-13 – Silver Decorated Ware		Ebony
646	5" Candlesticks D/971-S pr.	100.00
1070	36 oz. Pinch Bottle D/970-S	200.00
1242	10" Vase D/970-S	190.00
3400/4	12" Bowl, Flared D/970-S	205.00
3400/5	12" Bowl D/971-S	100.00
3400/10	10" Sandwich Tray D/971-S	90.00
3400/14	7" Tall Compote D/971-S	125.00
3400/38	80 oz. Ball Jug D/971-S	330.00
3400/1185	10" 2-Handled Bowl D/971-S	100.00
3400/1186	12½" 2-Hdl. Plate D/970-S	95.00

Page 31-14 – Ice Tea Sets		Crystal	Pastel
3400/27	67 oz. Jug, E Lorna	70.00	110.00
3400/27	12 oz. Tumbler, E Lorna	15.00	20.00
3400/27	67 oz. Jug, E Gloria	95.00	155.00
3400/27	12 oz. Tumbler, E Gloria	25.00	28.00
3400/27	67 oz. Jug, E Apple Blossom	100.00	160.00
3400/27	12 oz. Tumb., E Apple Blossom.	20.00	28.00
3400/38	80 oz. Jug, E Apple Blossom	110.00	185.00
3400/38	12 oz. Tumb., E Apple Blossom.	22.00	30.00
3400/38	80 oz. Jug, E Lorna	85.00	140.00
3400/38	12 oz.Tumbler, E Lorna	35.00	60.00
3400/38	80 oz. Jug, E Gloria	110.00	190.00
3400/38	12 oz. Tumbler, E Gloria	20.00	28.00
3400/27	67 oz. Jug	45.00	75.00
3400/27	12 oz. Tumbler	10.00	12.00
3400/38	80 oz. Jug	40.00	75.00
3400/38	12 oz. Tumbler	10.00	12.00

Page 31-15 – Vases		Crystal	Pastel
1233	9½" Vase, E Lorna	50.00	65.00
1234	12" Vase, E Apple Blossom	60.00	75.00
1237	9" Vase, E Lorna	50.00	65.00
1238	12" Vase, E Gloria	65.00	95.00
1239	14" Vase, E Gloria	75.00	140.00
1305	10" Vase, E Gloria	95.00	165.00
1308	6" Vase, E Apple Blossom	40.00	65.00
1309	5" Vase, E Apple Blossom	35.00	55.00

Page 31-16 – Vases		Crystal	Pastel
1283	8" Vase, E Apple Blossom	30.00	50.00
1284	10" Vase, E Gloria	35.00	60.00
1295	10" Vase, E Lorna	35.00	65.00
1296	12" Vase, E Apple Blossom	55.00	75.00
1297	11" Vase, E Gloria	65.00	135.00
1298	13" Vase, E Lorna	55.00	75.00
1299	11" Vase, E Gloria	65.00	125.00
1300	8" Vase, E Apple Blossom	35.00	50.00
1301	10" Vase, E Apple Blossom	55.00	75.00
1303	7" Vase, E Lorna	45.00	65.00

Page 31-17 – Business Stimulators		Crystal	Pastel
397	5-Comp. Celery and Relish	25.00	40.00
489	4-Piece Boudoir Set	65.00	80.00
862	4-Compartment Relish	20.00	25.00
955	62 oz. Jug with Cover	35.00	60.00
1095	3-Piece Sugar and Cream Set	30.00	50.00
1223	5" Candlesticks pr.	35.00	50.00
1224	11" Oval Bowl	15.00	20.00
1252	10" Vase	45.00	85.00
1253	12" Vase	55.00	95.00
1256	11" Oval Bowl	35.00	65.00
		Crystal	**Ebony**
1043	8½" Swan w/2¾" Block	85.00	195.00

Page 31-18 – Business Stimulators		Crystal	Pastel
214	10" Tray	15.00	25.00
880/8701	5-Piece Bridge Set	45.00	65.00
880/8701	5-Piece Bridge Set E 740	65.00	85.00
882	Tobacco Humidor w/Moistener	45.00	85.00
1025	Cigar Humidor & Cover w/Moistener	35.00	90.00
		Crystal	**Ebony**
607	Cigarette Box and Cover	55.00	160.00
		Crystal	**CR-RB**
1070	36 oz. Pinch Decanter	35.00	85.00
1070	2 oz. Pinch Tumbler	5.00	15.00
3145	32 oz. Decanter	30.00	85.00
3145	2½ oz. Tumbler	5.00	15.00
3145	84 oz. Jug, Ice Lipped	45.00	85.00
3145	14 oz. Tumbler	10.00	18.00

Page 31-19 – Business Stimulators		Crystal	Pastel
197	6 oz. Tall Oil, E Cleo	55.00	95.00
532	6½ oz. Compote, E 731	25.00	55.00
608	6½ oz. Low Compote, E 731	20.00	35.00
871	2-Handled Mayonnaise and Ladle, E 731	20.00	35.00
1012	8½" Bowl, E Cleo	20.00	45.00
1147	Ice Tub, Open Handles, E 731	30.00	50.00
1308	6" Vase, E 731	20.00	35.00
3077	22 oz. Jug and Cover, E Cleo	65.00	145.00
3400/13	4-Toed Compote, E Cleo	20.00	35.00
3400/90	2-Handled 2 Compartment Relish, E Cleo	15.00	25.00

Page 31-20 – Sport Novelties		Crystal
320	7 oz. Tumbler D/983	65.00
320	7 oz. Tumbler D/985	45.00
320	7 oz. Tumbler D/987	45.00
320	7 oz. Tumbler D/989	25.00
693/3000	2-Piece Canape Set D/983	65.00
693/3000	2-Piece Canape Set D/985	55.00
693/3000	2-Piece Canape Set D/987	55.00
693/3000	2-Piece Canape Set D/989	35.00
9403	14 oz. Tumbler D/983	75.00
9403	14 oz. Tumbler D/985	55.00

9403	14 oz. Tumbler D/988	60.00	
9403	12 oz. Tumbler D/984	56.00	
9403	12 oz. Tumbler D/986	50.00	
9403	12 oz. Tumbler D/987	50.00	
9403	12 oz. Tumbler D/989	25.00	

Page 31-21 – Miscellaneous		**Crystal**	**Pastel**
1071	9" 2-Handled Tray	15.00	25.00
1076	Sugar and Cream, E Lorna	25.00	45.00
1230	Cigarette Box and Ash Tray	30.00	55.00
1259	3-Piece Salt and Pepper Set	20.00	40.00
1268	2-Light Candelabrum	ea. 65.00	75.00
1274	13½" Candelabrum	ea. 150.00	
1274	13½" Candelabrum, Eng 560 ea.	185.00	
1315	Small "Bunny" Box and Cover	175.00	325.00
1316	Large "Bunny" Box and Cover	225.00	375.00

Page 31-22 – Plate Etched 746 Gloria		**Crystal**	**Pastel**
1071	9" Handled Tray	15.00	26.00
3025	Fingerbowl	24.00	42.00
3400/28	7" Low Compote	45.00	70.00
3400/29	7" Tall Compote	60.00	90.00
3400/30	9½" 2-Handled Footed Bowl	75.00	165.00
3400/34	9½" 2-Handled Bowl	35.00	55.00
3400/35	11" 2-Handled Plate	30.00	40.00
3400/39	Tall Cream or Syrup	45.00	75.00
3400/40	Sugar Shaker with Glass Top	75.00	125.00
3400/50	Square 4-Toed Cup & Saucer	35.00	65.00
3400/79	Tall Oil, G.S.	85.00	130.00
3400/86	8¾" 2-Handled Pickle	25.00	45.00
3400/88	8¾" 2-Hdl. 2 Comp. Relish	25.00	45.00

Page 31-23 – 3011 Stemware Plate Etched 746 Gloria		**Crystal**
3011	11 oz. Banquet Goblet	*
3011	11 oz. Table Goblet	*
3011	7 oz. Tall Sherbet	*
3011	3½ oz. Cocktail	*
3011	7" Compote, Flared	*
Stemware Plate Etched 744 Apple Blossom		**Crystal**
3011	11 oz. Banquet Goblet	*
3011	11 oz. Table Goblet	*
3011	7 oz. Tall Sherbet	*
3011	3½ oz. Cocktail	*
3011	7" Compote, Cupped	*

*No suggested values due to lack of trading

Page 31-24 – Early American Glassware Mount Vernon Pattern		**Crystal**	**CR-RB**
MT.V.1	9 oz. Goblet	18.00	30.00
MT.V.2	6½ oz. Tall Sherbet	14.00	24.00
MT.V.3	10 oz. Footed Tumbler	12.00	20.00
MT.V.4	6" Bread and Butter Plate	10.00	12.00
MT.V.5	8½" Salad Plate	12.00	16.00
MT.V.6	5¼" Fruit Saucer	10.00	18.00
MT.V.7	Cup and Saucer	12.00	28.00
MT.V.9	1 lb. Candy Jar and Cover	65.00	135.00
MT.V.10	7" Footed, Bon Bon	20.00	35.00
MT.V.11	7½" Footed Compote	25.00	45.00
MT.V.12	4½" Footed Rose Bowl	30.00	60.00
MT.V.8	Sugar and Cream	30.00	50.00

Page 31-25 – Early American Glassware Mount Vernon Pattern		**Crystal**	**CR-RB**
MT.V.13	3 Pint Jug	65.00	150.00
MT.V.13	1½ Pint Jug	45.00	100.00
MT.V.61	11½" Bowl, Shallow	15.00	45.00
MT.V.68	11½" Bowl, Belled	20.00	50.00
MT.V.105	8½" 2-hdl. 2-Comp. Sweetmeat	20.00	55.00
MT.V.106	6½" Rose Bowl	25.00	65.00
MT.V.107	6½" Squat Vase	25.00	65.00
MT.V.126	10" Bowl, Shallow	15.00	45.00
MT.V.128	10" Bowl, Belled	20.00	45.00

Page 31-26 – Early American Glassware Mount Vernon Pattern		**Crystal**	**CR-RB**
MT.V.42	5" Vase	20.00	55.00
MT.V.46	10" Vase	50.00	95.00
MT.V.50	6" Vase	25.00	60.00
MT.V.54	7" Vase	25.00	65.00
MT.V.58	7" Vase	30.00	75.00
MT.V.65	8" Pickle	15.00	35.00
MT.V.73	5" Butter Tub and Cover	35.00	90.00
MT.V.74	Honey Jar and Cover	25.00	65.00
MT.V.77	5½" 2-Handled Compote	38.00	75.00
MT.V.79	10½" Celery Tray	20.00	45.00
MT.V.100	9" Oval Compote	30.00	90.00
MT.V.102	Oval Salt Dip	15.00	35.00
MT.V.16	3" Vanity Box and Cover	15.00	

Page 31-27 – Ebony Silver Decorated Ware – Sport Novelties		**Ebony**
103	Candy Box w/Cover D/989-S	50.00
693/1021	2-Piece Canape Set D/987-S	45.00
851	Ice Pail D/983-S	145.00
862	4-Comp. Hdl. Relish D/989-S	45.00
972	11" 2-Handled Plate D/990-S	100.00
973	5-Piece Bridge Set D/983-S Ebony Tray, Crystal Tumblers	175.00
1020	Cocktail Shaker D/987-S	125.00
1021	2½ oz. Tumbler, Crystal with Ebony Foot D/987-S	35.00
1066	3½ oz. Cocktail D/985-S	17.00
1070	36 oz. Decanter D/985-S	150.00
1093	2-Comp. Relish D/987-S	85.00
1095	3-Piece Sugar & Cream D/987	120.00
1179	5½" Bon Bon D/983-S	60.00
1181	6" Plate D/987-S	45.00
3400/17	12" Vase D/990-S	275.00
3400/38	80 oz. Jug D/983-S	300.00
3400/38	12 oz. Tumbler D/983-S	55.00
3400/68	Sugar and Cream D/983-S	135.00
3400/92	32 oz. Decanter D/983-S	175.00
3400/92	2½ oz. Tumbler D/983-S	20.00

Page 31-28 – Ebony Silver Decorated Ware – Sport Novelties		**Ebony**
388	4" Ash Tray D/985-S	35.00
390	6" Ash Tray D/987-S	40.00
391	8" Ash Tray D/990-S	75.00
413	Cigarette Box D/983-S	100.00
430	Cigarette Box D/989-S	45.00
615	Cigarette Box D/983-S	65.00
616	Cigarette Box D/987-S	80.00
617	Cigarette Jar D/983-S	225.00
641	4" Ash Well, 2-Piece D/987-S	95.00
643	6" Ash Well, 2-Piece D/983-S	125.00
882	Tobacco Humidor D/990-S	275.00
885	Cigarette Jar D/985-S	140.00
1025	Cigar Humidor D/985-S	265.00
1025	Ash Tray D/989-S	45.00

Page 31-29 – Sport Novelties – Color Decorations		**Crystal**
388	4" Ash Tray D/987	30.00
390	6" Ash Tray D/983	50.00
391	8" Ash Tray D/985	60.00
601	Coaster D/Lines	8.00
615	Cigarette Box D/985	65.00
616	Cigarette Box D/983	95.00
617	Cigarette Jar D/983	125.00
851	Ice Pail D/985	120.00
882	Tobacco Humidor D/985	150.00
885	Cigarette Box D/985	95.00
1025	Cigar Humidor D/990	175.00
1066	3½ oz. Cocktail D/983	12.00
1231	32 oz. Decanter D/987	100.00
1322	26 oz. Decanter D/985	125.00
1323	28 oz. Decanter D/983	145.00
1324	22 oz. Decanter D/986	65.00
3000	3 oz. Tumbler D/985	50.00
3400/8	11" 2-Handled Plate D/987	50.00
3400/90	2-Compartment Relish D/986	45.00
3400/91	3-Compartment Relish D/983	95.00
3400/92	32 oz. Decanter D/984	125.00
8151	2½ oz. Tumbler D/Lines	15.00
8161	2½ oz. Tumbler D/Lines	15.00

Page 31-30 – 3122 Stemware Plate Etched 752 Diane		**Crystal**
3122	12 oz. Footed Tumbler	27.00
3122	9 oz. Footed Tumbler	22.00
3122	7 oz. Low Sherbet	17.00
3122	5 oz. Footed Tumbler	20.00
3122	2½ oz. Footed Tumbler	35.00
3122	4½ oz. Oyster Cocktail	20.00
3122	Finger Bowl and Plate	35.00
3122	9 oz. Goblet	30.00
3122	7 oz. Tall Sherbet	20.00
3122	4½ oz. Claret	35.00
3122	2½ oz. Wine	35.00
3122	3 oz. Cocktail	25.00
3122	1 oz. Cordial	75.00

Page 31-31 – 3400 Dinnerware Plate Etched 752 Diane		**Crystal**
3400/51	10" Baker	50.00
3400/53	6" Cereal	27.00
3400/54	Cup and Saucer	33.00
3400/55	Cream Soup and Saucer	33.00
3400/58	13½" Platter	80.00
3400/62	8½" Plate	18.00
3400/68	Sugar and Cream	35.00
3400/77	Salt and Pepper	45.00
3400/1174	6" Bread and Butter Plate	15.00

Page 31-32 – 3400 Dinnerware Plate Etched 752 Diane		**Crystal**
3400/4	12" 4-Toed Bowl	70.00
3400/45	11" Bowl	70.00
3400/638	Candelabra	pr. 100.00
3400/646	Candlesticks	pr. 70.00
3400/647	Candelabra	pr. 100.00
3400/1240	12" Oval Bowl	70.00

Page 31-33 – 1066 Stemware Plate Etched 752 Diane		**Crystal**
1066	12 oz. Footed Tumbler	30.00
1066	9 oz. Footed Tumbler	25.00
1066	7 oz. Low Sherbet	22.00
1066	5 oz. Footed Tumbler	28.00
1066	3 oz. Footed Tumbler	28.00
1066	3 oz. Low Cocktail	22.00
1066	5 oz. Oyster Cocktail	20.00
1066	11 oz. Goblet	33.00
1066	7 oz. Tall Sherbet	20.00
1066	4½ oz. Claret	35.00
1066	3 oz. Wine	35.00
1066	3½ oz. Tall Cocktail	25.00
1066	1 oz. Cordial	75.00

Page 31-34 – 1066 Stemware Plate Etched 752 Diane		**Crystal**
1066	14 oz. Tumbler	28.00
1066	12 oz. Tumbler	28.00
1066	10 oz. Tumbler	22.00
1066	7 oz. Tumbler	22.00
1066	5 oz. Tumbler	28.00
1066	2½ oz. Tumbler	34.00
3135	12 oz. Footed Tumbler	30.00
3135	10 oz. Footed Tumbler	25.00
3135	8 oz. Footed Tumbler	25.00
3135	5 oz. Footed Tumbler	20.00
3135	2½ oz. Footed Tumbler	35.00

Page 32-1 – 3126 Stemware Etched Portia		**Crystal**
3126	3 oz. Cocktail	28.00
3126	9 oz. Goblet	30.00
3126	7 oz. Tall Sherbet	30.00
3126	7 oz. Low Sherbet	25.00
3126	4½ oz. Claret	45.00
3126	1 oz. Cordial	65.00
3126	4½ oz. Oyster Cocktail	40.00
3126	10 oz. Footed Tumbler	28.00
3126	13 oz. Footed Tumbler	28.00
3126	5 oz. Footed Tumbler	25.00
3126	2½ oz. Footed Tumbler	35.00

3126	2½ oz. Wine	30.00
3126	1 oz. Brandy	65.00
3126	Finger Bowl and Plate	50.00

Page 32-2 – 3121 Stemware Etched Portia		Crystal
3121	3 oz. Cocktail	28.00
3121	10 oz. Goblet	35.00
3121	6 oz. Tall Sherbet	25.00
3121	6 oz. Low Sherbet	20.00
3121	4½ oz. Claret	40.00
3121	1 oz. Cordial	65.00
3121	4½ oz. Oyster Cocktail	25.00
3121	10 oz. Footed Tumbler	30.00
3121	12 oz. Footed Tumbler	35.00
3121	5 oz. Footed Tumbler	25.00
3121	2½ oz. Footed Tumbler	35.00
3121	2½ oz. Wine	35.00
3121	1 oz. Brandy	50.00
3121	Finger Bowl and Plate	50.00

Page 32-3 – 3124 Stemware Etched Portia		Crystal
3124	10 oz. Goblet	35.00
3124	7 oz. Tall Sherbet	25.00
3124	3 oz. Cocktail	28.00
3124	7 oz. Low Sherbet	22.00
3124	4½ oz. Claret	40.00
3124	3 oz. Footed Tumbler	35.00
3124	3 oz. Wine	35.00
3124	5 oz. Footed Tumbler	28.00
3124	4½ oz. Oyster Cocktail	22.00
3124	10 oz. Footed Tumbler	25.00
3124	12 oz. Footed Tumbler	35.00
3124	Finger Bowl and Plate	50.00

Page 32-4 – Plate Etched Portia		Crystal
119	7" Basket	220.00
193	6 oz. Oil	110.00
652	11" Celery Tray	45.00
968	Sea Food or Fruit Cocktail	55.00
3400/41	3-Piece Frappe Set	55.00
3400/49	3½" Cranberry	35.00
3400/50	Square Cup and Saucer	35.00
3400/80	3½" Cranberry	35.00
3400/89	2-Compartment Relish	40.00
3400/93	Ivy Ball	85.00
3400/94	3½" Puff Box	165.00
3400/97	2 oz. Cologne	140.00
3400/98	Sugar and Cream	75.00
3400/99	6 oz. Oil	95.00
3400/108	80 oz. Cocktail Shaker	220.00
3400/109	6" Grapefruit	35.00
3400/1176	8½" Salad Plate	18.00
3400/1188	11" Bowl	55.00

Page 32-5 – Ten-Piece Assortment E 758		Crystal	Pastel
135	10½" Cheese and Cracker	30.00	45.00
138	Sugar and Cream	30.00	37.00
168	10½" Handled Sandwich Tray	22.00	28.00
315	20 oz. Decanter	75.00	125.00
531	7¼" Tall Compote	25.00	34.00
533	3-Piece Mayonnaise Set	35.00	50.00
628	3½" Candlestick ea.	15.00	25.00
676	11½" Bowl	20.00	25.00
782	8" Vase	25.00	35.00
988	11½" Bowl	22.00	22.00

Page 32-6 – Ten-Piece Assortment E 760		Crystal	Pastel
197	Tall Oil, G.S.	50.00	65.00
532	6½" Tall Compote	25.00	34.00
608	6½" Compote	15.00	20.00
871	2-Piece Mayonnaise Set	20.00	35.00
1012	8½" Bowl	20.00	30.00
1147	Ice Tub	25.00	40.00
1308	6" Vase	20.00	40.00
3077	22 oz. Jug and Cover	75.00	165.00
3400/13	6" 4-Toed Compote	15.00	20.00
3400/90	8" 2-Part Relish	15.00	20.00

Page 32-7 – Decorate 996 (Orange Trim)		Crystal
851	Ice Pail	45.00
864	Candy Box and Cover	45.00
1076	Sugar and Cream	25.00
1093	6" Handled Relish	23.00
1225	9" 2-Handled Bowl	25.00
1226	10" 2-Handled Plate, D/997	20.00
1284	10" Vase	30.00
1303	7" Vase	45.00
3400/28	7" Compote	40.00
3400/87	11" Celery	25.00
3400/88	8¾" 2-Compartment Relish	20.00
3400/102	5" Globe Jar	40.00

Page 32-8 – Console Sets		Crystal	Pastel
842	12½" Bowl, Eng 648	30.00	
842	12½" Bowl, E/755	30.00	35.00
992	12½" Bowl, E/756	25.00	35.00
993	12½" Bowl, D/997	25.00	35.00
993	12½" Bowl, D/999	25.00	35.00
993	12½" Bowl, Eng 649	30.00	
993	12½" Bowl, D/998	25.00	35.00
993	12½" Bowl, E/757	30.00	35.00
1307	Candelabra, D/997 ea.	30.00	35.00
1307	Candelabra, D/999 ea.	30.00	35.00

Page 32-9 – Cambridge Two Tone Quick Sellers		Crystal	CR-RB
119	7" Basket, 12" High	65.00	230.00
489	4-Piece Boudoir Set	85.00	160.00
627	4" Candlesticks pr.	35.00	
993	12½" Bowl	20.00	60.00
1070	36 oz. Pinch Decanter	40.00	95.00
1095	3-Piece Sugar and Cream Set	35.00	65.00
1234	12" Vase	30.00	75.00
1236	8" Ivy Ball	50.00	85.00
3400/28	7" Compote	30.00	65.00

Page 32-10 – Miscellaneous		Crystal	Pastel
319	8 oz. Georgian Tumb., E Grape	40.00	
320	7 oz. O.F. Cocktail, Eng 629	15.00	
321	9 oz. Tumbler	10.00	15.00
493	14 oz. Tumbler	10.00	15.00
496	2½ oz. Tumbler, Eng 625	12.00	
497	8 oz. Tumbler, E Gloria	15.00	35.00
498	12 oz. Tumb., E Apple Blossom	18.00	45.00
499	21 oz. Tumbler, Eng 629	16.00	
1197/1066	5-Piece Set, Eng Laurel Wreath	75.00	100.00
1198/1066	5-Piece Set, D/992	75.00	
1201	2½ oz. Georgian Tumbler, E Grape	50.00	
1202	12 oz. Georgian Tumbler, E Grape	40.00	
1212	Bitter Bottle, D/992	30.00	
1403	10 oz. Pilsner	15.00	
3400/100	14 oz. Tumbler, E Gloria	18.00	45.00

		Crystal	CR-RB
320	7 oz. O.F. Cocktail	10.00	
601	3" Coaster	5.00	12.00
602	5¼" Coaster	6.00	15.00
603	4" Coaster	6.00	15.00
604	5¼" Coaster	6.00	15.00
1066	7 oz. O.F. Cocktail, Eng Laurel Wreath	15.00	
1206	12 oz. Tumbler, Spiral Optic	10.00	20.00
1306	20 oz. Tumbler	10.00	
1404	6 oz. Ginger ale	10.00	
3400/107	14 oz. Stein	17.00	35.00
9024	16 oz. Tumbler	8.00	
9024	14 oz. Tumbler	8.00	
9024	10 oz. Tumbler	8.00	
9024	5 oz. Tumbler	8.00	
9024	2½ oz. Tumbler	10.00	
M.W.49	10 oz. Tumbler	12.00	24.00
M.W.49	12 oz. Stein	18.00	48.00

Page 32-11 – Vases and Urns		Crystal	Pastel
1238	12" Vase, Eng 639	50.00	
1297	11" Vase, Eng 640	50.00	
1299	11" Vase, Eng 615	55.00	
1304	11" Urn, Eng 618	150.00	
1305	10" Vase, Eng 560	95.00	
1318	14" Vase, Eng 639	150.00	
1335	12" Vase, E 758	45.00	60.00
3400/102	5" Vase, Eng 641	35.00	
3400/103	6½" Vase, Eng 640	35.00	

		Crystal	CR-RB
1319	4½" Vase	20.00	70.00
1330	5" Sweet Potato Vase	15.00	40.00

Page 32-12 – Stemware and Tumblers Etched Old Fashioned Grape 401		Crystal
1203	14 oz. Tumbler	15.00
1203	12 oz. Tumbler	15.00
1203	10 oz. Tumbler	12.00
1203	8 oz. Tumbler	12.00
1203	2½ oz. Tumbler	12.00
1203	7 oz. O.F. Cocktail	12.00
1203	5 oz. Juice	10.00
1204	14 oz. Tumbler	15.00
1400	10 oz. Goblet	18.00
1401	10 oz. Footed Tumbler	16.00
1401	5 oz. Footed Tumbler	14.00
1401	10 oz. Goblet	18.00
1401	6 oz. Tall Sherbet	15.00
1401	4½ oz. Claret	16.00
1401	3 oz. Cocktail	15.00
1401	3 oz. Wine	16.00
1401	1 oz. Cordial	50.00
1401	Finger Bowl	12.00

Page 32-13 – Rock Crystal Engraved 646		Crystal
1203	14 oz. Tumbler	15.00
1203	12 oz. Tumbler	15.00
1203	10 oz. Tumbler	12.00
1203	8 oz. Tumbler	12.00
1203	2 oz. Tumbler	12.00
1203	7 oz. O.F. Cocktail	12.00
1203	5 oz. Juice	10.00
1204	14 oz. Tumbler	14.00
1401	10 oz. Goblet	18.00

Rock Crystal Engraved 643		Crystal
1400	12 oz. Footed Tumbler	15.00
1400	5 oz. Footed Tumbler	14.00
1400	10 oz. Goblet	18.00
1400	7 oz. Tall Sherbet	15.00
1400	5½ oz. Sherbet	15.00
1400	3½ oz. Cocktail	15.00
1400	2½ oz. Wine	16.00
1400	1 oz. Cordial	45.00
1404	6 oz. Hollow Stem Ginger ale	18.00

Page 32-14 – Rock Crystal Eng Stemware		Crystal
1066	12 oz. Ftd. Tumbler Eng 622	22.00
1066	12 oz. Ftd. Tumbler Eng 629	22.00
3035	9 oz. Goblet, Eng 621	22.00
3120	9 oz. Goblet, Eng 622	22.00
3120	9 oz. Goblet, Eng 628	22.00
3120	9 oz. Goblet, Eng 637	22.00
3120	9 oz. Goblet, Eng 638	22.00
3121	10 oz. Goblet, Eng 640	22.00
3122	9 oz. Goblet, Eng 603	22.00
3122	9 oz. Goblet, Eng 621	22.00
3122	9 oz. Goblet, Eng 623	22.00
3122	9 oz. Goblet, Eng 640	22.00
3122	9 oz. Goblet, Eng 641	22.00
3124	10 oz. Goblet, Eng 611	22.00
3124	10 oz. Goblet, Eng 618	22.00

Page 32-15 – Rock Crystal Eng Stemware		Crystal
3035	9 oz. Goblet, Eng 613	22.00
3035	9 oz. Goblet, Eng 614	22.00
3035	9 oz. Goblet, Eng 616	22.00
3121	10 oz. Goblet, Eng 654	22.00
3121	10 oz. Goblet, Eng 655	22.00
3122	9 oz. Goblet, Eng 661	22.00
3124	10 oz. Goblet, Eng 615	22.00

3124	10 oz. Goblet, Eng 639	22.00
3126	9 oz. Goblet, Eng 642	22.00
3126	9 oz. Goblet, Eng 651	22.00
3130	8 oz. Goblet, Eng 538	22.00
3130	8 oz. Goblet, Eng 541	22.00
3130	8 oz. Goblet, Eng 652	22.00
3130	8 oz. Goblet, Eng 656	22.00
3130	8 oz. Goblet, Eng 657	22.00

Page 32-16 – Rock Crystal Engraved 644		**Crystal**
103	3-Compartment Candy Box	35.00
627	4" Candlestick ea.	15.00
647	Candelabrum ea.	30.00
842	12¼" Bowl	25.00
856	11" Bowl	25.00
868	11" Cheese and Cracker	25.00
870	11" Handled Sandwich Tray	20.00
873	3-Piece Mayonnaise Set	30.00
877	9½" Compote	26.00
984	10" Bowl	25.00
1090	7" Tall Compote	35.00
1147	Ice Tub	30.00
1225	9" Bowl	25.00
1226	10½" Plate	18.00
1242	10" Vase	50.00
3400/90	2-Compartment Relish	16.00
3400/91	3-Compartment Relish	25.00

Page 32-17 – Rock Crystal Engraved 650		**Crystal**
103	7" Candy Box	35.00
489	22 oz. Jug and Cover	55.00
532	6½" Tall Compote	35.00
639	4" Candlesticks pr.	35.00
864	Candy Box	45.00
871	5½" 2-Handle Compote	20.00
983	2-Piece Mayonnaise Set	30.00
988	11½" Bowl	25.00
1012	8½" Bowl	20.00
1076	Cream and Sugar	25.00
1147	Ice Pail	30.00
1169	Bon Bon, Chrome Handle	25.00
1225	9" Bowl	20.00
1226	10½" Plate	20.00
1226	10½" Plate, Eng 647	20.00
1284	10" Vase	25.00
1308	6" Vase	25.00
3400/59	9" Celery Tray	15.00
3400/88	8¾" 2-Compartment Relish	20.00
3400/90	7½" 2-Compartment Relish	16.00
3400/102	5" Vase	35.00

Page 32-18 – Rock Crystal Engraved		**Crystal**
531	7" Tall Compote, Eng 622	40.00
533	5" Compote, Eng 629	25.00
652	11" Celery Tray, Eng 628	25.00
851	Ice Pail, Eng 622	65.00
993	12½" Bowl, Eng 629	40.00
1228	9" Vase, Eng 629	85.00
1268	6" Prism Candelabrum Eng 629.	95.00
1272	10½" Candlestick, Eng 629	65.00
3400/35	11" 2-Handled Plate, Eng 628	40.00
3400/67	12" Celery & Relish, Eng 628	40.00
3400/862	8" 4-Comp. Relish, Eng 628	40.00
3400/1185	10" Bowl, Eng 637	40.00
3400/1186	12½" 2-Hdl. Plate, Eng 628	40.00
3400/1240	12" Oval Bowl, Eng 622	55.00

Page 32-19 – Rock Crystal Engraved		**Crystal**
1268	Candelabrum, Eng 621 ea.	95.00
3400/1	13" Bowl, Eng 615	35.00
3400/3	11" Footed Compote, Eng 560	40.00
3400/4	12" Bowl, Eng 611	35.00
3400/6	11" Cheese & Cracker, Eng 624	30.00
3400/10	11" Sandwich Plate, Eng 623	25.00
3400/28	7" Low Compote, Eng 611	55.00
3400/29	7" Tall Compote, Eng 615	65.00
3400/32	11½" Bowl, Eng 652	30.00
3400/67	12" Celery & Relish, Eng 621	40.00
3400/91	8" 3-Comp. Relish, Eng 624	25.00
3400/862	8" Relish, Eng 615	40.00

Page 32-20 – Rock Crystal Engraved		**Crystal**
1261	French Dress. Bottle, Eng 641	55.00
1263	French Dress. Bottle, Eng 639	40.00
3400/1	13" Bowl, Eng 640	35.00
3400/4	12" Bowl, Eng 641	50.00
3400/14	7" Tall Compote, Eng 641	50.00
3400/18	Shaker, Chrome Top, Eng 560	17.00
3400/21	9" Bowl, Eng 640	30.00
3400/32	11½" Bowl, Eng 642	35.00
3400/34	9½" Bowl, Eng 641	35.00
3400/36	Shaker, Chrome Top, Eng 642	12.00
3400/37	Shaker, Chrome Top, Eng 641	15.00
3400/77	Shaker, Glass Top, Eng 642	22.00
3400/79	6 oz. Oil, G.S., Eng 611	75.00
3400/88	8¾" 2-Comp. Relish, Eng 642	22.00
3400/89	11" 2-Comp. Relish, Eng 642	25.00
3400/90	2-Comp. Relish, Eng 611	22.00
3400/1093	Handled Relish, Eng 615	28.00
3400/1192	6" Candlestick, Eng 642	30.00

Page 32-21 – Rock Crystal Engraved Laurel Wreath		**Crystal**
324	6-Piece Relish Set	55.00
531	7¼" Compote	25.00
556	8" Plate	15.00
647	5½" Candelabrum ea.	27.00
922	Cream Soup and Saucer	18.00
993	12½" Bowl	25.00
1066	12 oz. Footed Tumbler	15.00
1066	9 oz. Footed Tumbler	12.00
1066	5 oz. Footed Tumbler	12.00
1066	11 oz. Goblet	20.00
1066	7 oz. Tall Sherbet	15.00
1066	3 oz. Tall Cocktail	18.00
1304	11" Urn	95.00
3400/8	11½" Sandwich Plate	20.00
3400/77	Shaker, Glass Top	16.00
3400/79	6 oz. Oil	65.00
3400/100	76 oz. Jug	75.00
3400/100	14 oz. Tumbler	10.00
3400/102	5" Globe Jar	30.00

Page 32-22 – Rock Crystal Engraved		**Crystal**
556	8" Salad Plate, Eng 628	15.00
660/94/97	4-Piece Dresser Set, Eng 639	175.00
968/698	3-Piece Sea Food, Eng 639	50.00
1070	36 oz. Decanter, Eng 639	65.00
1070	2 oz. Tumbler, Eng 639	15.00
1205	64 oz. Jug, Eng 560	95.00
3011	9" Candlestick w/Prisms, Eng 639 ea.	250.00
3011	9" Candlestick, Eng 639 ea.	225.00
3130	2½ oz. Ftd. Tumbler, Eng 611	15.00
3135	12 oz. Ftd. Tumbler, Eng 560	18.00
3400/38	80 oz. Ball Jug, Eng 639	95.00
3400/38	12 oz. Tumbler, Eng 639	15.00
3400/39	Cream, Eng 611	45.00
3400/40	Sugar Shaker, Eng 611	65.00
3400/54	Cup and Saucer, Eng 642	17.00
3400/55	Cream Soup & Saucer, Eng 615	20.00
3400/62	8½" Plate, Eng 640	15.00
3400/68	Cream and Sugar on 1071 Tray, Eng 621	50.00
3400/78	Cocktail Shakers, Eng 611	165.00
3400/92	32 oz. Decanter, Eng 639	90.00
3400/96	3-Piece Vinegar & Oil, Eng 639	75.00
3400/98	Ball Cream & Sugar, Eng 639	60.00
3400/99	6 oz. Oil, Eng 639	50.00
3400/100	13 oz. Tumbler, Eng 639	15.00
3400/101	76 oz. Jug, Eng 639	80.00
3400/106	Marmalade Jar, Eng 639	75.00
3400/1176	8½" Plate, Eng 638	18.00
8161	2 oz. Tumbler, Eng 639	10.00

Page 32-23 – Martha Washington Stemware		**Crystal**	**CR-RB**
1203	14 oz. Tumbler	12.00	25.00
1203	12 oz. Tumbler	12.00	25.00
1203	10 oz. Tumbler	12.00	25.00
1203	8 oz. Tumbler	10.00	22.00
1203	7 oz. O.F. Cocktail	10.00	22.00
1203	5 oz. Tumbler	10.00	20.00
1203	2½ oz. Tumbler	8.00	20.00
1204	14 oz. Tumbler	14.00	30.00
1400	12 oz. Footed Tumbler	12.00	24.00
1400	5 oz. Footed Tumbler	12.00	25.00
1400	10 oz. Goblet	12.00	25.00
1400	7 oz. Tall Sherbet	12.00	25.00
1400	7 oz. Low Sherbet	12.00	25.00
1400	3½ oz. Cocktail	15.00	30.00
1400	2 oz. Wine	15.00	30.00
1400	1 oz. Cordial	25.00	60.00
1400	5½ oz. Sherbet	15.00	26.00
1400	Finger Bowl and Plate	15.00	30.00
1401	10 oz. Footed Tumbler	15.00	28.00
1401	10 oz. Goblet	15.00	28.00
1401	6 oz. Tall Sherbet	12.00	25.00
1401	5 oz. Footed Tumbler	10.00	24.00
1401	4½ oz. Claret	15.00	30.00
1401	3 oz. Cocktail	15.00	30.00
1401	3 oz. Wine	15.00	30.00
1401	1 oz. Cordial	25.00	60.00
1401	Finger Bowl	10.00	22.00
1404	6 oz. Ginger Ale	15.00	

Page 32-24 – Martha Washington		**Crystal**	**CR-RB**
1400	6" Compote	18.00	35.00
M.W.1	Sugar and Cream	24.00	65.00
M.W.10	5½" Compote	14.00	35.00
M.W.14	Sugar and Cream	24.00	60.00
M.W.15	5½" Compote	18.00	45.00
M.W.19	Sugar and Cream	26.00	60.00
M.W.20	6⅜" Bread & Butter Plate	8.00	18.00
M.W.21	8⅜" Bread & Butter Plate	17.00	
M.W.34	9 oz. Goblet	17.00	30.00
M.W.35	10 oz. Footed Tumbler	17.00	30.00
M.W.36	6 oz. Sherbet	14.00	25.00
M.W.42	Cup and Saucer	14.00	25.00
M.W.45	7 oz. Tall Sherbet	17.00	30.00
M.W.46	5 oz. Footed Tumbler	13.00	24.00
M.W.47	7 oz. Fruit Salad	12.00	20.00
M.W.48	8 oz. Footed Tumbler	14.00	24.00
M.W.49	10 oz. Footed Tumbler	14.00	24.00
M.W.50	12 oz. Tumbler, E Grape	19.00	
M.W.51	10 oz. Goblet	19.00	35.00
M.W.52/53	Finger Bowl and Plate	18.00	30.00
M.W.54	8 oz. Stein	22.00	48.00
M.W.55	Stein	22.00	48.00
M.W.56	12 oz. Stein	22.00	48.00
M.W.57	5¼" Fruit Saucer	12.00	15.00

Page 32-25 – Martha Washington		**Crystal**	**CR-RB**
1269	10" Candlestick w/Prisms ea.	75.00	125.00
M.W.2	4" Candlestick ea.	15.00	25.00
M.W.3	9" Candlestick ea.	45.00	65.00
M.W.4	9" Bowl	15.00	55.00
M.W.5	10½" Bowl	18.00	60.00
M.W.6	10" Bowl	18.00	60.00
M.W.7	12½" Bowl	18.00	60.00
M.W.8	12½" Bowl, E Grape	30.00	
M.W.9	10" Compote	25.00	65.00
M.W.11	13" Bowl	20.00	60.00
M.W.12	9½" Bowl	20.00	55.00
M.W.13	7½" Bowl	25.00	60.00
M.W.16	10" Vase	35.00	115.00
M.W.17	7½" Fan Vase	25.00	65.00
M.W.18	11" Vase	35.00	95.00
M.W.23	12½" Plate, E Grape	35.00	
M.W.25	10½" Plate, E Grape	30.00	
M.W.26	13½" Plate, E Grape	30.00	
M.W.27	8½" Bowl	20.00	50.00
M.W.28	12" Bowl	20.00	50.00
M.W.39	12" Urn	55.00	130.00
M.W.40	14½" Urn	75.00	175.00
M.W.41	9½" Urn	55.00	130.00
M.W.43	7½" 3-Comp. Candy Box	45.00	110.00
M.W.44	11½" Sandwich Plate	15.00	40.00

M.W.58	6½" Ice Tub	25.00	85.00

Page 32-25A – Miscellaneous		Crystal	CR-RB
M.W.22	7½" Coupe Salad	15.00	25.00
M.W.30	80 oz. Jug	65.00	165.00
M.W.56	12 oz. Stein	20.00	55.00
M.W.59	5 oz. Footed Sherbet	12.00	20.00
M.W.60	4½" Oyster Cocktail	12.00	20.00
M.W.61	3½" Cocktail	18.00	30.00
M.W.66	11" Cheese and Cracker	45.00	100.00
MT.V.72	7½" Coupe Salad	15.00	25.00
MT.V.84	14 oz. Stein	20.00	55.00
MT.V.91	86 oz. Jug	65.00	165.00

Page 32-26 – Mount Vernon		Crystal	CR-RB
MT.V.1	9 oz. Goblet	18.00	30.00
MT.V.2	6½ oz. Tall Sherbet	14.00	24.00
MT.V.3	10 oz. Footed Tumbler	12.00	20.00
MT.V.5	8½" Salad Plate	12.00	16.00
MT.V.7	Cup and Saucer	12.00	28.00
MT.V.8	Sugar and Cream	30.00	50.00
MT.V.13	3 Pint Jug	65.00	150.00
MT.V.13	12 oz. Tumbler	6.00	16.00
MT.V.14	14 oz. Tumbler	12.00	20.00
MT.V.19	6⅜" Bread and Butter Plate	8.00	15.00
MT.V.20	12 oz. Footed Tumbler	12.00	22.00
MT.V.21	5 oz. Footed Tumbler	12.00	22.00
MT.V.22	3 oz. Footed Tumbler	12.00	22.00
MT.V.24	Individual Salt	8.00	18.00
MT.V.28	Shaker, Glass Top	12.00	25.00
MT.V.29	2½ oz. Mustard	20.00	65.00
MT.V.40	10½" Dinner Plate	25.00	55.00
MT.V.52	40 oz. Decanter	45.00	145.00
MT.V.84	14 oz. Stein	18.00	48.00
MT.V.102	Individual Salt, Oval	14.00	35.00
MT.V.74	Honey Jar and Cover	25.00	75.00

Page 32-27 – Mount Vernon		Crystal	CR-RB
1340	2½" Cologne	35.00	
MT.V.6	5¼" Fruit Saucer	10.00	18.00
MT.V.15	4½" Toilet Box	38.00	
MT.V.16	3" Toilet Box	28.00	
MT.V.17	4" Toilet Box	38.00	60.00
MT.V.18	7 oz. Toilet Bottle	65.00	110.00
MT.V.23	Finger Bowl and Plate	15.00	28.00
MT.V.31	4½" Fruit Saucer	10.00	20.00
MT.V.32	6" Cereal	14.00	22.00
MT.V.76	6" Preserve	12.00	22.00
MT.V.78	6" Handled Pickle	15.00	25.00
MT.V.79	12" Celery Tray	18.00	30.00
MT.V.80	12" 2-Part Relish	30.00	60.00
MT.V.101	6" Handled Relish	20.00	35.00
MT.V.103	8" Relish	20.00	45.00
MT.V.104	6" Celery and Relish	30.00	60.00
MT.V.105	6" 4-Compartment Sweetmeat	35.00	65.00

Page 32-28 – Mount Vernon		Crystal	CR-RB
MT.V.9	8" Urn	65.00	135.00
MT.V.10	7" Bon Bon	20.00	35.00
MT.V.11	7½" Compote	25.00	45.00
MT.V.12	4½" Rose Bowl or Ivy Ball	30.00	60.00
MT.V.30	Sauce Boat and Ladle	60.00	95.00
MT.V.33	4½" Compote	20.00	45.00
MT.V.34	6" Compote	20.00	45.00
MT.V.46	10" Vase	50.00	95.00
MT.V.50	6" Vase	25.00	60.00
MT.V.54	7" Vase	35.00	70.00
MT.V.77	6" Compote	20.00	45.00
MT.V.96	6½" Compote	25.00	45.00
MT.V.97	6½" Compote	25.00	45.00
MT.V.99	9½" Compote	30.00	60.00

Page 32-29 – Mount Vernon		Crystal	CR-RB
MT.V.35	8" Candlestick	25.00	60.00
MT.V.36	8½" Candlestick w/Prisms	55.00	90.00
MT.V.37	11½" Plate	20.00	35.00
MT.V.38	13½" Candelabrum	ea. 150.00	
MT.V.39	10" Bowl	20.00	35.00
MT.V.43	10½" Bowl	30.00	50.00
MT.V.44	12½" Bowl	35.00	65.00
MT.V.45	12½" Bowl	35.00	65.00
MT.V.100	9" Oval Compote	30.00	55.00
MT.V.129	12" Bowl	35.00	65.00
MT.V.130	4" Candlestick	ea. 15.00	25.00
MT.V.135	11" Oval Bowl	25.00	50.00

Page 32-30 – Missing

Page 32-31 – Varsity Sport Glassware		Crystal
9403	14 oz. Tumblers	55.00
	(Price is the same on all decorations)	

Page 32-32 – Varsity Sport Glassware		Crystal
	(See Catalog or Decorations)	
320	7 oz. O.F. Cocktail	25.00
390	6" Ash Tray	25.00
499	20 oz. Tumbler, Cut Flute	55.00
601	Coaster	10.00
616	Cigarette Box	75.00
617	Cigarette Jar	75.00
623/8701	5-Piece Bridge Set	200.00
693/3000	3 oz. Canape Set	50.00
851	Ice Pail	75.00
882	Tobacco Humidor	125.00
885	Cigarette Jar	75.00
973/8701	10 oz. 5-Piece Bridge Set	200.00
1020	Cocktail Shaker	125.00
1021	2½ oz. Footed Tumbler	10.00
1025	Cigar Humidor	150.00
1070	Pinch Decanter	95.00
1321	Decanter	95.00
1322	Decanter	95.00
1324	Decanter	95.00
3000	3 oz. Footed Tumbler	25.00
3000/1198	3 oz. Footed Tumbler Set	120.00
3135	12 oz. Footed Tumbler	45.00
3400/8	11½" Plate	35.00
3400/38	Jug	175.00
3400/91	Relish	65.00
3400/92	Decanter	175.00
8151	2½ oz. Tumbler	10.00
8161	2½ oz. Tumbler	10.00
9403	12 oz. Tumbler	55.00

Page 32-33 – 1402 Tally-Ho Line		Crystal	CR-RB
1402/1	18 oz. Goblet, E Imperial Hunt Scene	75.00	
1402/2	14 oz. Goblet, E Catawba	45.00	
1402/3	10 oz. Goblet, Eng 690	35.00	
1402/4	10 oz. Lunch Goblet	15.00	35.00
1402/5	7½ oz. Tall Sherbet	12.00	30.00
1402/6	6½ oz. Low Sherbet	10.00	25.00
1402/7	6 oz. Tall Stem Juice	15.00	35.00
1402/8	5 oz. Low Stem Juice	12.00	30.00
1402/9	4½ oz. Claret	18.00	50.00
1402/10	3 oz. Cocktail	16.00	45.00
1402/11	4 oz. Low Oyster Cocktail	12.00	30.00
1402/12	2½ oz. Wine	18.00	50.00
1402/13	1 oz. Cordial	20.00	50.00
1402/14	Finger Bowl	12.00	25.00
1402/15	Finger Bowl Plate	10.00	20.00

Page 32-34 – 1402 Tally-Ho Line		Crystal	CR-RB
1402/17	Sauce Boat, Plate & Ladle	30.00	65.00
1402/19	Cup and Saucer	15.00	35.00
1402/21	6" Bread and Butter Plate	10.00	15.00
1402/22	7" Tea Plate, D/1007	25.00	
1402/23	8" Salad Plate	12.00	18.00
1402/24	9½" Dinner Plate	20.00	35.00
1402/25	10½" Service	25.00	60.00
1402/28	18" Buffet Lunch Plate	55.00	165.00
1402/30	4½" Footed Fruit Saucer	12.00	20.00
1402/31	6½" Footed Cereal	15.00	25.00
1402/32	6½" Grapefruit	15.00	25.00
1402/33	Sugar and Cream	30.00	60.00
1402/34	11½" 2-Hdl. Sandwich Plate	25.00	45.00
1402/60	4½" Low Footed Compote	20.00	35.00
1402/61	Low Footed Mint, D/1008	20.00	
1402/62	7" Low Footed Compote	20.00	45.00
1402/65	4½" Tall Compote	20.00	45.00
1402/66	6" High Footed Mint	20.00	45.00
1402/67	6½" Tall Compote	25.00	50.00

Page 32-35 – Tally-Ho Line		Crystal	CR-RB
1402/35	12 oz. Handled Stein	18.00	50.00
1402/36	14 oz. Handled Stein	18.00	50.00
1402/44	15 oz. Tumbler	15.00	25.00
1402/45	14 oz. Tumbler	15.00	25.00
1402/47	4" Coaster	5.00	12.00
1402/48	50 oz. Footed Cocktail Shaker	75.00	175.00
1402/49	88 oz. Jug	65.00	150.00
1402/50	74 oz. Tankard Jug	65.00	165.00
1402/51	Handled Cocktail Shaker	75.00	195.00
1402/52	Ice Pail	45.00	125.00
1402/53	Tall Frappe Cocktail & Liner	20.00	40.00
1402/54	5" Frappe Cocktail & Liner	20.00	40.00
1402/55	6" Iced Fruit or Salad	25.00	45.00
1402/56	7" Iced Fruit or Salad	25.00	45.00
1402/58	6" Footed Iced Fruit	30.00	60.00
1402/59	7" Footed Iced Fruit	30.00	60.00

Page 32-36 – 1402 Tally-Ho Line		Crystal	CR-RB
1402/64	10½" Low Footed Bowl	65.00	125.00
1402/68	8" Bowl	25.00	55.00
1402/69	9" Bowl	25.00	55.00
1402/70	10½" Bowl	30.00	65.00
1402/71	10½" 2-Handled Bowl	25.00	60.00
1402/72	9" Pan Bowl	20.00	50.00
1402/73	10" Pan Bowl	20.00	50.00
1402/74	12½" Pan Bowl	20.00	55.00
1402/75	17" Pan Bowl	35.00	95.00
1402/76	5" Candlestick	ea. 25.00	65.00
1402/77	13" Footed Punch Bowl	375.00	800.00
1402/78	Footed Punch Cup	12.00	25.00
1402/79	12" Footed Vase	50.00	145.00

Page 33-1 – 1402 Tally-Ho Line		Crystal
1402/34	Sandwich Plate, E Elaine	40.00
1402/34	Sandwich Plate, E Minerva	40.00
1402/34	Sandwich Plate, E Valencia	40.00
1402/100	Wine, E Elaine	40.00
1402/100	Goblet, E Elaine	35.00
1402/100	Goblet, E Valencia	30.00
1402/100	Tall Sherbet, E Elaine	25.00
1402/100	Low Sherbet, E Elaine	22.00
1402/100	Oyster Cocktail, E Valencia	21.00
1402/100	Tall Sherbet, E Valencia	24.00
1402/100	Goblet, E Minerva	30.00
1402/100	Claret, E Minerva	30.00
1402/100	Cocktail, E Minerva	26.00

Page 33-2 – 1402/100 Tally-Ho Line		Crystal	CR-RB
1402/100	Low Sherbet	17.00	32.00
1402/100	Goblet	25.00	46.00
1402/100	Oyster Cocktail	17.00	32.00
1402/100	Tall Sherbet	21.00	41.00
1402/100	Claret	25.00	52.00
1402/100	Wine	25.00	52.00
1402/100	Brandy Inhaler (Tall)	29.00	52.00
1402/100	Cocktail	23.00	41.00
1402/100	Cordial	29.00	52.00

The following items are 1402/150 although not labeled as such on this page.

		Crystal	CR-RB
1402/150	16 oz. Footed Tumbler	18.00	30.00
1402/150	12 oz. Footed Tumbler	17.00	29.00
1402/150	5 oz. Footed Tumbler	14.00	23.00
1402/150	3 oz. Footed Tumbler	14.00	23.00
1402/150	Brandy Inhaler (Low)	21.00	35.00
1402/150	Finger Bowl and Plate	14.00	23.00

Page 33-3 – 1402 Tally-Ho Line		Crystal	CR-RB
1402/37	2½ oz. Handled Tumbler	12.00	25.00
1402/38	34 oz. Decanter	50.00	110.00
1402/39	34 oz. Decanter	55.00	135.00

1402/78	6 oz. Punch Mug	15.00	32.00
1402/80	6½" Candlestick ea.	25.00	50.00
1402/81	Candelabrum w/Prisms ea.	50.00	75.00
1402/82	10" Bowl	22.00	50.00
1402/87	Cookie Jar	85.00	175.00
1402/88	11" Bowl	25.00	55.00
1402/89	2-Handled Nappy	15.00	25.00
1402/90	2-Handled Relish	15.00	25.00
1402/92	4-Compartment Relish	30.00	60.00

Page 33-4 – 1402 Tally-Ho Line		**Crystal**	**CR-RB**
1066	Cigarette Holder (Oval)	28.00	55.00
1402/85	4" Ash Tray	17.00	35.00
1402/86	4" Ash Tray	25.00	55.00
1402/86	2-Piece Ash Well	40.00	70.00
1402/91	3-Compartment Relish	30.00	55.00
1402/94	12" Celery	20.00	50.00
1402/95	4-Piece Twin Salad Dressing	65.00	100.00
1402/96	3-Piece Salad Dressing Set	60.00	95.00
1402/98	6½" 2-Handled Nappy	15.00	29.00
1402/99	7" Handled Plate	15.00	25.00
1402/101	18" Cheese and Cracker	55.00	125.00
1402/104	14" Cheese and Cracker	45.00	110.00

Page 33-5 – 1402 Tally-Ho Line		**Crystal**	**CR-RB**
1402/77/78/29	14-Piece Set	610.00	1285.00
1402/29	17½" Tray	55.00	150.00
1402/77	Footed Punch Bowl	375.00	750.00
1402/78	6 oz. Punch Mug	15.00	32.00

Page 33-6 – 1402 Tally-Ho Line		**Crystal**	**CR-RB**
1402/28	18" Buffet Plate	55.00	150.00
1402/29	17½" Cabaret Plate	55.00	150.00
1402/96/102	4-Piece Salad Set	110.00	235.00
1402/97	4-Piece Set, 18"	110.00	235.00
1402/101/102	Cheese and Cracker	65.00	125.00

Page 33-7 – 3400 Ball Shaped Line		**Crystal**	**CR-RB**
1341	1 oz. Cordial	12.00	21.00
3400/38	5 oz. Tumbler	7.00	16.00
3400/38	12 oz. Tumbler	12.00	18.00
3400/38	80 oz. Jug with Ice Lip	46.00	110.00
3400/76	Salt and Pepper	25.00	86.00
3400/92	2½ oz. Tumbler	6.00	12.00
3400/92	32 oz. Decanter	40.00	110.00
3400/93	5½" Ivy Ball	29.00	110.00
3400/94	3½" Puff Box	29.00	86.00
3400/95	4½" Puff Box	35.00	98.00
3400/96	2 oz. Oil	23.00	40.00
3400/96	3-Piece Oil & Vinegar Set	63.00	105.00
3400/97	2 oz. Perfume	29.00	52.00
3400/98	Sugar and Cream	35.00	70.00
3400/99	6 oz. Oil	29.00	52.00
3400/100	14 oz. Tumbler	9.00	18.00
3400/106	Marmalade	29.00	86.00
3400/107	14 oz. Stein	16.00	35.00
3400/108	80 oz. Cocktail Shaker	58.00	145.00
3400/111	5½" Candy Box	63.00	110.00
3400/112	8 oz. Tumbler	12.00	18.00
3400/113	35 oz. Decanter	40.00	110.00
3400/114	64 oz. Jug with Ice Lip	40.00	98.00
3400/115	14 oz. Tumbler	9.00	18.00
3400/116	14 oz. Stein	18.00	35.00
3400/118	35 oz. Decanter	40.00	109.00
3400/119	Cordial Decanter	23.00	63.00
3400/120	64 oz. Cocktail Shaker	45.00	130.00
3400/127	2½ oz. Handled Tumbler	14.00	23.00
3400/128	8 oz. Stein	16.00	32.00
3400/132	9" Vase	40.00	80.00
3400/133	11" Vase	52.00	105.00
3400/134	13" Vase	63.00	127.00
3400/140	Marmalade	29.00	86.00

Page 33-8 – 3500 Gadroon Line		**Crystal**
3500	Low Sherbet, E Valencia	18.00
3500	Goblet, E Elaine	35.00
3500	Goblet, E Valencia	30.00
3500	Footed Tumbler, E Elaine	20.00
3500	Cocktail, E Elaine	29.00
3500	Goblet, E Minerva	31.00
3500	Wine, E Minerva	31.00
3500	Tall Sherbet, E Valencia	21.00
3500	5 oz. Footed Tumbler, E Minerva	18.00
3500	10 oz. Footed Tumbler, E Minerva	23.00
3500/39	Sandwich Plate, E Elaine	52.00
3500/39	Sandwich Plate, E Minerva	40.00
3500/39	Sandwich Plate, E Valencia	40.00

Page 33-9 – 3500 Gadroon Stemware		**Crystal**	**CR-RB**
3500	Goblet, Long Bowl	21.00	50.00
3500	Goblet, Short Bowl	21.00	50.00
3500	Tall Sherbet	16.00	40.00
3500	Cocktail	18.00	45.00
3500	Low Sherbet	14.00	35.00
3500	Finger Bowl and Plate	16.00	40.00
3500	Claret	21.00	52.00
3500	Wine	21.00	52.00
3500	2½ oz. Footed Tumbler	16.00	40.00
3500	Oyster Cocktail	14.00	40.00
3500	5 oz. Footed Tumbler	14.00	40.00
3500	10 oz. Footed Tumbler	18.00	45.00
3500	13 oz. Footed Tumbler	18.00	45.00
3500	Footed Finger Bowl and Plate	18.00	44.00

Page 33-10 – 3500 Gadroon Line		**Crystal**	
3500/1	Cup and Saucer	17.00	
3500/2	Cream Soup and Saucer	18.00	
3500/3	6" Bread and Butter Plate	7.00	
3500/4	7½" Dessert Plate	9.00	
3500/5	8½" Salad Plate	12.00	
3500/10	5" Fruit Saucer	7.00	
3500/11	6" Cereal	12.00	
3500/36	6" Tall Compote	23.00	63.00
3500/37	7" Tall Compote	40.00	98.00
3500/39	12" Tall Ftd. Sandwich Plate	29.00	

Page 33-11 – 3500 Gadroon Line		**Crystal**	**CR-RB**
3500/16	11" Bowl	30.00	65.00
3500/17	12" Bowl	30.00	65.00
3500/21	12" Oval Bowl	52.00	130.00
3500/25	9" Bowl	110.00	325.00
3500/28	10" Bowl	30.00	65.00

Page 33-12 – 3500 Gadroon Line		**Crystal**	**CR-RB**
3500/18	12" Fruit Basket	45.00	100.00
3500/19	11" Bowl	50.00	110.00
3500/26	12" Fruit Basket	100.00	310.00
3500/27	8" Bowl	100.00	310.00
3500/67	12" 6-Piece Relish Set	65.00	

Page 33-13 – 3500 Gadroon Line		**Crystal**	**CR-RB**
3500/59	3-Piece Mayonnaise Set	38.00	
3500/60	5½" Hdl. 2-Comp. Relish	14.00	28.00
3500/61	6½" Hdl. 2-Comp. Relish	18.00	40.00
3500/62	7½" 2-Hdl. 4-Comp. Relish	22.00	45.00
3500/63	10" No Compartments Relish	18.00	34.00
3500/64	10" 3-Compartment Relish	28.00	55.00
3500/65	10" 4-Compartment Relish	28.00	55.00
3500/68	5½" 2-Compartment Relish	14.00	28.00
3500/69	6½" 3-Compartment Relish	15.00	34.00
3500/70	7½" 4-Compartment Relish	17.00	34.00

Page 33-14 – 3500 Gadroon Line		**Crystal**	**CR-RB**
3500/13	Sugar Basket	20.00	50.00
3500/14	Sugar and Cream	22.00	34.00
3500/15	Sugar and Cream, Individual	22.00	39.00
3500/38	13" Torte Plate	22.00	
3500/47	5" Bon Bon	14.00	28.00
3500/49	5" Handled Nappy	14.00	28.00
3500/50	6" Handled Nappy	14.00	28.00
3500/51	5" Handled Basket	28.00	55.00
3500/52	6" Handled Basket	28.00	55.00
3500/54	6½" Low Compote	17.00	34.00
3500/55	6" Basket	17.00	34.00
3500/56	7" Basket	17.00	34.00
3500/67	12" Tray	25.00	

Page 33-15 – 3500 Gadroon Line		**Crystal**	**CR-RB**
1338	Candelabrum ea.	37.00	120.00
3500/31	6½" Candlestick ea.	30.00	85.00
3500/32	Candelabrum with Prisms ea.	55.00	110.00
3500/41	10" Urn or Candy Jar	75.00	160.00
3500/42	12" Urn or Candy Jar	90.00	275.00
3500/44	8" Footed Vase	40.00	85.00
3500/45	10" Footed Vase	50.00	145.00

Page 33-16 – Missing

Page 33-17 – 3078 Stemware		**Crystal**	**CR-RB**
3078	15 oz. Tumbler	10.00	20.00
3078	10 oz. Goblet	18.00	30.00
3078	Tall Sherbet	12.00	20.00
3078	Low Sherbet	10.00	18.00
3078	Oyster Cocktail	10.00	18.00
3078	Cocktail	14.00	28.00
3078	Wine	14.00	28.00
3078	3 oz. Footed Tumbler	10.00	20.00
3078	5 oz. Footed Tumbler	10.00	20.00
3078	9 oz. Footed Tumbler	12.00	24.00
3078	12 oz. Footed Tumbler	14.00	28.00
3078	Claret	15.00	28.00
3078	5 oz. Tumbler	5.00	14.00
3078	84 oz. Jug	45.00	135.00
3078	12 oz. Tumbler	8.00	16.00
3078	Finger Bowl and Plate	12.00	25.00
3078	2½ oz. Tumbler	5.00	14.00
3078	32 oz. Decanter	30.00	95.00

Page 33-18 – Vases		**Crystal**
1336	18" Vase, E Diane	350.00
1336	18" Vase, Eng 698	350.00

Page 33-19 – Console Sets		**Crystal**	**Pastel**
628	3½" Candlestick, E 758 ea.	18.00	28.00
993	12½" Bowl, E Lorna	25.00	50.00
1307	Candelabrum, E 764 ea.	60.00	
1348	11" Bowl, E 758	35.00	50.00
1349	12" Bowl, E 764	75.00	
3400/135	9" Bowl	20.00	35.00
3400/136	6" Bowl	20.00	35.00

		Crystal	**CR-RB**
3500/31	6" Candlestick ea.	30.00	85.00
3500/32	6½" Candelabrum w/Prisms	55.00	110.00

Page 33-20 – Miscellaneous		**Crystal**	**CR-RB**
306	3" Vase	15.00	45.00
308	4½" Vase	15.00	45.00
309	4½" Vase	15.00	45.00
379	3" Vase	15.00	45.00
1066	5½" Low Compote	30.00	65.00
1332	6" Plate	5.00	
1333	7½" Plate	6.00	
1334	8½" Plate	7.00	
1352	Handled Frog Vase	225.00	
1361	7" Coupe Salad or Coaster	10.00	
1362	8" Coupe Salad or Coaster	10.00	
3122	5½" Tall Compote	35.00	75.00
3126	5½" Tall Compote	35.00	75.00
3400/129	6" Lemon Tray	25.00	
6004	5" Vase	12.00	40.00
6004	6" Vase	15.00	45.00

Page 33-21 – Beverage Accessories		**Crystal**	**CR-RB**
270	1 oz. Cordial	8.00	16.00
1066	Cafe Parfait	18.00	30.00
1069	11 oz. Goblet	20.00	
1070	14 oz. Pinch Tumbler	10.00	22.00
1070	36 oz. Pinch Decanter	75.00	150.00
1213	8 oz. Bitter Bottle	25.00	60.00
1217	4 oz. Bitter Bottle	25.00	60.00
1321	32 oz. Decanter, Jigger Stop	75.00	150.00
1322	26 oz. Decanter, No. 1 Jigger	75.00	150.00
1323	28 oz. Decanter, No. 1 Jigger	75.00	150.00
1324	22 oz. Decanter, No. 1 Jigger	75.00	150.00
1327	1 oz. Cordial	18.00	25.00

1329	4½ oz. Mustard	35.00	75.00
1337	Cigarette Holder	25.00	50.00
1344	1 oz. Cordial	8.00	
1405	16 oz. Stein	20.00	45.00
1406	6 oz. O.F. Stein	12.00	
1407	9 oz. O.F. Stein	12.00	
1408	60 oz. Cocktail Mixer	95.00	
3187	4 oz. Cocktail	12.00	25.00
3400/46	Cabinet Flask	45.00	100.00
3400/121	38 oz. Cocktail Shaker	60.00	135.00
3400/122	5 oz. Juice Tumbler	8.00	15.00
3400/122	38 oz. Juice Jug	75.00	165.00
3400/130	11 oz. Tumbler	12.00	25.00
NO. 1	Muddler	15.00	20.00

Page 33-22 – Leaf Line		**Crystal**	**Pastel**
1207	11" Bowl	55.00	185.00
1209	Candlestick ea.	25.00	85.00
1210	Flower Holder	65.00	145.00
1211	Candelabrum ea.	50.00	225.00
1216	Flower Holder	100.00	325.00

Page 33-23 – Novelty Sets in Display Boxes		**Crystal**	**CR-RB**
925/1327	18-Piece After Dinner Coffee and Cordial Set	290.00	350.00
1327	6-Piece Cordial Set	155.00	190.00
3011	6-Piece Cocktail Set	660.00	885.00
3400/107	6-Piece Stein Set	120.00	225.00
3500/15	Individual Sugar and Cream	35.00	50.00

Page 33-24 – Novelty Sets in Display Boxes		**Crystal**	**CR-RB**
925	After Dinner Coffee Set	160.00	190.00
1402/39/37	7-Piece Decanter Set	135.00	265.00
3011	3-Piece Smoker Set	465.00	625.00
3400/92	7-Piece Decanter Set	95.00	195.00

Page 33-25 – Everglade		**Crystal**	**CR-RB**
EVGL.20	10½" Vase	45.00	
EVGL.21	7½" Vase	35.00	
EVGL.22	6" Vase	30.00	58.00
EVGL.23	5" Vase	25.00	45.00

		Crystal	**CR**
EVGL.24	Sherbet	15.00	28.00
EVGL.25	8" Plate	14.00	40.00
EVGL.26	Sugar and Cream	40.00	70.00
EVGL.27	7½" Bowl	15.00	40.00

Page 33-26 – Everglade		**Crystal**	**CR**
EVGL.1	10" Bowl	45.00	175.00
EVGL.2	Candlesticks pr.	50.00	170.00
EVGL.3	Candelabrum pr.	100.00	450.00
EVGL.19	12" Oval Bowl	40.00	145.00

Page 33-27 – Everglade		**Crystal**	**CR**
EVGL.5	2-Piece Flower Holder	65.00	145.00
EVGL.6	3-Piece Flower Holder	100.00	325.00
EVGL.7	11" Bowl	35.00	95.00
EVGL.8	12" Bowl	40.00	100.00
EVGL.10	4" Candlesticks pr.	45.00	95.00
EVGL.28	16" Bowl	85.00	175.00

Page 33-28 – Everglade		**Crystal**	
EVGL.15	11" Bowl	60.00	125.00
EVGL.16	12" Bowl	60.00	130.00
EVGL.17	13" Bowl	65.00	125.00
EVGL.18	14" Bowl	70.00	125.00

Page 33-29 – Everglade		**Crystal**	
EVGL.11	10½" Bowl	50.00	130.00
EVGL.12	12" Bowl	50.00	130.00
EVGL.13	13" Bowl	52.00	140.00
EVGL.14	14" Bowl	52.00	140.00

Page 33-29A – Everglade		**Crystal**	**CR**
EVGL.32	Candlestick ea.	35.00	90.00
EVGL.33	Candlestick ea.	35.00	90.00
EVGL.37	13" 2-Piece Oval Epergne	63.00	290.00
EVGL.38	11" Footed Vase	60.00	150.00
EVGL.39	14½" Oval Footed Plate	35.00	80.00
EVGL.43	12 oz. Beer Mug	40.00	65.00
EVGL.51	2-Piece Epergne	105.00	150.00
EVGL.53	2-Piece Epergne	105.00	150.00
EVGL.55	14½" Oval Epergne	115.00	230.00

Page 33-29B – Everglade		**Crystal**	**CR**
EVGL.30	16" Plate	58.00	145.00
EVGL.31	16" Plate	52.00	130.00
EVGL.40	6" Compote	23.00	95.00
EVGL.41	7" Compote	23.00	95.00
EVGL.45	2-Piece Flower Holder	70.00	160.00
EVGL.48	10" Bowl	40.00	90.00
EVGL.49	11" Bowl	40.00	90.00
EVGL.56	13" Sandwich Plate	45.00	100.00
EVGL.57	15" Sandwich Plate	45.00	100.00
EVGL.58	3-Piece Flower Holder	150.00	350.00

Page 33-30 – Crown Tuscan		**Crown**
518	Figure Flower Holder	1,200.00
1040½	3" Swan	45.00
1043	8½" Swan	500.00
1240	12" Bowl, D/1012	250.00
1307	Candelabrum D/1001 ea.	125.00
3011	Candlestick, w/Prism D/1007-8	500.00
3011	Ash Tray D/1007-8	450.00
3011	Cigarette Box D/1007-8	650.00
3011	Compote D/1007-8	950.00
3400/45	11" Bowl, D/1001	225.00
3400/114	64 oz. Jug, D/995	800.00
3500/41	10" Urn, D/995	500.00
3500/42	12" Urn, D/1007-8	700.00

Page 33-31 – Crown Tuscan		**Crown**
1130	11" Vase, D/1007-8	300.00
1228	9" Vase, D/1001	550.00
1238	12" Vase, D/1007-8	275.00
1297	11" Vase, D/1001	300.00
1298	13" Vase, D/995	350.00
1299	11" Vase, D/1012	250.00
1300	8" Vase, D/1012	165.00
1301	10" Vase, D/995	250.00
1302	9" Vase, D/1007-8	800.00
1309	5" Vase, D/1012	125.00
3400/102	5" Vase, D/995	125.00
3400/103	6" Vase, D/1001	150.00

Page 33-32 – Missing

Page 33-33 – New Buffet or Sunday Evening Supper Sets		**Crystal**
1402/101/101/8	3-Piece Set E Elaine	165.00
1402/101	18" Buffet Plate E Elaine	85.00
1402/101	9" Compote E Elaine	50.00
1402/8	5 oz. Cocktail E Elaine	25.00
1402/102/101/33	3-Piece Set E Minerva	160.00
1402/102	17½" Cabaret Plate E Minerva	85.00
1402/101	9" Compote E Minerva	50.00
1402/33	Whipped Cream or Small Mayonnaise E Minerva	25.00

Page 33/34 – 7801 Line Stemware		**Crystal**
7801	6 oz. Hollow Stem Champagne	12.00
7801	4 oz. Hollow Stem Champagne (7927)	12.00
7801	5 oz Hollow Stem Champagne (7927½)	12.00
7801	5½ oz. Tall Champagne (7516)	10.00
7801	6 oz. Low Sherbet	8.00
7801	6 oz. Hollow Stem Champagne Cut Stem	14.00
7801	4 oz. Hollow Stem Champagne Cut Stem (7927)	14.00
7801	5 oz. Hollow Stem Champagne Cut Stem (7927½)	14.00
7801	6 oz. Low Stem Saucer Champagne	10.00
7801	6 oz. Tall Stem Saucer Champagne	10.00

Page 33-35 – 7801 Line Stemware		**Crystal**
7801	1 oz. Cordial	16.00
7801	¾ oz. Brandy	16.00
7801	1 oz. Pousse Cafe	16.00
7801	4½ oz. Parfait (7982)	10.00
7801	5 oz. Hot Whiskey (7858)	10.00
7801	4½ oz. Rhine Wine (7516)	10.00
7801	5 oz. Roemer	10.00
7801	6 oz. Hoch (3104)	20.00
7801	9 oz. Tall Stem Goblet	10.00
7801	10 oz. Goblet	10.00
7801	9 oz. Low Stem Goblet	10.00
7801	5 oz. Claret	10.00
7801	4 oz. Claret	10.00
7801	3 oz. Wine	10.00
7801	2 oz. Wine	10.00

Page 33-36 – 7801 Line Stemware		**Crystal**
2900	5 oz. Punch Cup	6.00
7801	3½ oz. Cocktail	10.00
7801	2 oz. Sherry (7966)	10.00
7801	1½ oz. Sherry (7966)	10.00
7801	1 oz. Cordial (7966)	18.00
7801	4½ oz. Claret (7901)	10.00
7801	4½ oz. Claret (3280)	10.00
7801	4½ oz. Oyster Cocktail (7608)	10.00
7801	2½ oz. Creme De Menthe (7967)	10.00
7801	3½ oz. Cocktail (7966)	10.00
7801	3 oz. Cocktail (7911)	10.00
7801	4 oz. Side Car Cocktail (7911)	10.00
7801	4½ oz. Side Car Cocktail (7911)	10.00

Page 33B-1 – Beer and Bar Glassware (Mugs and Steins, Pressed)		**Crystal**
550	10 oz. Mug	15.00
593	8 oz. Mug	10.00
595	12 oz. Mug	12.00
611	8 oz. Mug	12.00
1402/35	12 oz. Stein	15.00
1402/36	14 oz. Stein	15.00
1405	16 oz. Mug	15.00
3400/149	13 oz. Mug	15.00
3400/150	12 oz. Mug	15.00
3400/151	13 oz. Mug	15.00
M.W.54	8 oz. Stein	18.00
M.W.55	10 oz. Stein	18.00
M.W.56	12 oz. Stein	18.00
MT.V.84	14 oz. Mug	18.00

Page 33B-2 – Beer and Bar Glassware (Mugs and Pilsners, Blown)		**Crystal**
1206	12 oz. Footed Tumbler Spiral	10.00
1402/113	16 oz. Stein	16.00
3135	10 oz. Footed Tumbler	8.00
3400/107	14 oz. Mug	15.00
3400/116	14 oz. Mug	15.00
3400/128	8 oz. Mug	15.00
7857	12 oz. Pilsner	12.00
7857	10 oz. Pilsner	12.00
7857	8 oz. Pilsner	12.00
7857	6½ oz. Pilsner	12.00
7857½	12 oz. Pilsner Low Footed	11.00
7857½	10 oz. Pilsner Low Footed	11.00
7857½	8 oz. Pilsner Low Footed	11.00
7857½	6½ oz. Pilsner Low Footed	11.00

Page 33B-3 – Beer and Bar Glassware (Pilsner and Weiss Beer Goblets, Pressed)		**Crystal**
575	34 oz. Weiss Beer	14.00
971	8 oz. Goblet	12.00
972	9 oz. Goblet	12.00
973	11 oz. Goblet	12.00
1041½	12 oz. Weiss Beer	12.00
1055	31 oz. Weiss Beer	15.00
1057½	14 oz. Weiss Beer	12.00
1403	10 oz. Pilsner	10.00

1403	8 oz. Pilsner	10.00
1403½	8 oz. Pilsner Low Footed	10.00

Page 33B-4 – Beer and Bar Glassware (Goblets, Pressed)

		Crystal
552	8 oz. Goblet Low Footed	10.00
665	8 oz. Goblet	12.00
667	8 oz. Goblet	12.00
690	8 oz. Goblet	12.00
690½	11 oz. Goblet, Optic	12.00
690½	9½ oz. Goblet, Optic	12.00
690½	8 oz. Goblet, Optic	12.00
691	8 oz. Goblet Long Stem	12.00
694½	10 oz. Goblet, Optic	12.00
694½	8 oz. Goblet, Optic	12.00
800	8 oz. Goblet	12.00
964	10 oz. Goblet, Optic	12.00
995½	8 oz. Goblet, Optic	12.00
1069	11 oz. Goblet	16.00
1400	10 oz. Goblet	15.00
1401	10 oz. Goblet	15.00
1402/1	18 oz. Goblet	20.00
1402/2	14 oz. Goblet	18.00
1402/3	10 oz. Goblet	16.00
M.W.51	10 oz. Goblet	16.00
MT.V.1	10 oz. Goblet	15.00

Page 33B-5 – Beer and Bar Glassware (Goblets, Blown)

		Crystal
301	9 oz. Goblet Low Foot	12.00
1066	11 oz. Goblet Low Foot	16.00
1402/100	16 oz. Goblet Low Foot	16.00
1402/100	12 oz. Goblet Low Foot	16.00
3078	12 oz. Goblet Low Foot	14.00
3078	10 oz. Goblet	14.00
3078	9 oz. Goblet Low Foot	16.00
3226	9 oz. Goblet	12.00
3226	8 oz. Goblet	12.00
3234	7 oz. Goblet	12.00
7607	10½ oz. Goblet	12.00
7796	9½ oz. Goblet	12.00
7796	9½ oz. Goblet	12.00
7796	8 oz. Goblet	12.00
7797	8 oz. Goblet	12.00
7798	8 oz. Goblet	12.00
7803	10 oz. Goblet	12.00
7825	9 oz. Goblet	12.00
7828	10 oz. Goblet	12.00
7841	11 oz. Goblet	12.00
7865	8 oz. Goblet	12.00
7973	10 oz. Goblet	12.00
7974	8½ oz. Goblet	12.00
9072	8 oz. Goblet Low Foot	12.00

Page 33B-6 – Beer and Bar Glassware (Miscellaneous, Pressed)

		Crystal
599	5¼" Coaster	8.00
601	3" Coaster	4.00
602	5¼" Coaster	5.00
603	4" Coaster	4.00
690½	4 oz. Claret, Optic	12.00
695	3 oz. Wine, Optic	12.00
764	3 oz. Cocktail	12.00
764½	3½ oz. Cocktail	12.00
765	4 oz. Cocktail	12.00
769	2½ oz. Creme de Menthe	12.00
827	5 oz. Hot Whiskey	12.00
828	4½ oz. Hot Whiskey	12.00
848	2 oz. Wine	12.00
901	4½ oz. Rhine Wine	12.00
903	4½ oz. Rhine Wine	12.00
922½	2½ oz. Sherry	12.00
924	1½ oz. Sherry	12.00
935	1 oz. Pousse Cafe	12.00
1402/47	4" Coaster	6.00
1404	6 oz. Hollow Stem Champagne	12.00

Page 33B-7 – Beer and Bar Glassware (Miscellaneous, Blown)

		Crystal
300	4 oz. Claret	12.00
300	3 oz. Wine	12.00
300	2½ oz. Creme de Menthe	12.00
300	1½ oz. Sherry	12.00
300	1 oz. Cordial	20.00
300	1 oz. Pousse Cafe	20.00
7801	10 oz. Goblet	12.00
7801	9 oz. Goblet	12.00
7801	4 oz. Claret	12.00
7801	3½ oz. Cocktail	12.00
7801	3 oz. Wine	12.00
7801	1 oz. Cordial	20.00
7801	¾ oz. Brandy	20.00
7805	1 oz. Pousse Cafe	20.00
7901	4½ oz. Claret	12.00
7911	3 oz. Cocktail	12.00
7927½	5 oz. Hollow Stem Champagne	12.00
7958	5 oz. Hot Whiskey	12.00
7966	2 oz. Sherry	12.00
7967	2½ oz. Creme de Menthe	12.00
7980	4 oz. Cocktail	12.00

Page 33B-8 – Beer and Bar Glassware (Tumblers, Pressed)

		Crystal
19	2½ oz. Tumbler	10.00
22	7 oz. Old Fashioned Cocktail	8.00
270	1 oz. Tumbler, Sham	10.00
317	5 oz. Georgian Tumbler	12.00
319	9 oz. Georgian Tumbler	16.00
468	12 oz. Tumbler	10.00
469	14 oz. Tumbler	10.00
517	7 oz. Tumbler	8.00
1201	2½ oz. Georgian Tumbler	16.00
1202	12 oz. Georgian Tumbler	16.00
1203	14 oz. Tumbler	10.00
1203	12 oz. Tumbler	10.00
1203	10 oz. Tumbler	10.00
1203	8 oz. Tumbler	10.00
1203	7 oz. O.F. Cocktail, Sham	10.00
1203	5 oz. Tumbler	8.00
1203	2½ oz. Tumbler, Sham	10.00
1204	14 oz. Tumbler, Sham	10.00
1402/44	15 oz. Tumbler	12.00
1402/45	14 oz. Tumbler	12.00
1406	7 oz. Tumbler	8.00
1407	9 oz. Tumbler	8.00
3400/130	11 oz. Tumbler	12.00
M.W.48	8 oz. Footed Tumbler	12.00
M.W.49	10 oz. Footed Tumbler	12.00
M.W.50	12 oz. Footed Tumbler	14.00
MT.V.14	14 oz. Tumbler	12.00

Page 33B-9 – Beer and Bar Glassware (Tumblers, Blown)

		Crystal
318	4 oz. Tumb., Sham, Cut Flute	10.00
320	7 oz. O.F. Cocktail, Cut Flute	8.00
321	9 oz. Tumb., Sham, Cut Flute	8.00
493	14 oz. Tumb., Sham, Cut Flute	10.00
496	2½ oz. Tumb., Sham, Cut Flute	10.00
497	8 oz. Tumb., Sham, Cut Flute	10.00
498	12 oz. Tumb., Sham, Cut Flute	10.00
499	20 oz. Tumb., Sham, Cut Flute	10.00
1066	14 oz. Tumbler, Light	12.00
1066	12 oz. Tumbler, Light	10.00
1066	10 oz. Tumbler, Light	10.00
1066	7 oz. Tumbler, Light	8.00
1066	5 oz. Tumbler, Light	8.00
1066	2½ oz. Tumbler, Light	10.00
1402/112	16 oz. Tumbler	15.00
3078	15 oz. Tumbler, Half Sham	8.00
3078	12 oz. Tumbler, Half Sham	8.00
3078	5 oz. Tumbler, Half Sham	5.00
3078	2½ oz. Tumbler	5.00
3400/100	13 oz. Tumbler	10.00
3400/115	14 oz. Tumbler	10.00
9024	16 oz. Tumbler	10.00
9024	14 oz. Tumbler	10.00
9024	10 oz. Tumbler	10.00
9024	8 oz. Tumbler	10.00
9024	2½ oz. Tumbler	10.00

Page 33B-10 – Beer and Bar Glassware (Tumblers, Blown)

		Crystal
107	13 oz. Tumbler	6.00
119	13 oz. Tumbler	6.00
318	4 oz. Tumbler, Sham	4.00
320	7 oz. O.F. Cocktail, Sham	6.00
321	9 oz. Tumbler, Sham	6.00
493	14 oz. Tumbler, Sham	6.00
496	2½ oz. Tumbler, Sham	6.00
497	8 oz. Tumbler, Sham	6.00
498	12 oz. Tumbler, Sham	6.00
499	20 oz. Tumbler, Sham	6.00
1306	20 oz. Tumbler	8.00
3400/27	12 oz. Tumbler	10.00
3400/38	12 oz. Tumbler	10.00
3400/38	5 oz. Tumbler	8.00
8401	12 oz. Tumbler	6.00
8401	10 oz. Tumbler	6.00
8401	8 oz. Tumbler	6.00
8401	5 oz. Tumbler	6.00
8401	3½ oz. Tumbler	6.00
8401	2½ oz. Tumbler	6.00
8401	1½ oz. Tumbler	6.00
8701	14 oz. Tumbler	6.00
8701	12 oz. Tumbler	6.00
8701	10 oz. Tumbler	6.00
8701	8 oz. Tumbler	6.00

Page 33B-11 – Beer and Bar Glassware (Jugs, Pretzel Jars, Etc.)

		Crystal
96	69 oz. Tankard Jug	35.00
96	59 oz. Tankard Jug	35.00
96	40 oz. Tankard Jug	30.00
96	32 oz. Tankard Jug	30.00
96	18 oz. Tankard Jug	25.00
395	Shaker, Chromium Plated Top	10.00
396	Shaker, Chromium Plated Top	10.00
1212	11 oz. Bitter Bottle w/Tube	25.00
1213	8 oz. Bitter Bottle w/Tube	25.00
1217	4 oz. Bitter Bottle w/Tube	20.00
1229	Shaker C.M. Top	10.00
1402/49	88 oz. Jug	60.00
1402/50	75 oz. Tankard Jug	75.00
1402/87	Covered Pretzel Jar	85.00
1402/93	Covered Pretzel Jar	65.00
3400/38	80 oz. Ball Shape Jar	45.00
3400/76	Shaker with Glass Top	12.00
3400/77	Shaker with Glass Top	12.00
3400/101	76 oz. Jug	40.00
3400/141	80 oz. Jug	75.00
M.W.67	Covered Pretzel Jar	60.00

Page 34-1 – 3450 Nautilus		**Crystal**	**CR-RB**
3450	84 oz. Jug	60.00	160.00
3450	40 oz. Decanter, G.S.	55.00	115.00
3450	28 oz. Decanter, G.S.	50.00	115.00
3450	Sugar and Cream	35.00	75.00
3450	9" Footed Vase	45.00	120.00
3450	2 oz. Wine	10.00	30.00
3450	1 oz. Cordial	30.00	55.00
3450	1 oz. Tumbler	6.00	20.00
3450	2 oz. Tumbler	5.00	15.00
3450	2½ oz. Tumbler	6.00	18.00
3450	5 oz. Tumbler	6.00	18.00
3450	12 oz. Tumbler	12.00	25.00
3450	15 oz. Tumbler	12.00	25.00
3450	7" Footed Vase	25.00	75.00
3450	14 oz. Decanter, G.S.	30.00	100.00
3450	1½ oz. Perfume, G.S.	55.00	150.00
3450	3-Piece Oil and Vinegar Set	65.00	150.00
3450	3-Piece Salt and Pepper Set	35.00	80.00

Page 34-2 – 3011 Figure Stem Line		**Crystal**	**CR-RB**
3011	Covered Sweetmeat	600.00	800.00
3011	7" Compote, Flared	125.00	165.00
3011	Cigarette Holder	300.00	450.00

3011	9" Candlestick ea.	200.00	400.00
3011	Covered Cigarette Box, Short	200.00	225.00
3011	9" Candlestick w/Bobeche and Prisms ea.	225.00	450.00
3011	Covered Cigarette Box, Tall	250.00	350.00
3011	7" Compote, Cupped	125.00	165.00
3011	Ash Tray	150.00	200.00
3011/1	Banquet Goblet	250.00	350.00
3011/2	Table Goblet	125.00	150.00
3011/3	Saucer Champagne	125.00	150.00
3011/5	6 oz. Hoch	250.00	400.00
3011/6	5 oz. Roemer	250.00	400.00
3011/7	4½ oz. Claret	100.00	125.00
3011/8	4½ oz. Sauterne	250.00	400.00
3011/9	3 oz. Cocktail	200.00	400.00
3011/10	3 oz. Cocktail	200.00	400.00
3011/11	3 oz. Cocktail	80.00	125.00
3011/12	3 oz. Wine	150.00	250.00
3011/13	1 oz. Brandy	85.00	135.00
3011/14	1 oz. Cordial	350.00	450.00

Page 34-3 – 7966 Stemware Plate Etched Bacchus		**Crystal**
7966	3½ oz. Cocktail	22.00
7966	9 oz. Goblet	22.00
7966	3 oz. Cocktail	22.00
7966	3 oz. Tall Champagne	19.00
7966	2 oz. Sherry	22.00
7966	4 oz. Claret	22.00
7966	1½ oz. Sherry	22.00
7966	3 oz. Wine	22.00
7966	1 oz. Cordial	75.00
7966	6 oz. Hollow Stem Champagne Cut Flute Stem	25.00
7966	6 oz. Hollow Stem Champagne	24.00
7966	6 oz. Saucer Champagne	20.00
7966	Finger Bowl and Plate	30.00

Page 34-4 – 1402/150 Stemware Etched Elaine 1402/200 Stemware Etched 766 Chintz		**Crystal**
1402/150	12 oz. Tall Footed Tumbler	34.00
1402/150	12 oz. Footed Tumbler	34.00
1402/150	9 oz. Footed Tumbler	29.00
1402/150	5 oz. Claret	29.00
1402/150	3 oz. Wine	29.00
1402/150	Finger Bowl and Plate	30.00
1402/150	Low Sherbet	29.00
1402/150	3½ oz. Cocktail	29.00
1402/150	1 oz. Cordial	100.00
1402/200	Finger Bowl and Plate	30.00
1402/200	10 oz. Footed Tumbler	29.00
1402/200	5 oz. Footed Tumbler	29.00
1402/200	6 oz. Low Sherbet	26.00
1402/200	3 oz. Footed Tumbler	26.00
1402/200	3½ oz. Cocktail	26.00
1402/200	1 oz. Pousse Cafe	100.00

Page 34-5 – Rnd Dinner Plate Etched 766 Chintz		**Crystal**	**Pastel**
103	6" 3-Comp. Covered Candy	50.00	65.00
135	10" Cheese and Cracker	35.00	45.00
168	10" Handled Sandwich Tray	24.00	30.00
242	13½" Plate	26.00	34.00
441	10½" Low Footed Compote	30.00	40.00
531	7" Compote	25.00	40.00
533	3-Piece Mayonnaise Set	25.00	40.00
556	8" Plate	10.00	15.00
628	3½" Candlesticks pr.	30.00	40.00
652	12" Celery	20.00	25.00
668	6" Plate	5.00	12.00
851	Ice Pail Chrome Handle	55.00	70.00
993	12½" Bowl	25.00	40.00

Page 34-6 – 3129 Stemware Plate Etched Vichy (765)		**Crystal**
3129	5 oz. Tall Champagne	30.00
3129	10 oz. Goblet	28.00
3129	5 oz. Roemer	28.00
3129	6 oz. Tall Hoch	28.00
3129	4 oz. Claret	28.00
3129	6 oz. Saucer Champagne	30.00
3129	3½ oz. Cocktail	28.00
3129	6 oz. H.S. Champagne	30.00
3129	4 oz. H.S. Sparkling Burgundy	30.00
3129	6 oz. H.S. Champagne, Cut Flute Stem	35.00
3129	4 oz. H.S. Sparkling Burgundy Cut Flute Stem	35.00
3129	6 oz. Low Sherbet	20.00
3129	2 oz. Sherry (7966)	30.00
3129	2 oz. Burgundy Wine	25.00
3129	2 oz. Sherry, Cut Flute (7966)	30.00
3129	2 oz. Wine	30.00
3129	1½ oz. Sherry (7966)	30.00
3129	1 oz. Cordial	75.00
3129	1½ oz. Sherry, Cut Flute (7966)	25.00
3129	1 oz. Pousse Cafe	75.00
3129	¾ oz. Brandy	75.00
3129	Fingerbowl and Plate	22.00

Page 34-7 – 3109 Stemware Plate Etched Vintage		**Crystal**
3109	9 oz. Goblet	20.00
3109	6 oz. H.S. Champagne	20.00
3109	6 oz. H.S. Champagne Cut Flute Stem	22.00
3109	6 oz. Saucer Champagne	15.00
3109	6 oz. Low Sherbet	12.00
3109	5 oz. Sherbet, Tall Bowl	15.00
3109	6 oz. Tall Ale	18.00
3109	5 oz. H.S. Sparkling Burgundy	18.00
3109	4 oz. H.S. Sparkling Burgundy Cut Flute Stem	20.00
3109	5½ oz. Tall Champagne	18.00
3109	5 oz. Tall Champagne	18.00
3109	4 oz. Claret	18.00
3109	2½ oz. Creme de Menthe	18.00
3109	3 oz. Wine	20.00
3109	2 oz. Wine	20.00
3109	4 oz. Cocktail	18.00
3109	3½ oz. Cocktail	18.00
3109	3 oz. Cocktail	18.00
3109	1 oz. Cordial	65.00
3109	1 oz. Pousse Cafe	65.00

Page 34-8 – 3109 Stemware Plate Etched Vintage		**Crystal**
3109	14 oz. Tumbler	15.00
3109	12 oz. Tumbler	15.00
3109	10 oz. Tumbler	15.00
3109	8 oz. Tumbler	15.00
3109	9 oz. Tumbler	15.00
3109	5 oz. Tumbler	15.00
3109	Fingerbowl and Plate	20.00
3109	6 oz. Fruit Salad	12.00
3109	4½ oz. Oyster Cocktail	12.00
3109	1 oz. Tumbler	20.00
3109	2 oz. Tumbler	15.00
3109	3 oz. Tumbler	15.00
3109	5 oz. Cafe Parfait	18.00
3109	3 oz. Footed Tumbler	12.00
3109	5 oz. Footed Tumbler	12.00
3109	10 oz. Footed Tumbler	12.00
3109	12 oz. Footed Tumbler	14.00

Page 34-9 – Crown Tuscan		**Crown**
615	Cigarette Box & Cover D/1012	200.00
862	8" 4-Comp. Handled Relish	125.00
1066	Cigarette Holder D/1012	200.00
1311	4" Footed Ashtray D/1012	200.00
1312	Footed Cigarette Box & Cover	175.00
1337	Cigarette Holder D/1001	200.00
3400/67	12" 5-Comp. Celery D/1012	300.00
3400/91	8" 3-Compartment 3-Handled Relish D/1001	125.00
3400/54	6½" 2-Handled Low Compote	60.00
3400/55	6" 2-Handled Square Basket	60.00
3400/57	8" 3-Compartment Candy Box and Cover D/1001	150.00
3400/60	5½" 1-Handled Relish D/1001	185.00
3400/61	6½" 1-Hdl. 3-Comp. Relish	45.00
3400/64	10" 2-Handled 3-Compartment Relish D/1015	180.00
3400/68	5½" 2-Compartment Relish	40.00
3400/69	6½" 3-Compartment Relish	40.00

Page 34-10 – Crown Tuscan		**Crown**
626	3½" Candlestick ea.	40.00
647	2 Holder Candelabrum ea.	85.00
3011	9" Candlestick ea.	200.00
3400/4	12" 4-Toed Bowl	90.00
3400/32	11½" Bowl, Flared	80.00
3400/136	6" 4-Toed Bowl, Fancy	200.00
3500/16	11" Footed Bowl	300.00
3500/21	12" Handled and Footed Bowl Oval D/1015	600.00
3500/26	12" Fruit Bowl (Ram's Head)	450.00
3500/28	10" 2-Handled Bowl	200.00
3500/39	11" Footed Cake Plate	80.00
3500/74	4" Candlestick ea.	50.00
3500/110	13" Torte Plate D/1001	225.00

Page 34-11 – Crown Tuscan		**Crown**
79	8" Vase	50.00
80	10" Vase	80.00
82	10" Vase	85.00
83	12" Vase D/1001	225.00
119	7" Handled Basket D/1001	550.00
274	10" Vase D/1007/8	110.00
1066	5⅝" Compote	125.00
1236	Ivy Ball	65.00
1321	28 oz. Decanter, Footed D/1015	700.00
1402/52	Ice Pail, Chrom. Handle	500.00
1418	5½" Vase	60.00
1430	8" Vase	80.00
3400/152	76 oz. Jug	900.00
3500/36	6" Tall Compote	100.00
7966	2 oz. Sherry D/1015	200.00

Page 34-12 – Crown Tuscan with Ebony Foot		**Crown**
274	10" Vase	100.00
1066	5⅝" Compote	225.00
1066	Cigarette Holder Oval	180.00
1283	8" Vase	90.00
1300	8" Vase	95.00
1311	4" Footed Ash Tray	125.00
1312	Footed Cigarette Box & Cover	200.00
1314	3" Footed Ash Tray	180.00
1337	Cigarette Holder	200.00
3011	Cigarette Box and Cover	500.00
3011	Ash Tray	425.00
3011	7" Compote	400.00
6004	6" Vase	80.00

Page 34-13 – Decanters		**Crystal**	**CR-RB**
1320	14 oz. Decanter, Cut Neck	40.00	80.00
1321	28 oz. Decanter	40.00	100.00
1324	22 oz. Decanter	35.00	85.00
1378	26 oz. Decanter	40.00	100.00
1379	26 oz. Decanter	40.00	100.00
1380	26 oz. Square, E Scotch	95.00	
1380	26 oz. Square, E Rye	95.00	
1380	26 oz. Square, E Gin	95.00	
1382	14 oz. Square Decanter	30.00	65.00
1383	24 oz. Decanter	30.00	100.00
1385	28 oz. Decanter	30.00	125.00
1387	14 oz. Decanter	40.00	125.00
1388	28 oz. Decanter Cut Neck	50.00	125.00
1402/38	34 oz. Decanter	50.00	125.00
1402/39	34 oz. Decanter	55.00	145.00
3400/46	12 oz. Cabinet Flask	40.00	120.00
3400/156	12 oz. Decanter	30.00	65.00
3450	40 oz. Decanter, Nautilus	55.00	115.00
3450	28 oz. Decanter, Nautilus	50.00	115.00
3450	14 oz. Decanter, Nautilus	30.00	100.00

Page 34-14 – Decanters		**Crystal**	**CR-RB**
1070	36 oz. Decanter, Pinch	35.00	95.00
1121	2 oz. Bitter Bottle	12.00	30.00
1121	1¼ oz. Bitter Bottle	12.00	30.00
1322	26 oz. Decanter, Cut Flute	35.00	90.00

1323	28 oz. Decanter, Cut Neck	35.00	90.00
1325	30 oz. Decanter	30.00	65.00
1375	10 oz. Decanter	25.00	60.00
1376	16 oz. Decanter	25.00	60.00
1377	32 oz. Decanter, Cut Flute	35.00	90.00
1381	28 oz. Decanter	25.00	90.00
1381	28 oz. Bar Bottle, Cut Flute	20.00	65.00
1386	30 oz. Decanter, Cut Neck	35.00	90.00
1389	30 oz. Decanter	45.00	115.00
2764	1½ oz. Bitter Bottle	12.00	30.00
3078	32 oz. Decanter	30.00	115.00
3400/92	32 oz. Decanter, Ball Shape	35.00	115.00
3400/113	35 oz. Decanter	35.00	115.00
3400/118	35 oz. Decanter	35.00	115.00
3400/119	12 oz. Decanter, Ball Shape	20.00	65.00
MT.V.52	40 oz. Decanter	70.00	165.00

Page 34-15 – Candelabra		**Crystal**
1355	2-Holder Candelabra ea.	75.00
1356	2-Holder w/Bobeches & Prisms	135.00
1357	3-Holder Candelabra ea.	80.00
1358	3-Holder w/Bobeches & Prisms	140.00
3500/94	2-Holder Candelabra ea.	65.00
3500/95	2-Holder w/Bobeches & Prisms	115.00

Page 34-16 – Liquor Sets		**Crystal**	**CR-RB**
	14-Piece Set	122.00	335.00
3500/112	Tray	30.00	55.00
3400/119	Decanter	20.00	65.00
3109	1 oz. Tumbler	6.00	18.00
	8-Piece Set	180.00	270.00
3500/112	Tray	30.00	55.00
3400/156	Decanter	30.00	65.00
1327	1 oz. Cordial	20.00	25.00
	10-Piece Set	100.00	315.00
3500/112	Tray	30.00	55.00
3450	14 oz. Decanter	30.00	100.00
3450	1 oz. Tumbler	6.00	20.00
	11-Piece Set	145.00	315.00
3500/113	Tray	35.00	55.00
1382	14 oz. Decanter	30.00	65.00
3109	1 oz. Tumbler	6.00	16.00
	9-Piece Set	100.00	190.00
3500/113	Tray	35.00	55.00
No. 1	Muddler	10.00	18.00
1203	7 oz. Old Fashioned Cocktail	8.00	16.00
	9-Piece Set	144.00	270.00
3500/100	Tray	20.00	47.00
1393	Mixer with No. 1 Spoon	40.00	90.00
1402/200	3½ oz. Cocktail	14.00	22.00
	10-Piece Set	215.00	465.00
3500/72	Tray	20.00	50.00
MT.V.52	Decanter	70.00	165.00
MT.V.57	7 oz. Old Fashioned Cocktail	15.00	30.00
MT.V.62	Bitter Bottle	25.00	50.00
No. 1	Muddler	10.00	18.00
	5-Piece Set	155.00	315.00
3500/113	Tray	35.00	55.00
1382	14 oz. Decanter	30.00	65.00

Page 34-17 – Miscellaneous Blown Ware		**Crystal**
0431	18 oz. Tumbler	12.00
0431	15 oz. Tumbler	10.00
0431	9 oz. Tumbler	8.00
0431	2½ oz. Tumbler	6.00
1066	2 oz. Sherry	35.00
1066	1 oz. Pousse Cafe	35.00
1066	3¼ oz. Brandy	35.00
1402/100	12 oz. Tumbler	18.00
3101	¾ oz. Pousse Cafe	20.00
3126	12 oz. Footed Tumbler	18.00
3129	12 oz. Footed Tumbler	12.00
3129	10 oz. Footed Tumbler	10.00
3500	12 oz. Footed Tumbler	18.00
7801	12 oz. Footed Tumbler	8.00
7801	10 oz. Footed Tumbler	8.00
7801	8 oz. Footed Tumbler	8.00
7801	5 oz. Footed Tumbler	6.00
7801	2 oz. London Duck	12.00
7801	5" Grapefruit	16.00
7801	5" Low Compote	12.00
7801	6" Low Compote	14.00
7801	7" Low Compote	16.00
7801	8" Low Compote	18.00
7801	6" Tall Compote	16.00
7801	8" Bowl	18.00
7801	5½" Fruit	12.00
7801	5" Fruit	10.00
7801	4" Fruit	10.00
7966	12 oz. Footed Tumbler	14.00
7966	10 oz. Footed Tumbler	14.00
7966	8 oz. Footed Tumbler	12.00
7966	5 oz. Footed Tumbler	10.00
7966	2½ oz. Footed Tumbler	10.00

Page 34-18 – Rose Bowls, Vases and Novelties		**Crystal**	**CR-RB**
705	Flower Pot	20.00	55.00
1409	4½" Rose Bowl	20.00	50.00
1410	6" Rose Bowl	20.00	50.00
1411	7" Rose Bowl	25.00	60.00
1412	8" Rose Bowl	25.00	60.00
1413	10" Rose Bowl	28.00	67.00
1417	8" Vase	18.00	65.00
1430	8" Vase	18.00	65.00
1431	Bulb Vase	30.00	115.00
1446	6" Vase	20.00	75.00
1447	8" Vase	25.00	90.00
1448	10" Vase	28.00	100.00

		Crystal	**Pastel**
	Frog	34.00	50.00
	Squirrel	34.00	50.00
No. 1	Bird	55.00	80.00
No. 1	Butterfly	50.00	70.00
No. 2	Bird	55.00	80.00
No. 2	Butterfly	50.00	70.00
No. 3	Bird	55.00	80.00
No. 3	Butterfly	50.00	70.00

Page 34-19 – Miscellaneous		**Crystal**	**CR-RB**
1351	10" Bowl	25.00	55.00
1359	10½" Bowl	20.00	55.00
1402/80	6" Candlestick ea.	18.00	42.00
1402/121	14½" Bowl	25.00	70.00
3400/160	12" Bowl	35.00	
3400/168	10½" Bowl	30.00	
3500/118	12" Bowl	40.00	100.00
Evlg. 60	16" Cheese and Cracker	85.00	

Page 34-20 – Miscellaneous		**Crystal**	**CR-RB**
1402/119	18" Footed Plate	25.00	90.00
1402/122	11" 3-Compartment Bowl	25.00	75.00
1439	Ladle	25.00	
2750	16" Punch Bowl and Foot	150.00	
3500/119	13" Punch Bowl	110.00	
M.W.79	15" 2-Piece Buffet Set	45.00	110.00

Page 34-21 – Miscellaneous		**Crystal**	**CR-RB**
393	10" 5-Compartment Relish	22.00	48.00
394	10" 5-Compartment Relish	22.00	48.00
1121	2 oz. Bitter Bottle	24.00	50.00
1365	6" Ash Tray	10.00	26.00
1371	Bridge Hound	20.00	100.00
1374	10 oz. Bitter Bottle	22.00	48.00
1378	2½ oz. Tumbler	6.00	15.00
1393	Cocktail Mixer	40.00	110.00
1394	Cocktail Mixer	40.00	110.00
1395	Cocktail Mixer	40.00	110.00
1425	4" Ash Receiver E Minerva	30.00	
3400/157	Cocktail Shaker	48.00	110.00
3400/158	Cocktail Shaker	48.00	110.00
3400/159	Cocktail Shaker	60.00	120.00
3400/161	6 oz. Oil	40.00	100.00
3500/139	Honey Jar and Cover	30.00	95.00
M.W.76	Salt and Pepper Shaker	12.00	34.00
MT.V.62	Bitter Bottle w/Chrome Tube	25.00	50.00
MT.V.90	50 oz. Jug	80.00	160.00
No. 1	Muddler	10.00	18.00
No. 2	Muddler	20.00	60.00

Page 34-22 – 3102 Stemware Etched Marlene		**Crystal**
3102	9 oz. Goblet	22.00
3102	6 oz. Tall Sherbet	19.00
3102	4½ oz. Claret	25.00
3102	3 oz. Wine	25.00
3102	2 oz. Sherry	25.00
3102	5 oz. Oyster Cocktail	17.00
3102	6 oz. Low Sherbet	17.00
3102	2½ oz. Creme de Menthe	20.00
3102	3 oz. Cocktail	20.00
3102	12 oz. Footed Tumbler	15.00
3102	1 oz. Cordial	65.00
3102	¾ oz. Brandy	65.00
3102	1 oz. Pousse Cafe	65.00
3102	Finger Bowl and Plate	20.00

Page 34-23 – 3103 Stemware Etched Marlene		**Crystal**
3103	9 oz. Goblet	22.00
3103	6 oz. Low Sherbet	17.00
3103	4½ oz. Claret	25.00
3103	2 oz. Sherry	25.00
3103	3 oz. Wine	25.00
3103	2½ oz. Creme de Menthe	20.00
3103	3 oz. Cocktail	20.00
3103	5 oz. Oyster Cocktail	17.00
3103	12 oz. Footed Tumbler	15.00
3103	1 oz. Pousse Cafe	65.00
3103	¾ oz. Brandy	65.00
3103	1 oz. Cordial	65.00
3103	Fingerbowl and Plate	20.00

Page 34-24 – 3104 Stemware Etched Elaine		**Crystal**
3104	5 oz. Roemer	75.00
3104	9 oz. Goblet	85.00
3104	2 oz. Sherry	90.00
3104	7 oz. Tall Sherbet	55.00
3104	3 oz. Wine	90.00
3104	5 oz. Hoch	90.00
3104	2½ oz. Creme de Menthe	90.00
3104	4½ oz. Claret	90.00
3104	3½ oz. Cocktail	65.00
3104	1 oz. Cordial	125.00
3104	¾ oz. Brandy	125.00
3104	1 oz. Pousse Cafe	125.00
3104	Finger Bowl and Plate	35.00

Page 34-25 – 3106 Stemware Etched Diane		**Crystal**
3106	10 oz. Goblet, Low Bowl	26.00
3106	9 oz. Goblet, Tall Bowl	26.00
3106	7 oz. Tall Sherbet	20.00
3106	4½ oz. Claret	30.00
3106	2½ oz. Wine	30.00
3106	2 oz. Sherry	35.00
3106	7 oz. Low Sherbet	18.00
3106	1 oz. Cordial	65.00
3106	¾ oz. Brandy	65.00
3106	1 oz. Pousse Cafe	65.00
3106	2½ oz. Creme de Menthe	24.00
3106	3 oz. Cocktail	24.00
3106	12 oz. Footed Tumbler	20.00
3106	9 oz. Footed Tumbler	18.00
3106	5 oz. Footed Tumbler	14.00
3106	3 oz. Footed Tumbler	15.00
3106	5 oz. Oyster Cocktail	16.00
3106	Finger Bowl and Plate	35.00

COLLECTOR BOOKS

Informing Today's Collector

DOLLS, FIGURES & TEDDY BEARS

2079 **Barbie** Doll Fashion, Volume I, Eames $24.95
3957 **Barbie** Exclusives, Rana $18.95
4557 **Barbie,** The First 30 Years, Deutsch $24.95
3810 **Chatty Cathy** Dolls, Lewis $15.95
4559 Collectible **Action Figures,** 2nd Ed., Manos $17.95
1529 Collector's Encyclopedia of **Barbie** Dolls, DeWein/Ashabraner $19.95
2211 Collector's Encyclopedia of **Madame Alexander Dolls,** 1965-1990, Smith $24.95
4863 Collector's Encyclopedia of **Vogue Dolls,** Stover/Izen $29.95
4861 Collector's Guide to **Tammy,** Sabulis/Weglewski $18.95
3967 Collector's Guide to **Trolls,** Peterson $19.95
1799 **Effanbee Dolls,** Smith $19.95
5253 Story of **Barbie,** 2nd Ed., Westenhouser $24.95
1513 **Teddy Bears & Steiff** Animals, Mandel $9.95
1817 **Teddy Bears & Steiff** Animals, 2nd Series, Mandel $19.95
2084 **Teddy Bears, Annalee's & Steiff** Animals, 3rd Series, Mandel $19.95
1808 Wonder of **Barbie,** Manos $9.95
1430 World of **Barbie** Dolls, Manos $9.95
4880 World of **Raggedy Ann Collectibles,** Avery $24.95

TOYS, MARBLES & CHRISTMAS COLLECTIBLES

3427 **Advertising Character** Collectibles, Dotz $17.95
2333 Antique & Collectible **Marbles,** 3rd Ed., Grist $9.95
4934 **Breyer Animal** Collector's Guide, Identification and Values, Browell ..$19.95
4976 **Christmas** Ornaments, Lights & Decorations, Johnson $24.95
4737 **Christmas** Ornaments, Lights & Decorations, Vol. II, Johnson $24.95
4739 **Christmas** Ornaments, Lights & Decorations, Vol. III, Johnson $24.95
2338 Collector's Encyclopedia of **Disneyana,** Longest, Stern $24.95
4958 Collector's Guide to **Battery Toys,** Hultzman $19.95
5038 Collector's Guide to **Diecast Toys** & Scale Models, 2nd Ed., Johnson ..$19.95
4566 Collector's Guide to **Tootsietoys, 2nd Ed,** Richter $19.95
3436 Grist's Big Book of **Marbles** $19.95
3970 Grist's Machine-Made & Contemporary **Marbles,** 2nd Ed. $9.95
5267 **Matchbox** Toys, 3rd Ed., 1947 to 1998, Johnson $19.95
4871 **McDonald's Collectibles,** Henriques/DuVall $19.95
1540 **Modern Toys** 1930–1980, Baker $19.95
3888 **Motorcycle** Toys, Antique & Contemporary, Gentry/Downs $18.95
5168 Schroeder's Collectible **Toys,** Antique to Modern Price Guide, 5th Ed ..$17.95
1886 Stern's Guide to **Disney** Collectibles $14.95
2139 Stern's Guide to **Disney** Collectibles, 2nd Series $14.95
3975 Stern's Guide to **Disney** Collectibles, 3rd Series $18.95
2028 **Toys,** Antique & Collectible, Longest $14.95

JEWELRY, HATPINS, WATCHES & PURSES

1712 Antique & Collectible **Thimbles** & Accessories, Mathis $19.95
1748 Antique **Purses,** Revised Second Ed., Holiner $19.95
1278 Art Nouveau & Art Deco **Jewelry,** Baker $9.95
4850 Collectible **Costume Jewelry,** Simonds $24.95
3875 Collecting Antique **Stickpins,** Kerins $16.95
3722 Collector's Ency. of **Compacts, Carryalls & Face Powder Boxes,** Mueller $24.95
4940 **Costume Jewelry,** A Practical Handbook & Value Guide, Rezazadeh ..$24.95
1716 Fifty Years of Collectible **Fashion Jewelry,** 1925-1975, Baker $19.95
1424 **Hatpins** & Hatpin Holders, Baker $9.95
1181 100 Years of Collectible **Jewelry,** 1850-1950, Baker $9.95
3830 Vintage **Vanity Bags & Purses,** Gerson $24.95

FURNITURE

1457 American **Oak** Furniture, McNerney $9.95
3716 American **Oak** Furniture, Book II, McNerney $12.95
1118 Antique **Oak** Furniture, Hill $7.95
2132 Collector's Encyclopedia of **American** Furniture, Vol. I, Swedberg $24.95
2271 Collector's Encyclopedia of **American** Furniture, Vol. II, Swedberg ..$24.95
3720 Collector's Encyclopedia of **American** Furniture, Vol. III, Swedberg ...$24.95
1755 Furniture of the **Depression Era,** Swedberg $19.95
3906 **Heywood-Wakefield** Modern Furniture, Rouland $18.95
1885 **Victorian** Furniture, Our American Heritage, McNerney $9.95
3829 **Victorian** Furniture, Our American Heritage, Book II, McNerney $9.95

INDIANS, GUNS, KNIVES, TOOLS, PRIMITIVES

1868 Antique **Tools,** Our American Heritage, McNerney $9.95
1426 **Arrowheads** & Projectile Points, Hothem $7.95
2279 **Indian** Artifacts of the Midwest, Hothem $14.95
3885 **Indian** Artifacts of the Midwest, Book II, Hothem $16.95
5162 Modern **Guns,** Identification & Values, 12th Ed., Quertermous $12.95
2164 **Primitives,** Our American Heritage, McNerney $9.95
1759 **Primitives,** Our American Heritage, Series II, McNerney $14.95
4730 Standard **Knife** Collector's Guide, 3rd Ed., Ritchie & Stewart $12.95

PAPER COLLECTIBLES & BOOKS

4633 **Big Little Books,** A Collector's Reference & Value Guide, Jacobs $18.95
4710 Collector's Guide to **Children's Books,** 1850 to 1950, Jones $18.95
1441 Collector's Guide to **Post Cards,** Wood $9.95
2081 Guide to Collecting **Cookbooks,** Allen $14.95
2080 Price Guide to **Cookbooks & Recipe Leaflets,** Dickinson $9.95
3973 **Sheet Music** Reference & Price Guide, 2nd Ed., Pafik & Guiheen $19.95
4654 **Victorian Trade Cards,** Historical Reference & Value Guide, Cheadle .$19.95
4733 **Whitman Juvenile Books,** Brown $17.95

OTHER COLLECTIBLES

2269 Antique **Brass & Copper** Collectibles, Gaston $16.95
1880 Antique **Iron,** McNerney $9.95
3872 Antique **Tins,** Dodge $24.95
1128 **Bottle** Pricing Guide, 3rd Ed., Cleveland $7.95
3718 Collectible **Aluminum,** Grist $16.95
4560 Collectible **Cats,** An Identification & Value Guide, Book II, Fyke $19.95
4852 Collectible **Compact Disc** Price Guide 2, Cooper $17.95
2018 Collector's Encyclopedia of **Granite Ware,** Greguire $24.95
3430 Collector's Encyclopedia of **Granite Ware,** Book II, Greguire $24.95
4705 Collector's Guide to Antique **Radios,** 4th Ed., Bunis $18.95
4857 Collector's Guide to **Art Deco,** 2nd Ed., Gaston $17.95
4933 Collector's Guide to **Bookends,** Identification & Values, Kuritzky $19.95
3880 Collector's Guide to **Cigarette Lighters,** Flanagan $17.95
4887 Collector's Guide to **Creek Chub Lures** & Collectibles, Smith $24.95
3966 Collector's Guide to **Inkwells,** Identification & Values, Badders $18.95
3881 Collector's Guide to **Novelty Radios,** Bunis/Breed $18.95
4652 Collector's Guide to **Transistor Radios,** 2nd Ed., Bunis $16.95
4864 Collector's Guide to **Wallace Nutting Pictures,** Ivankovich $18.95
1629 **Doorstops,** Identification & Values, Bertoia $9.95
3968 **Fishing Lure** Collectibles, Murphy/Edmisten $24.95
5259 **Flea Market Trader,** 12th Ed., Huxford $9.95
4945 **G-Men and FBI Toys,** Whitworth $18.95
3819 **General Store Collectibles,** Wilson $24.95
2216 **Kitchen Antiques,** 1790–1940, McNerney $14.95
4950 The **Lone Ranger,** Collector's Reference & Value Guide, Felbinger ...$18.95
2026 **Railroad** Collectibles, 4th Ed., Baker $14.95
1632 **Salt & Pepper Shakers,** Guarnaccia $9.95
5091 **Salt & Pepper Shakers** II, Guarnaccia $18.95
2220 **Salt & Pepper Shakers** III, Guarnaccia $14.95
3443 **Salt & Pepper Shakers** IV, Guarnaccia $18.95
5007 **Silverplated Flatware,** Revised 4th Edition, Hagan $18.95
1922 Standard **Old Bottle** Price Guide, Sellari $14.95
3892 **Toy & Miniature Sewing Machines,** Thomas $18.95
5144 Value Guide to **Advertising Memorabilia,** 2nd Ed., Summers $19.95
3977 Value Guide to **Gas Station** Memorabilia, Summers $24.95
4877 Vintage **Bar Ware,** Visakay $24.95
4935 The W.F. Cody **Buffalo Bill** Collector's Guide with Values, Wojtowicz $24.95
5281 **Wanted to Buy,** 7th Edition $9.95

GLASSWARE & POTTERY

4929 **American Art Pottery,** 1880 – 1950, Sigafoose $24.95
4938 Collector's Encyclopedia of **Depression Glass,** 13th Ed., Florence ...$19.95
5040 Collector's Encyclopedia of **Fiesta,** 8th Ed., Huxford $19.95
4946 Collector's Encyclopedia of **Howard Pierce Porcelain,** Dommel $24.95
1358 Collector's Encyclopedia of **McCoy Pottery,** Huxford $19.95
2339 Collector's Guide to **Shawnee Pottery,** Vanderbilt $19.95
1523 Colors in **Cambridge Glass,** National Cambridge Society $19.95
4714 **Czechoslovakian Glass** and Collectibles, Book II, Barta $16.95
3725 **Fostoria,** Pressed, Blown & Hand Molded Shapes, Kerr $24.95
4726 **Red Wing Art Pottery,** 1920s – 1960s, Dollen $19.95

This is only a partial listing of the books on collectibles that are available from Collector Books. All books are well illustrated and contain current values. Most of our books are available from your local bookseller, antique dealer, or public library. If you are unable to locate certain titles in your area, you may order by mail from COLLECTOR BOOKS, P.O. Box 3009, Paducah, KY 42002-3009. Customers with Visa, MasterCard, or Discover may phone in orders from 7:00–5:00 CST, Monday–Friday, Toll Free 1-800-626-5420. Add $3.00 for postage for the first book ordered and $0.40 for each additional book. Include item number, title, and price when ordering. Allow 14 to 21 days for delivery.

cb

www.collectorbooks.com

**You Are Cordially Invited
To Become A Member Of The
NATIONAL CAMBRIDGE COLLECTORS, INC.**

Benefits derived from membership include: receipt of our club publication, The Cambridge *Crystal Ball*; informative Quarterly Meetings; Antique Shows; Auctions; and other special events.

The Cambridge *Crystal Ball* is published the first of each month. This newsletter contains educational and interesting articles, questions and answers, information on reproductions and reissues, notices of all club functions, classified advertisements, dealers' directory, and many other features of interest to collectors of Cambridge glass.

Yearly dues are $17.00 for individual members and $3.00 for each associate member. All members have voting rights, but only one issue of the *Crystal Ball* will be mailed per household.

Name (please print) ______________________________ $17.00

Mailing Address ______________________________

City ____________________ State ____________ Zip ________

Associate Members: (Must be at least 12 years of age and living in the same household.)

1. Name ______________________________

2. Name ______________________________

3. Name ______________________________

Associate Members @ $3.00 each $____________

Please made check payable to: National Cambridge Collectors, Inc.

TOTAL AMOUNT ENCLOSED: $ ____________

Schroeder's ANTIQUES Price Guide

Without doubt, you'll find
SCHROEDER'S ANTIQUES PRICE GUIDE
the only one to buy for reliable information and values.

. . . is the #1 best-selling antiques & collectibles value guide on the market today, and here's why . . .

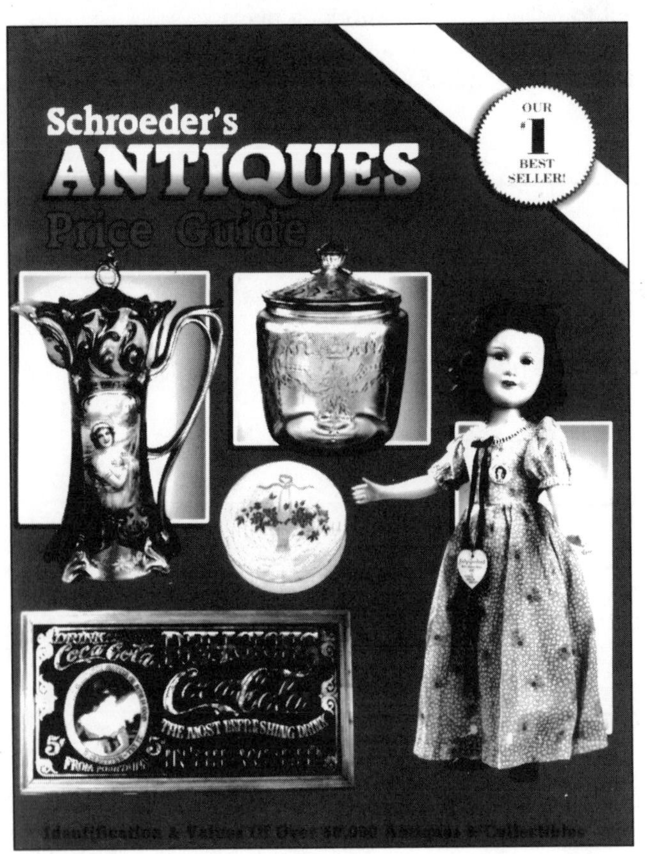

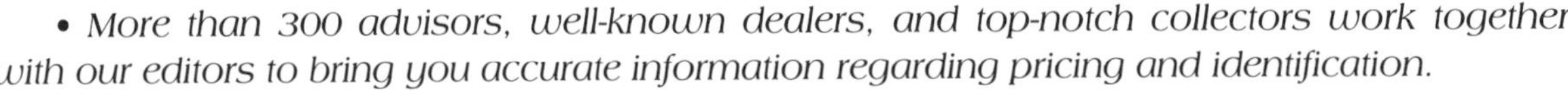

• *More than 300 advisors, well-known dealers, and top-notch collectors work together with our editors to bring you accurate information regarding pricing and identification.*

• *More than 45,000 items in almost 500 categories are listed along with hundreds of sharp original photos that illustrate not only the rare and unusual, but the common, popular collectibles as well.*

• *Each large close-up shot shows important details clearly. Every subject is represented with histories and background information, a feature not found in any of our competitors' publications.*

• *Our editors keep abreast of newly-developing trends, often adding several new categories a year as the need arises.*

If it merits the interest of today's collector, you'll find it in *Schroeder's*. And you can feel confident that the information we publish is up to date and accurate. Our advisors thoroughly check each category to spot inconsistencies, listings that may not be entirely reflective of market dealings, and lines too vague to be of merit. Only the best of the lot remains for publication.

8½ x 11, 608 Pages, $12.95

COLLECTOR BOOKS
A Division of Schroeder Publishing Co., Inc.